JOURNEYS IN THE SONGSCAPE

Journeys in the Songscape

Space and the Song of Songs

Christopher Meredith

Sheffield Phoenix Press

2013

Copyright © 2013 Sheffield Phoenix Press

Published by Sheffield Phoenix Press
Department of Biblical Studies, University of Sheffield
Sheffield S3 7QB

www.sheffieldphoenix.com

A CIP catalogue record for this book
is available from the British Library

Typeset by CA Typesetting Ltd
Printed on acid-free paper by Lightning Source

ISBN-13 978-1-907534-85-0
ISSN 1747-9614

To Rebecca Jamieson
for the careful pouring of lavender tea

Space is a doubt:
I have constantly to mark it,
to designate it.
It's never mine, never given to me,
I have to conquer it.
My spaces are fragile.
—Georges Perec, *Species of Spaces*

CONTENTS

ACKNOWLEDGEMENTS

Apparently it is customary to confess at the outset that this book is an adaptation of my doctoral thesis, and there seems no reason to break with that tradition here. But, truth be told, I was always more sorcerer's apprentice than PhD student, imagining—poor, young and foolish thing that I am—that I could simply conjure up a few texts, bend them to my will and get a shiny new title for the credit card. As it turns out (and as a good many people tried to warn me), summoning texts is far easier than making them do your bidding. I am thus horrendously indebted to all those who have so willingly helped me over the years to pin my thoughts down and wrestle these infernal pages in the general direction of the bindery.

First, there are a number of financial benefactors to whom I owe a great deal. Without the generous award of a fellowship from the Arts and Humanities Research Council this project simply would never have been completed. Private funds also came (at particularly daunting times) from the Browns, the Clarkes, the Carlisles, and the Morrises. I am also extremely grateful to the AHRC and to the Learned Societies Fund at the University of Sheffield for releasing the resources that let me test out much of this material at various conferences and gatherings around the world. Those trips have been a crucial part of the process. And fun, if I'm honest.

True to form, the Department of Biblical Studies in Sheffield has proved to be a rich and stimulating environment to work in. Without its quirks this project would have ended up in a very different shape, and, without its personnel, so would I. Thanks go to Cynthia Shafer-Elliott for keeping me sane in the early days, to James Crossley for playing poker on my behalf with the powers that be (let the reader understand), and to Alison Bygrave, for both her saintlike patience in the face of my administrative torpor and for her unflagging personal support—as well as the hockey tickets.

My thanks also go to numerous scholars whom I have encountered on my travels, and who continue to take an interest in what I'm typing. David Gunn and Claudia Camp made some extremely helpful suggestions during the very early stages of my work, and, most memorably, welcomed a young postgraduate to the table without flinching. At the other end of the process, Yvonne Thöne, whose research topic coincides with mine, has been so helpful (and gracious) in contributing to my thinking on the project as a whole. I am also especially grateful to James Harding and John Lyons for their ongoing encouragement (and their refreshing blend of whimsy and cynicism), to

Miriam Bier (for the cyber cheerleading), and to Emma England (for the frank and graphic advice on how to 'finish up' properly). Warm and very special thanks also go to professors Francis Landy and Mary Mills, my PhD examiners, for their rigor, for taking such a genuine interest in the work, and for their kind and insightful comments on my feverish scribbles.

Since writing a PhD, or converting one into a book, seems not nearly so bothersome as living with me while I work, I also need to express my appreciation to all those with whom I have shared a roof during my research. This valiant band have put up with vacant stares, malaises, grumps, and general shortness of shrift with great sympathy and kindness: Jon and Lydia Haines, Beci Jamieson, Owen McCarthy, Jamie Fletcher, Kay Morrison, Rich Newman, the Dormands—Claire, Stu and young Master Jacob—and, most recently, Becca Woodthorpe (née Bluett-Duncan). Your support during what has been on reflection quite a tumultuous few years has been more important to me than you know. Also, it is quite possible that I would have starved without some of you.

Significant recognition goes to Val Bruce, who not only paid a considerable sum for the oh-so-sparkly laptop on which all these words were written, but has been a constant source of comfort, wisdom and hard liquor during the years of writing. Thanks too to Linda Harding for her guidance, encouragement and indefatigable optimism, and for donating her Northumbrian homestead for a time so I could finish off Chapter 5. I would be so much poorer without the love and care you both offer so freely.

Three names warrant special mention. Katie Edwards, whose folksy northern charm and wayward sense of propriety keeps me (pointing and) laughing. Hugh Pyper, longtime friend and Jedi Master, who has fed me invaluable comments and suggestions throughout the process of writing this, and whose unique manner and mind continue to inspire me to sit back down at my keyboard. And Cheryl Exum, my long-suffering supervisor; without her time, passion, unparalleled expertize, rigorous questioning and heartfelt support, this project would have been impossible. It is difficult to express how much I appreciate the advice, the investment, and the unflagging support that has come my way. It is not taken for granted.

Finally, I want to thank my mother and father, Janet and Graham Meredith. I vividly remember a conversation with my dad, in the children's seating area of Crawley's McDonalds (circa 1994), about how I might be interested in the maps of *The Hobbit*, with their strange runes and sigils and their inky trees. Believe it or not, this book is an outgrowth of that conversation, and I am tremendously grateful for it. The first seeds of my predilection for literary space, though, are a little older. They come from somewhere among the boughs of *The Magic Faraway Tree*, and I appreciate my mother taking me there to find them (and Moonface) more than I have ever expressed. I could not have found the Songscape without you, much less traveled there.

ABBREVIATIONS

AB	Anchor Bible Series
BDB	Francis Brown, S.R. Driver and Charles Briggs, *A Hebrew and English Lexicon of the Old Testament* (7th edn.; Peabody, MA: Hendrickson, 2000 [1907]).
BibInt	*Biblical Interpretation*
DCH	David J.A. Clines (ed.), *Dictionary of Classical Hebrew* (8 vols.; Sheffield: Sheffield Phoenix Press, 1993–2011).
IB	*Interpreter's Bible*
JAAR	*Journal of the American Academy of Religion*
JAOS	*Journal of the American Oriental Society*
JHS	*Journal of Hebrew Scriptures*
JPS	Jewish Publication Society Bible
JQR	*Jewish Quarterly Review*
JSNTSup	Journal for the Study of the New Testament: Supplement Series
JSOT	*Journal for the Study of the Old Testament*
JSOTSup	Journal for the Study of the Old Testament: Supplement Series
JTS	*Journal of Theological Studies*
MT	Masoretic Text
NGC	*New German Critique*
NJB	New Jerusalem Bible
TQ	*Theologische Quartalschrift*
VT	*Vetus Testamentum*
ZAW	*Zeitschrift für die alttestamentliche Wissenschaft*

Chapter 1

TOWARDS A CARTOGRAPHY OF READING

> Toy is handtool—not artwork
> —Walter Benjamin[1]

This book is a response to an afternoon's failed doodling. Sitting in a café (at around +53° 49' 13.09", -1° 34' 34.91"), I tried to draw what the first cartographers would have undoubtedly called *a moftlie true and accurate mappe* of the Song of Songs. I failed several times over. I have since lost those preliminary sketches of the Songscape, but if memory serves correctly some were circular, like those charts of the constellations that track the wheeling movements of the heavens.[2] Others were thin rambling lanes peppered with landmarks, similar to countless itinerant's maps hastily rendered on the backs of envelopes. Others were like the huge brightly coloured affairs one usually finds at the thresholds to theme parks, with separate zones of intensity (buildings, gardens, etc.) moored to one another by arrows, by vague representations of possible connections. These divers maps of the Song were highly contrived, impossible to complete, and suspiciously partial.

The Song's resistance to my naive cartographic advances was, I now realize, quite curious. Other spaces, even atypical ones, welcome the attention. Tolkien's Middle Earth for instance is an imaginary space that has never existed as a concrete world, and yet it can be—and has been—extensively mapped. The same holds for Narnia; I could quite easily ink in the contours of Stormness Head, or give Cair Paravel flags that flutter in the breeze off the Eastern Sea. If I wanted, I could trace imaginary (that is, never written) journeys through the Hundred Acre Wood with Pooh Bear. And though the results would be historically contested, I could map out Solomon's temple too, and trace Joshua's apportioning of the Promised Land to the tribes of Israel, or give shape to Ezekiel's fetish for cubits. Like all maps these projects would require decisions and omissions of course—that is what a map

---

1. Walter Benjamin, *Walter Benjamin's The Archive: Images, Texts, Signs* (London: Verso: 2007), p. 72 (**Ms.** 604).
2. Though of course the heavens do not move at all, or at least not like that; they merely fool us into thinking that they do.

is: a collection of omissions, as London's tube map aptly demonstrates—but these worlds would nevertheless form on the page without too much of a struggle. The Song simply refused me.

The difficulties I faced in trying to map the Song would be easier to understand if the text were simply ambivalent about space, if space were not among its concerns. But the Song is a profoundly spatial text. It consists of royal rooms and palanquins, secret tree houses, wine barns, sun-scorched vineyards, dappled springtime vistas, the incense-dusted wilderness, lush botanical gardens, and cities in perpetual nightscape. Moreover, the poem dashes between these scenes at such a breakneck pace that the whirlwind romance and the spinning dance of settings seems to become one and the same. Of course, the poem's spatiality goes beyond mere setting though. The text relies on the spatiality of absence too, on relocations, and on the shifts in perception that spatial repositioning allows. Space is a crucial aspect of the text, even on a cursory reading, but the centrality of the Song's spatial sensitivities does not necessarily make them easy to apprehend as critical categories, let alone easy to pin down on a mapmaker's coffee table.

How, for instance, would one chart the spatial connection between city and garden in the Song, since there is no intervening space implied by the text? The city just ceases to be and the garden replaces it. The lovers do not travel; they are simply, and effortlessly, relocated. Should the literary cartographer *invent* spaces in order to map them? Such a move seems rather at odds with the mapmaker's usual role of cutting spaces down to size. What would it mean to have a map that was bigger than the world it described? There are other more pressing questions, however. Are the Song's two city scenes set in the same city? If not, how, where, would we plot them? What about the two (or is it three?) gardens? Even the idea of physical dimensions becomes a problem, since the lovers can be in a house and yet that structure's architecture can double as the bodies that inhabit it. How does one map that? What kind of scale might one use?

An important issue, it seemed to me (as I, and that café, whizzed around the sun at roughly thirty kilometers per second), is that we tend to fix spatialities only when it suits us. The Song is not perhaps a difficult space but an irritatingly candid one. The Song's world is profoundly relative, built as a site of the subjective. As a result it is always moving around under our gaze, not a quantity to be interpreted but a series of processes that readers must configure. And that kind of space requires an entirely different sort of mapping. The reader should be advised, then, that this 'volume' attempts something of that order, thinking about literary space not simply as a series of settings to be contrasted across two dimensions, but as a process by which relationships come into being: relationships between scenes, between characters, and, ultimately, between readers and pages. In other words, this book attempts to step away from the idea that accounts of literary space are synonymous with accounts of literary setting, and addresses instead the idea that space represents a dynamic field that makes literature, and lovers, possible. The result is not a map as I had originally envisaged it. It is instead a plotting of the forces of attraction and repulsion by which the Song's poetic world comes to be constituted, a labyrinthine account of the spatiality of the text as well as the individual scenes 'in' it. As we shall see, what emerges in the Song is actually a fusing, or better a (con)fusing, of the spatiality of the reading process with the spatiality of sexual relationships. It is this matrix of literary and spatial operations that gives rise to the Song's fluidity and which accounts for the troublesome spatiality of the text as a whole.

Notes in the Margins of Other Maps

At the time of my coffee fuelled cartography no dedicated studies on spatiality and the Song of Songs existed to help with these questions. Spatial contributions to Song scholarship were limited, in fact, to commentators' broad assertions about the unstable 'poetic world' of the text (statements that I shall look at in more detail in Chapter 2) and brief discussions on setting that appeared as small parts of bigger projects on the poem. One particular example of this latter phenomenon is Marcia Falk's sense of the Song's four primary 'contexts': the habitable countryside, the wild natural landscape, interior environments (houses, rooms etc.), and city streets.[3] Falk attempts to grade each of the contexts in terms of their hospitableness to love, with the countryside and garden most readily supporting the lovers and the city being most antagonistic to them. While there are some notable problems and inconsistencies in Falk's discussion of these contexts,[4] it is

---

3. Marcia Falk, *Love Lyrics from the Bible: A Translation and Literary Study of the Song of Songs* (Bible and Literature, 4; Sheffield: Almond Press, 1982), p. 88.

4. Falk's notion of the habitable countryside as a consistent platform for the 'pastoral idyll' is undermined by the familial anger of the brothers in 1.6, which actually has most resonance with the violent characteristics of Falk's hostile city. Similarly, the view that tamed nature operates as an unswerving setting for intimacy breaks down as early as 1.7 when the young shepherd, separated from her lover, becomes worried about becoming lost on the hills with her flocks. Falk admits that 'although the lovers are often separated in the countryside, reunions always seem to be expected there' (p. 88). But reunions are an equally important feature of the two developed searching/finding sequences, which both use public urban space (Falk's most disruptive and antagonistic category). Moreover, the supposedly 'distant or overwhelming forces' of the wild natural landscape, as Falk would have them, can in fact be hospitable to love and function with a sense of proximity: 'Moreover, our daybed is green, the joists of our house are cedar, our rafters are pine' (1.16b). By giving specific contexts different jobs to perform for (or against) the lovers, Falk presents spatial-thematic categories that are either too specific to encompass the whole raft of the text's images, or else are too broad to be of genuine interpretative use. A prime example of this latter problem lies in Falk's

noticeable, first, that spatiality and setting can very quickly become synony-mous in literary discussions, and, second, that the Song's characteristic flu-idity is largely erased by the standardizing rhetoric of Falk's analysis. This begs the question of whether my café-based cartography was an attempt to get to know the poem better, or an attempt to subjugate the Songworld to my orderly sensibilities (such as they are). Moreover, while the question of how the Song's spaces relate in terms of *ideology* is addressed by Falk's contexts, the question of how they are imagined to relate *in space* hangs still in the air.

Recently, there has been more sustained interest in the Song's spaces, and in space as a critical concept more generally. Some discussions about the Song's literary space have coped with the kinds of problems I have described here by keeping analysis at a purely descriptive level, as the very recently published essays by Meik Gerhards and Stefan Fischer do.[5] This approach is useful, but this presents rather limited opportunities for critical engagement with the questions of textual space as such.

More recent still is a book length study by Yvonne Sophie Thöne, enti-tled *Liebe zwischen Stadt und Feld: Raum und Geschlecht im Hohelied.*[6] Essentially Thöne's thesis is that scenes in the text have an intrinsic rela-tionship with certain emotional, sexual or gendered responses; they act as carefully defined affective fields for the poem's characters. 'Sexy spaces' (*sexy Räume*) are those spaces that are suitable for an erotic meeting of the lovers. These spaces, says Thöne, are always gendered feminine, are enclosed, and are hidden from public view: the maternal dwelling, the garden, some parts of the countryside, the vineyard. This gives rise to a

summary comment on the wild natural landscape: 'intimacy is not supported by this con-text; here nature can keep the lovers apart or be an awesome backdrop to their union'. The two ideas, surely, are not simply divergent but mutually exclusive. And because some parts of the Song (most strikingly 1.5-6) are implicated in all four of Falk's con-textual discussions, these spatial-thematic categories seem limited as tools for properly considering the controlling moods of Falk's poetic units, or even individual snippets of text within them. Indeed, this is a crucial problem in thinking about space in the Song: all purpose nostrums that cure the text of its idiosyncrasies violate a particular quality of the text itself, a quality that many commentators would call oneiric, though I prefer the phantasmagorical (see my discussion in Chapter 2).

5. Meik Gerhards, *Das Hohelied: Studien zu seiner literarischen Gestalt und the-ologischen Bedeutung* (Leipzig: Evangelische Verlagsanstalt, 2010), pp. 349-61, and Stefan Fischer, *Das Hohelied Salomos zwischen Poesie und Erzählung: Erzähltextanal-yse eines poetischen Textes* (Tübingen: Mohr Siebeck, 2010), pp. 173-206.

6. Yvonne Sophie Thöne, *Liebe zwischen Stadt und Feld: Raum und Geschlecht im Hohelied* (Berlin: Lit Verlag, 2012). My sincerest thanks go to Dr. Thöne for kindly allowing me access to the proofs during a recent trip to Germany in order that I may make some brief comments here—and for her hospitality, given my rude incursions into her area of expertize.

correlation in the poem between the teasing of physical boundaries and the act of penetrative sex. Thöne thus sees a clear distinction between certain qualities of space in the text (the most notable of which is the distinction between the good garden and the sinister city again) and looks for what pre-determined meanings those spaces delineate for readers.[7]

While at first glance *Liebe zwischen Stadt und Feld* seems to share certain affinities with Falk's work, it is worth stressing that Thöne's full length study is of course far more detailed, and thus more attentive to the variegated quality of space in the Song. Thöne is also more methodologically attuned, treating each literary scene as a product of performative action, using Michel de Certeau's idea that spaces are constituted by social practice as her starting point.[8] Despite these crucial differences, however, what seems to remain in Thöne's rigorous analysis is the broader exercise of resisting the Song's spatial fluidity by means of categorization: sexy, not sexy, masculine, feminine. The divisions beg the question of why the text is more spatially coherent in analysis than it is in reading. Thöne's spatial analysis addresses the ideological relationships of the Song's scenes adroitly, but is it possible to go beyond the ideological relationships between spaces and address the difficulties we face when we try to think about their *spatial* relationships? To put it another way, there is a question that remains, and which draws attention to the difference between the textual sceneographies of Falk, Thöne and others and the textual spatialities that I have been alluding to. What is it about the text that makes these scenes impossible to put on a map? That is, what fundamental spatial operations text exist in the text that sustain these mixtures between spatial clarity and spatial ambiguity and so make the poem's world so difficult to pin down?

Furthermore, certain key questions emerge from Thöne's utilizing of de Certeau's 'performative space' to read texts that require further attention.[9] In short, one could point out that the characters on the biblical page are not the only actors embroiled in enacting the Songscape. There is a spatial performance on the part of the reader too since reading space is also a spatial practice. How does that spatial relationship—the gap between reader and text—affect the ways in which literary spaces come into being? Is the enactment of the Song's literary spaces limited to the actions of textual characters, or do readerly practices shape the Songscape as well? If so, the (now long recognized) openness and subjectivity of the reading process may well

---

7. Thöne's analysis also benefits from a wider study of how the Song's toponyms function in the rest of the Hebrew Bible. This gives her scope to argue that a particular set of gender politics are at work in the poem; Thöne sees the Song as being radical and countercultural in its affirmation of women and female sexuality.

8. See Michel De Certeau, *The Practice of Everyday Life* (trans. Steven Rendall; Berkeley, CA: University of California Press, 1984).

9. A stance that is not limited to de Certeau, as we shall see.

affect the degree to which we could ascribe definitive ideological meanings to the Song's spaces, including even the idea of the garden as a positive ideological space or the city as a sinister one.

These questions and problems are all very well, and pertinent to the particular idiosyncrasies of the Song, but how do we go about addressing them? If existing approaches to the Song's imaginative world have not concentrated on spatial performativity as broadly as we require, and if the openness of the reading process or the frustrations of fluid biblical space are yet to be theorized, how do we begin? What does the wider field of biblical spatial analysis have to offer me in my attempt to map the Songscape, and thus to think about the spatiality of texts in general?

Outside of scholarship on the Song, biblical spatial analysis has flourished in distinct ways of course, though its main development has come through interdisciplinary analyses that employ particular spatial theorists. By far the most trumpeted of these is Henri Lefebvre and his work on the production of space (published in his seminal 1974 work *La production de l'espace),* as well as the rather less important—though no less cited—works of Edward Soja on Thirdspace.[10] For anyone familiar with the available material on biblical space, these two names will be immediately familiar. Indeed, most studies on biblical space (and we shall look at few below) have claimed one or other of this pair as their intellectual pedigree. Thus, suitably theoretically attuned work on space would seem to be ready and to hand for a journey across the Song.[11]

Here though we come up against a particular methodological problem, namely, that our methodological mainstays, Soja and Lefebvre, are spectacularly ill suited to textual analysis, and particularly unsuited to reading the Song of Songs. To anyone familiar with the literature this may seem like quite a claim. After all, to be a writer on biblical spatial was, for a time, to be a reader of Soja and Lefebvre.[12] But there is a case to be made (and I am

10. Henri Lefebvre, *The Production of Space* (trans. Donald Nicholson-Smith; Oxford: Blackwell, 1991); Edward Soja, *Post-modern Geographies: The Reassertion of Space in Critical Social Theory* (London: Verso, 1989); Soja, *Thirdspace: Journeys to Los Angeles and Other Real-and-Imagined-Places* (Oxford: Blackwell, 1996); Soja, *Postmetropolis: Critical Studies of Cities and Regions* (Oxford: Blackwell, 2000). For a handy introduction on Edward Soja and his terminology see Paula McNutt, 'Fathers of the Empty Space' and 'Strangers Forever': Social Marginality and the Construction of Space', in *"Imagining" Biblical Worlds: Studies in Spatial, Social and Historical Constructs in Honor of James W. Flanagan* (Sheffield: Sheffield Academic Press, 2002), p. 35.

11. Henri Lefebvre, *The Production of Space* (trans. Donald Nicholson-Smith; Oxford: Blackwell, 1991); Edward Soja, *Post-modern Geographies: The Reassertion of Space in Critical Social Theory* (London: Verso, 1989); Soja, *Thirdspace: Journeys to Los Angeles and Other Real-and-Imagined-Places* (Oxford: Blackwell, 1996); Soja *Postmetropolis: Critical Studies of Cities and Regions* (Oxford: Blackwell, 2000).

12. If, for example, one takes the three major collections of essays on biblical space

not the first to make it) that the application of Soja and Lefebvre to texts is more troublesome than has been previously been advertized. I want to take a quick look, then, at the Soja-Lefebvre animal (they seem to merge on the biblical scholar's page), if only to highlight some of the aspects of textual spatiality that remain as blind-spots in mainstream biblical spatial analysis, and to ground the very different approach(es) to spatial theory I intend to adopt in the rest of this volume.

Theorists Abroad: Lefebvre and Soja

Space is not even Lefebvre's subject. The very point of Lefebvre's work is to expose and decode modern capitalism in order to empower socialists in their struggle against a pervasive urban, capitalist project.[13] Space is Lefebvre's *means* of engaging with modern urban experience as a whole, but his project does not seek to ground a epistemological theory of space so much as ground a *theory incarnate in history.* Most importantly, the history (and thus the future) that Lefebvre wishes to advocate on these terms is emphatically Marxist. Naturally this is not an intrinsic problem, either for me, or

published to date—*Constructions of Space* I, *Constructions of Space* II, and *'Imagining' Biblical Worlds*—there is a total of thirty-five essays, twenty-three of which appeal beyond the discipline to 'critical' discourse, see Jon L. Berquist and Claudia V. Camp (eds.), *Constructions of Space.* I. *Theory, Geography and Narrative* (Library of Hebrew Bible/Old Testament Studies, 481; London: T. & T. Clark, 2007); Jon L. Berquist and Claudia V. Camp (eds.), *Constructions of Space* II. *The Biblical City and Other Imagined Spaces* (Library of the Hebrew Bible/Old Testament Studies, 490; London: T. & T. Clark, 2008); David Gunn and Paula McNutt (eds.), *'Imagining' Biblical Worlds: Studies in Spatial, Social and Historical Constructs in Honor of James W. Flanagan* (Sheffield: Sheffield Academic Press, 2002). Of these twenty-three essays no less than nineteen employ Soja's work as a methodology. Of the remaining four, three appeal directly to Lefebvre, albeit a Lefebvre of curiously Sojan construction; two utilize no particular theoretical framework pertaining to spatial relations, and the remaining one is Tina Pippin, 'The Ideological of Apocalyptic Space', in Berquist and Camp (eds.), *Constructions of Space*, II, pp. 156-70. Pippin seems to be the exception to this rule in these volumes in that she deals with a huge variety of spatial scholars from a variety of fields. There are, of course, a few other exceptions to this rule. A notable one is Jorunn Økland's book *Women in their Place: Paul and the Corinthian Discourse of Gender and Space* (JSNTSup, 269; London: T. & T. Clark, 2004), which adopts a far more nuanced approach to the question of spatial construction and inscription. Two major monographs on space in the Hebrew Bible have emerged in recent years as well: Christl Maier's *Daughter Zion, Mother Zion* (Minneapolis, MN: Fortress Press, 2008) and Mark George's *Israel's Tabernacle as Social Space* (Ancient Israel and its Literature, 2; Atlanta, GA: Society of Biblical Literature, 2009). The latter relies on Lefebvre's work, the former on a combination of Soja and Lefebvre. Maier's Lefebvre has a strangely Sojan flavor, as I discuss below.

13. Lefebvre, *The Production of Space*, p. 24.

for the rest of the vaguely leftish, theory-toting wing of academia. But it is worth noting that in importing Lefebvre into the biblical text we do not simply gain an informed thinker on space for biblical studies, we get quite a lot of Marxist historical preoccupation along with him.

One major theme underwriting *La production de l'espace* is that of Marxist periodization—Marx's claim that human history can be divided into discrete epochs, each of which is characterized by a particular mode of production, and which anticipate Socialism as their zenith.[14] *La production de l'espace* essentially constitutes a spatialization of Marx's first volume of *Kapital*,[15] Lefebvre's goal being to understand the determinate spatialities that concretize each of these epochs. Thus Lefebvre's work on space cannot really be posited outside of his Marxist preoccupations, at least not without an awful lot of ideological transposition.[16] The particular problem with a (faithfully applied) Lefebvran perspective is that such an approach can deal only with a society's major spaces, the spaces that define it as an epoch, or which help us understand the economic modes of production that mark it out as singular: temple, city-state, feudal manor, football pitch, and so on. Lefebvran theory is concerned with the bright lights of public historical

14. Boer offers a comprehensive summary of this in a handy tabulated form (Boer, 'Henri Lefebvre: The Production of Space in 1 Samuel', p. 86). These run from an 'absolute space' (a primal, natural space, and not to be confused with Kant's notion of Euclidean space) in Neolithic hunter/gatherer societies, then to 'sacred space' during the reign of divine ('despot-') kings, then to the historicized space of the Greco-Roman city-states. Lefebvre then tracks a return to a sacred space enmeshed in the hierarchies of feudalism before moving on to assess a kind of 'abstract space' (cf. Marx's *abstract labour*) at work in early capitalism. As Andy Merrifield puts it: 'Here [in capitalist abstract space] exigencies of banks, business centres, productive agglomerations, information networks, law and order, reign supreme—or try to.', Merrifield, 'Henri Lefebvre: A Socialist in Space', in Mike Crang and Nigel Thrift (eds.), *Thinking Space* (New York: Routledge, 2000), p. 176. This abstract space, Lefebvre insists, is also a *male* space, the phallic verticality of the skyscraper acting as the 'spatial expression of a potentially violent power' (Lefebvre, *The Production of Space*, p. 98). In turn, late capitalism produces contradictory space, a global community in which meaning remains localized, with the individual and the global locked into a centre-periphery jig of no mean ferocity. Communism is concretized in and as 'differential space', the space that celebrates particularity in body and experience.

15. Karl Marx, *Das Kapital: Kritik der Politischen Oekonomie* (Berlin: Otto Meisner, 1867).

16. He was actually expelled from the French Communist party in 1957 for being too unpredictable. For more see Roland Boer, 'Henri Lefebvre: The Production of Space in 1 Samuel', in Jon L. Berquist and Claudia V. Camp (eds.), *Constructions of Space, II. The Biblical City and Other Imagined Spaces* (Library of the Hebrew Bible/Old Testament Studies, 490; London: T. & T. Clark, 2008), p. 80; Merrifield, 'Henri Lefebvre: A Socialist in Space', p. 178: 'His Marxism is more about love and life than Five Year Plans. His Marxism sounds more like libertarian anarchism'.

space, not with the darker nooks, crannies and book alleys that constitute private life. What we do with our emotionally charged personal spaces, our marginal, our hidden and disused spaces is none of Lefebvre's concern. Economic approaches to space are important, naturally, but what do we do with the silly, the romantic, and the sexual? What do we do with the over-looked spaces that actually tend to constitute our everyday worlds?

This particularity in Lefebvre's approach to space is precisely what Holly Prescott calls attention to in her critique of the well-known appropriations of *La production de l'espace* in literary studies.[17] Literary spatial studies based on Lefebvre simply launch, she says, a 'commentary upon our era's dominant, authoritative representations of space'.[18] In other words, in literary analysis Lefebvran theory has simply, and predictably, become a mode of translating our 'real' relationships with space; properly decoded, textual spaces serve to interpret our non-literary contexts and little more. Fiction tells us about historical spatiality, but it does not constitute, epistemologically speaking, a real world of its own apparently. Prescott, by contrast, is concerned with the ways in which literary spaces function by 'exceeding human attempts to contain them either through imaginary containment or through available processes of mapping'.[19] She is interested in literary spaces as affective spaces in their own right, and with those literary spaces, and those literary responses to space, that simply refuse to fit into Lefebvre's historical schema. This is vital because in reality textual worlds are not simply determined by the economic conditions and social mores surrounding the text's production but by the demands of plot, by the imaginative impositions of the reader, and by a whole host of subjective factors by which we, as human beings, continually bring spaces into being and then cast them off.

If Lefebvre's work does not always adequately account for the phenomenological experience of reading, if it sometimes seems lacking as an approach to interpreting the gamut of literary spaces we come across as readers, it is because it was never designed for such a use. As Philip Davies notes in his (pointedly) non-theoretical approach to biblical space, Lefebvre famously cautioned against applying his work to literature: 'any search for

---

17. Prescott looks at the Lefebvran analyses of Andrew Thacker, *Moving Through Modernity: Space and Geography in Modernism* (Manchester: Manchester University Press, 2003); Ian Davidson, *Ideas of Space in Contemporary Poetry* (Basingstoke: Palgrave Macmillan, 2007); David Cooper, 'The Poetics of Place and Space: Wordsworth, Norman Nicholson and the Lake District', *Literature Compass* 5 (2008), pp. 807-21; Michael Wiley, *Romantic Geography: Wordsworth and Anglo-European Spaces* (Basingstoke: Palgrave, 1998); see, Holly Prescott, 'Rethinking Urban Space in Contemporary British Writing' (PhD Thesis: University of Birmingham, 2011).

18. Holly Prescott, 'Rethinking Urban Space', p. 43.

19. Prescott, 'Rethinking Urban Space', p. 43.

space in literary texts will find it everywhere and in every guise; encoded, described, projected, dreamt of, speculated about'.[20] This is not a reason to abandon either textual space (so Lefebvre), or theory (so Davies), since Lefebvre's sentiment actually neatly stresses the importance of textual space. We need to look though for ways of engaging with textual space that are not dependent on, as Prescott puts it, a 'theoretical standpoint that negates the potential of literature'.[21]

My objection to the use of Edward Soja's work as a methodological main-stay in biblical spatial studies is a more straightforward case to make, since Soja's theories have been so widely criticized in his own field (where, by all accounts, his work does not enjoy nearly so much prominence as it does among biblical scholars). Soja's 'experiential' analysis is widely perceived to be detached and partial by other geographers and usually needs bolster-ing with other theoretical methods, an allegation that Sojan approaches in biblical studies more than bear out.

Soja's work is an adaptation of Lefebvre's and Soja seeks to foreground the ways in which space and power collude in society. To this end, Soja uses a trialectic (a three-way dialectic, again borrowed and heavily adapted from Lefebvre), consisting of Firstspace, the physical aspect of space, space as a measurable empirical reality; Secondspace, space as imagined and ide-ologized, the conceptions of space that govern its use and its representa-tion (maps, cultural space-stereotypes etc.); and Thirdspace, space as lived and experienced. Thirdspace thus encompasses and transcends First and Sec-ondspace, reopening the dichotomy between physicality and ideology. Third-space is intended to disrupt the physical/ideological dichotomy and its claims to exhaustiveness by introducing embodied, experienced space as a third way. Soja famously sums up Thirdspace as a fairly all-encompassing arena:

> *Everything* comes together in Thirdspace: subjectivity and objectivity, the abstract and the concrete, the real and the imagined, the knowable and the unimaginable, the repetitive and the differential, structure and agency, mind and body, consciousness and unconsciousness, the disciplined and the trans-disciplinary, everyday life and unending history.[22]

In terms of the application of the Sojan trialectic to biblical texts, the sig-nificance of Soja's theory seems to vary between biblical scholars.[23] For

---

20. Lefebvre, *The Production of Space*, p. 15; Philip Davies, 'Space and Sects in the Qumran Scrolls', in David Gunn and Paula McNutt (eds.), *'Imagining' Biblical Worlds*, pp. 81-98 (81).

21. Prescott, 'Rethinking Urban Space', p. 43.

22. Soja, *Thirdspace*, pp. 56-57.

23. In Biblical scholars' dealings with Lefebvre, though, it often seems as if Lefeb-vre has been read through Soja's reductions. Jon Berquist's introduction to critical spa-tial theory says, for example: 'Soja followed Lefebvre's tripartite conceptualization of

instance, Susan Graham breaks down Justinian's Nea Ekklesia in Jerusalem into its physical dimensions (its Firstspace), the concepts and mapping projects that depict and codify it (its Secondspatial representations), and argues that the Nea Ekklesia's failure to enter into the cultural *Gestalt*—which she sees as corresponding to Soja's Thirdspace—accounts for its eventual disappearance from the city.[24] Whether or not the Nea's worshipping community, the patients in its two hospices, and the numerous builders who worked, and in all probability sometimes died, during its construction would attest to the idea that the Nea was 'non-experiential', however, is a question that hangs over this conclusion. Though perhaps this issue is less a problem with Graham's discussion than with the awkward, all-encompassing nature of Soja's Thirdspace itself.

Similarly, Kathryn Lopez uses Soja's model to map the spatiality of Jewish apocalyptic literature. For Lopez, Jewish Firstspace is 'the little strip of land on the shore of the eastern Mediterranean'; its Secondspaces are the numerous, controversial attempts to map ('or even name') this land.[25] So far this all seems clear, but in Lopez's discussion Thirdspace turns out to be synonymous with apocalyptic literature itself, which, says Lopez, creates an 'alternative lived space' within the tradition, a space beyond the everyday.[26] The term 'alternative' is suggestive, of course. It assumes there

space, but used different terminology' (Berquist, 'Critical Spatiality and the Uses of Theory', in Berquist and Camp [eds.], *Constructions of Space*, I, p. 3), but terminology is just one of several substantive differences between the two theorists' works. William Miller reads Lefebvre's 'lived space' as an equivalent to Soja's reductions (through the canny use of parenthesis): 'lived space (Soja's Thirdspace)'; see, William R. Miller, 'A Bakhtinian Reading of Narrative Space and its Relationship to Social Space', in Berquist and Camp (eds.), *Constructions of Space*, I, p. 132. Hui Jolly sums up Lefebvre's work as a series of conspicuously Sojan categories: 'Lefebvre understood spatial awareness as a potentially liberating dynamic process of interaction, a tensive movement within a threefold dialectical (trialectic) process, often encapsulated in the phrases perceived space (or spatial practice), conceived space, and lived space.' Marie Huie-Jolly, 'Language as Extension of Desire: The Oedipus Complex and Spatial Hermeneutics', in Berquist and Camp (eds.), *Constructions of Space*, I, p. 70. Huie-Jolly does acknowledge the fluidity of Lefebvre's discussion, though this mixedness seems not to touch her overall discussions, which treat Lefebvre's paradigm as epistemologically fixed. Claudia Camp is forced to resort to hyphenating the two names into a single encompassing neologism, 'Soja(-Lefebvre)', as though the theorists comprize a single bimorphic creature (Claudia Camp, 'Introduction', in Berquist and Camp [eds.], *Constructions of Space*, II, p. 4).

24. Susan Graham, 'Justinian and the Politics of Space', in Berquist and Camp (eds.), *Constructions of Space*, II, pp. 51-77.

25. Kathryn Lopez, 'Standing Before the Throne of God: Critical Spatiality in Apocalyptic Scenes of Judgement', in Berquist and Camp (eds.), *Constructions of Space*, II, pp. 139-55 (141).

26. Lopez, 'Standing Before the Throne of God', p. 141.

are other kinds of lived experience *outside* apocalyptic literature. This stands to reason but it introduces *two* types of Thirdspace—apocalyptic literature, and 'normal' life—which it would seem are vying for attention in Lopez's work. But Soja's Thirdspace is supposed to subvert binary oppositions; it is supposed to be their final and inexhaustible answer.[27] Is the trialectic categorizing space, or infinitely multiplying its own structures—and is this multiplication at odds with its value as a parsing tool? Again this is not a comment on Lopez's insightful essay but rather a query about whether Soja's paradigm—semantically *and* epistemologically—can work as hard as Lopez needs it to.

In fact, the common theme in all Sojan readings of biblical space is the drafting in of secondary theoretical ballast to make Thirdspace work as a critical model despite itself. Susan Graham uses Maurice Halbwachs to this end; Lopez calls upon Foucault; Marie Huie-Jolly recruits Winnicott and Freud; Miller: Bakhtin. Perhaps this accounts for the marked differences in how Thirdspace is imagined to function as a 'critical' term in each of these scholar's essays.[28] One cannot help but wonder if the difference between these Thirdspaces is a result of Thirdspace's own epistemological vagueness, its tendency to collapse when put into practice.[29]

These kinds of criticism are not novel. Other spatial theorists have long suggested that these problems are endemic in the Thirdspace model. Earlier I

---

27. Surely the view that apocalyptic literature acts as a 'representation of alternative religious and political realities', as Lopez puts it, is more an *ideological* stance than a lived one anyway.

28. Crucially, these secondary theorists are seldom allowed to speak on their own spatial terms. Each is subjected to a lengthy enculturation into Soja-Lefebvre's trialectic model, turning trispace—a theory of multiplicity—into a disconcertingly one-dimensional sub-specialism, and, arguably, forcing useful intellectual work into a mould that has been debunked in its own field.

29. Claudia Camp raises precisely this point in one of the earlier essays on biblical Thirdspace: 'I struggle with this formulation of Thirdspace as "lived" space. There are two issues here. First, in what we usually call "real life", lived space is infused with the ideologies that would in the spatial trialectic be categorized as Secondspatial. This is not simply true in the sense that Secondspace represents the power that Thirdspace resists…[r]esistance is also a form of power and requires its own ideologies, all the more so if it is to be used effectively… Secondly, oppressors also have lived spaces… living involves a lot of things, including the production of power that makes critique and resistance necessary… This more jaundiced approach to Thirdspace is not the result of abstract reflection on my part regarding Soja's theory of critical spatiality. It is, rather, the result of my attempt to apply this theory to the book of Sirach. Sirach has spatial discourse aplenty and seems ripe for this sort of analysis. Yet I have struggled in applying the spatial trialectic here, partly because the boundaries between one sort of place and another keep collapsing when the matter of power comes into play' (Camp, 'Storied Space, or, Ben Sira "Tells" a Temple', in Gunn and McNutt [eds.], *"Imagining" Biblical Worlds*, pp. 68-69).

quoted Soja's own attempt to define Thirdspace· '*Everything* comes together in Thirdspace...' This very definition prompted one expert reviewer, Clive Barnett, to enquire as to whether Elvis might still be alive in Thirdspace.[30] Though Barnett's tongue was obviously lodged firmly in his cheek, the remark is indicative of widespread scepticism about the efficacy of Soja's model. Thirdspace means far too much and, as a result, not nearly enough for it to be useful as a tool for critical reflection. Thirdspace seems in fact to function as an all-purpose nostrum, a formula that covers up a lack of phenomenology in a study that claims to privilege personal perspective. Alan Latham sums this diagnosis up perfectly:

> Thirdspace is claimed to encompass everything there is to say about anything (and perhaps, as a result, nothing at all?)... In his keenness to stress just how new his 'radical postmodernism' is, Soja seems to completely de-anchor himself from any established intellectual tradition. This compels him to work at a level of abstraction that undermines some of the most productive and interesting elements of his argument.[31]

A good example is Soja's discussion of 'Disneyfied' districts in Orange County. This discussion is one of the most compelling parts of *Thirdspace* and, obviously, focuses on real, specific communities, honing in on particular spaces and spatial responses. But nowhere does Soja discuss individual or on-the-ground experiences within these communities. In fact Soja assiduously avoids the embodied subject upon whom his theory relies and for whom it tries to win freedom. As Latham put it, 'a question remains about the connection between Soja's theoretical foundations and his empirical narratives'.[32] If Soja himself cannot marry theory, narrative and character in discussion, we should be asking some serious questions about whether Soja's model 'works' for biblical scholars—for whom narrative, text, and character are primary, and interlocked, concerns.[33]

---

30. Clive Barnett, 'Review of Thirdspace: Journeys to Los Angeles and Other Real-and-Imagined-Places', in *Transactions, Institute of British Geographers* (1997), pp. 529-30.

31. Alan Latham, 'Edward Soja', in Hubbard, Kitchen and Valentine (eds.), *Key Thinkers on Space and Place*, p. 273.

32. Latham, 'Edward Soja', p. 273.

33. The issue of gender refocuses these problems particularly well, since it is an issue in which particularity, ideology and social praxis are intimately connected. Soja's own relationship with gender criticism is famously uneasy of course. His first book, *Post-modern Geographies*, omits women entirely (bar an odd reference to those who conflate Marxism with totalitarianism and 'radical feminism [with]...the destruction of the family'). The omission drew the attention of his feminist colleagues, particularly Doreen Massey, who mounted serious charges against *Post-modern Geographies*, questioning its postmodern credentials and highlighting its narrow treatment of social inequality. Or, as Massey herself puts it, patriarchy does not appear in Soja's index. She writes: 'Racism

What underwrites this fleeting snapshot of mainstream biblical spatial scholarship and its antecedents is a fundamental epistemological assumption that has skewed work on literary space in a particular direction: that space exists to be summarily decoded. In the work of Soja, Lefebvre and their disciples, historical spaces are reduced to the state of inaccessible social texts that must be interpreted, with biblical texts being made to stand in for the textuality of their historical counterparts: city, temple, and so forth. What we find in much of biblical spatial studies is an equivalency between historicity and spatiality, where the focus seems to be on deciphering historical spaces through the ways in which (biblical) texts report them.[34] Textual space thereby becomes a kind of supplement to historical space, and space continues to be a term associated with the so-called 'real world', the concrete world of extra-textual experience. That literary spaces might be perceived as experiential worlds in their own right, spaces traversed by characters and readers alike, seems not to appear in the literature as a fully formed idea.[35] Is this perhaps a reason why the works of Lefebvre and Soja

and sexism, and the need to refer to them, is recognized [in *Post-modern Geographies*] but it is assumed throughout, either explicitly or implicitly, that the only axis of power which matters in relation to these distinct forms of domination is that which stems fairly directly from the relations of production. No other relations of power and dominance are seriously addressed.' See, Doreen Massey, *Space, Place and Gender* (Minneapolis, MN: University of Minnesota Press, 1994), pp. 221-22. Soja simply does not acknowledge diversity or individuality in society, content instead to sketch overarching mega-categories: 'peripheralized-and-oppressed' versus 'relations of production'. This single oppressed mass is not only ungendered but viewed from the exclusive vantage point of the white Western heterosexual male. The result is what some geographers have called a 'god's eye-view' of Los Angeles in the last chapters of *Post-modern Geographies*. Soja's attempt to illustrate thirdspatial emancipation becomes an example of hegemony-by-culture and of hegemony-by-gender, imbibing the very hierarchical dualisms that post-modern projects usually try to subvert.

34. Now, all this is not to say that historical issues are completely unimportant. The project of history, though itself a series of contested textualities, is not always narrating an orthodoxy. History can help us to destabilize meanings as well. There is always another story to be told. So I am not suggesting that we do away with every offering that history can make us (and I shall be putting some of the cultural history of gardens to work myself in Chapter 3), but the particular role that history has been playing in biblical spatial analysis—as a controling critical paradigm—needs to be renegotiated. The problems and blind spots I have been discussing necessitate that.

35. Claudia Camp's aforementioned article does briefly address this issue, noting, particularly, that texts are worlds inhabited by readers and characters alike. Her discussion of Ben Sira's retelling of the temple also treats the particular textual space narrated in Ben Sira as a legitimate edifice in its own right. It is worth bearing in mind, however, that Camp's specific comments on the inhabitability of textual worlds are made as a direct critique of Soja's position, and that Camp's overall conclusions on the text of Ben Sira are situated in terms of an historically attuned discussion rather than a purely

have gained so much ground in biblical circles? The idea of words being spatial is not so easy to champion as the idea of a historical city, temple or tabernacle operating as a world of meaning.

Other Cartographies

Naturally, there are other ways to theorize spatial relationships.[36] One particular perspective this volume will explore is that space is not merely a

literary one. That is, Camp's discussion does not directly evince the kinds of problems I am discussing here, but their traces are nevertheless still visible (Camp, 'Ben Sira Tells a Temple, p. 67).

36. I should point out that more explicit literary approaches to space do exist. These are usually smaller chapters in broader, introductory works on the Bible as Literature. This study does not quite sit comfortably in their mold. The two principle examples are the chapter 'Time and Space' in Shimon Bar-Efrat's book *Narrative Art in the Bible*, and a similarly named chapter, 'Time and Space, Entrances and Exits', in Jan Fokkelman's *Reading Biblical Narrative: An Introductory Guide*. Bar-Efrat overwhelmingly favors the temporal aspect of the text over the spatial, even when space is the stated object of his inquiry: '[There are] appreciable differences between the dimensions of time and space in narrative. First of all, there is no parallel relationship in the realm of space to that between narration time and narrated time. Space exists within narrative but the narrative does not exist within space, and therefore the internal space of the narrative is realized not in external space (as in a painting) but in external time (Bar-Efrat, *Narrative Art in the Bible* [London: T. & T. Clark, 2004 (1989)], p. 184). The subservience of space to time actually becomes clearer as one progresses through the relevant chapter until, by the closing paragraph, space has disappeared as an 'appreciable' category altogether: 'the biblical narrative is wholly devoted to creating a sense of time' Bar-Efrat writes, 'and this is inevitably achieved at the expense of the shaping of space' (p. 195).

Fokkelman's essay sees space and time quite differently. Moving away from the Kantian presuppositions of Bar Efrat, and toward more of an Einsteinian paradigm, Fokkelman acknowledges time and space as 'almost inseparable dimensions of one and the same coordinate system' (he actually makes casual reference to quantum mechanics!) But for Fokkelman's purposes a text's spatial and temporal markers are primarily useful as exegetical signposts that allow narratives to be subdivided for analysis: 'when we succeed in making a correct division of the text into its various parts,' he begins the chapter, 'everything comes together' (Fokkelman, *Reading Biblical Narrative: An Introductory Guide* [Louisville, KY: Westminster/John Knox Press, 1995], p. 97). What this 'structuration' inevitably produces is a set of neat chiastic patterns, of which Fokkelman gives various examples. These are, obviously, useful in literary critical analysis, but in fairly specific ways that do not especially intersect with my interests here.

A third, more recent, approach to spatiality in the Hebrew Bible is a slim volume by Luke Gärtner-Brereton rather loquaciously entitled, *The Ontology of Space in Biblical Hebrew Narrative: The Determinate Function of Narrative 'Space' within the Biblical Hebrew Aesthetic* (London: Equinox, 2008). A full exposition of Gärtner-Brereton's approach is not possible here. In short, Gärtner-Brereton's attitude toward space is symptomatic of a wider sense in non-specialist thought that textual spatiality does not transcend 'setting'. Perspective, gaze, affinities, experiences, movements, journeys,

'social text' so much as the necessary precondition of all social relationships. Doreen Massey proposes this when she sketches out her own basic
sense of what space is and how it should be understood in critical discourse:

> We [must] understand space as the sphere of contemporaneous plurality; as
> the sphere in which distinct trajectories coexist; as the sphere therefore of
> coexisting heterogeneity. Without space, no multiplicity; without multiplic-
> ity, no space.[37]

Space is the necessary precondition of contemporaneous plurality and contemporaneous pluralities, likewise, give rise to space. In other words, space
is the field of the simultaneous. This has significant implications for the
way we perceive space when we work with it as a critical category. For to
say that a focus on space allows us to seize upon multiplicitous and simultaneous relationships is the same as saying that spatiality gives us a view of
an overall system, and what makes that system possible. Where the axis of
time allows for an analysis that progresses in terms of *development*, then,
the axis of space allows for an analysis that opens up thinking on *systemicity*. To my mind, the most significant legacy of Soja and Lefebvre's in
biblical analysis has been to obscure this basic sense of space as the field
of contemporaneous simultaneity. Mainstream biblical spatial analysis has
thus also obscured the corollary of that thought: that text is an inherently
spatial enterprise.

For texts may describe spaces, but the text itself, and the language it is
written in, are systems of contemporaneousness as well. These systems presume and come to form spaces of their own. To think about literary space is
not simply to think about imaginative settings (though it certainly involves
that). Rather, to think about literary space is to think about the fact that
space makes language possible. To think about literary space is to think
about the systemicity of a text, and the systemicity of our engagements
with it as readers. Thus the task of spatial reading is not simply to decode
space, but to use space to get at the logic of 'decoding' itself. Every space
in the Bible is not a further text to be read and adorned with footnotes, but
each instance of us reading it is a spatiality that requires analysis. Analysis of literary space is not simply a matter of our affirming that space is textual and then *reading*, but of realizing that text is spatial and then *exploring*.

actions, vectors, bodies—all of which presuppose spatiality in a broader sense—not to
mention the spatiality of text itself, are entirely effaced from his discussion. Setting,
meanwhile, is reified to the point of textual dysmorphia. For a more detailed, if rather
honest, appraisal of Gärtner-Brereton's volume see Deane Galbraith, 'Review of Luke
Gärtner-Brereton, *The Ontology of Space in Biblical Hebrew Narrative: The Determinate Function of Narrative 'Space' within the Biblical Hebrew Aesthetic*' in *Bible and
Critical Theory* 5 (2009), pp. 45.1-45.3.

37. Doreen Massey, *For Space* (London: Sage, 2005), p. 9.

In the context of a spatial reading of the Song, these issues become paramount. If we are to engage with the space of the Song, it is not sufficient to parse out its spatial referents into First, Second and Thirdspaces, nor, indeed, to subordinate the whole text to a particular epoch in Karl Marx's grand plan. If we are to assess the spatiality of the Song without losing its sense of emotional affectation and fluidity, if we are to map its spaces without simply forcing it to succumb to our own orderly sensibilities, we need to think about its systemicity rather than just its layout. We need to consider the way in which it creates a sense of contemporaneous plurality rather than the way it creates a sense of contrast, and we must acknowledge the ways in which, as a love poem, it is duty-bound to evoke a sense of the simultaneous—since its lovers, like our leather-bound text, need space to exist at all.

Exploring Text and Con-Text with Derrida

This complex relationship between presence, textuality and spatiality is precisely what Jacques Derrida was referring to in his now infamous axiom, *il n'y a pas de hors-texte*, 'there is no outside-text'.[38] Contrary to popular misapprehensions, Derrida's axiom is neither an affirmation that only texts matter, nor that textuality is our only mode of engaging with reality, nor, indeed, that the mechanics of text give us a blueprint for how everyday life is endowed with meaning. Derrida's point is that any attempt to situate a text does not end up revealing a pure 'context' for it (as is usually hoped). Situating a text—historically, thematically, in terms of its genre, etc.—only uncovers more words, more attempts to open meaning using discourse. 'There has never been anything but writing', Derrida goes on, 'there have never been anything but supplements, substantive significations which could come forth only in a chain of differential references'. In other words, context cannot be apprehended without recourse to further textual fabrication and to further supplements, each woven from signs and symbols. Attempting to unravel a context gives rise only to more glyphs, every one composed of more intricate strands, more entangled 'texts' with their own frayed edges. 'And thus to infinity.' (Of course in these terms, like Derrida's text, space is also always already thought of. Space, like text, is impossible to circumscribe without generating its self-multiplication. If we drew a line around all space, enclosing space itself, we would succeed only in creating another frontier that begged exploration.) Finding the edge of textuality serves not to define text by means of history. The 'edge' of text, intended to define, only creates an interface that incites more reading.

38. Jacques Derrida, *Of Grammatology* (trans. Gayatri Chakravorty Spivak; Baltimore, MD: Johns Hopkins University Press, 1997 [1974]), pp. 158-59.

Written texts still have their own borders of course (the page, the margin, the dust-jacket), but these borders do not back onto a non-textual 'signified'—in Derrida's studies in *Of Grammatology*, a 'real' Rousseau or his 'real' world. The text's context and its author are simply incitements to meaning, contrary, plural and supplemental. Worlds breed texts, but it is also the case that texts themselves give rise to their literary contexts: we infer these contexts, retroactively posit them around books,[39] and, vitally, only explicate these worlds and their inhabitants by recourse to yet more text. In the same way, the Bible has its own canonical edges, disputed as they are, but it does not back onto a real context, or a set of transcendent historical spaces. Instead, the edges of our writings are interfaces that incite other textual operations: the never-ending 'supplements' of a richly embroidered con-text. The biblical landscape is as much a product of the textual worlds we find in the Bible, as its textual worlds are a product of the landscape. Derrida is not lionizing written text *per se* when he writes *il n'y a pas de hors-texte* but arguing that textuality is a system that relies upon and creates further textualities; there is no realm of 'outside-text' to which one can appeal without textual entanglement. We are always 'within' text already. Text knows no bounds.

The interplay between textualities and spatialities that is implicit within this kind of discourse 'on' texts raises problems for the idea that the Bible-as-text can map and explicate historical space. Such a project of historical spatial analysis turns out to be an infinite deferment of meaning, shuttling as it does between the claims of the textual upon the contextual and the claims of the contextual upon the text. To put it bluntly, the issue of space, history and text is an impossible triad to 'parse' out, even if the grammatology we were to employ were more dependable than Soja's. Textuality and spatiality are mutually formed modalities of meaning.

By demonstrating the illegitimacy of all that claims to be 'beyond' text, Derrida points us to the unavoidable synonymy between textuality and internality. If there cannot be an outside-text then it holds that to be textual is to be held within. In a bastardization of one of Merleau-Ponty's[40] phrases, we

---

39. The archetypal example, of course, is the English adjective 'Dickensian'.

40. Merleau-Ponty, and the Husserlian school of phenomenology, provided one of the intellectual frameworks that Lefebvre sought to open out to broader interdisciplinary treatment (see *The Production of Space*, pp. 21-22). In his key work *Phenomenology of Perception*, Merleau-Ponty essentially argues for a new way of understanding how we interact with the world. One of the most important considerations in understanding *Phenomenology of Perception* is Merleau-Ponty's re-consideration of the human body. Merleau-Ponty puts the body back into the centre of questions about self, other and space, figuring it as a living corporeal extension of consciousness rather than as a lump of meat occupied by the higher pilot of the mind or *cogito*. For Merleau-Ponty, the world is neither tethered facts nor a sustained illusion generated by the mind. Rather the

might say that *being readerly is synonymous with being situated*. Text is not a closed system, but, and as Derrida would have it, it is an enclosing one:

> The question therefore is not only of Rousseau's writing but also of our reading. We should begin by taking rigorous account of this *being held within* [*prise*] or this *surprise*: the writer writes *in* a language and *in* a logic whose proper system, laws and life his [sic] discourse by definition cannot dominate absolutely. He uses them only by letting himself, after a fashion and up to a point, be governed by that system. And the reading must always aim at a certain relationship, unperceived by the writer, between what he commands and what he does not command of the patterns of language that he uses. This relationship is not a certain qualitative distribution of shadow and light, of weakness or of force, but a signifying structure that critical reading should *produce*.

external world and the personal consciousness are part of a single whole, a mutually constituting pair. Perception is the process of this mutual constitution. We do not perceive the world either because the transcendental Ego is continually constructing it with no basis at all, or because it is empirically knowable as a series of impersonal facts (every fact is essentially an *experience*, Merleau-Ponty insists). Instead, the world constitutes my consciousness by inviting it to partake of its elements, while my consciousness summons images appropriate to the world's invitations. So, the body-subject constitutes the world—allowing it to become real through sensing it—and is constituted *by* the world, which invites it to sense, to perceive, to take action and thus to have power *as* a consciousness. Perception is thus the process by which subject and world enter a mutually enforcing dialectic of creation.

While Merleau-Ponty is not seeking a unified theory on space *per se*, his phenomenological reductions obviously have implications for the way we discuss and grasp space as an experience (not, one notes, as a thing, vessel, or container as in Plato). Merleau-Ponty's phenomenology rejects the idea of the dichotomous divide between space and object in favor of a singular, inclusive, dynamic system. The divide attacked in this instance, of course, is not the *cogito*/world divide but the Kantian assumption of a distinction between 'space' as a sort of ether and the 'objects' that it contains. If Being is characterized as a process of dialectical inter-creation as Merleau-Ponty is suggesting, my body wears the world thrown around it and the world also prompts my body to respond towards it. As Merleau Ponty puts it in *Phenomenology of Perception*, 'This means instead of imaging it [space] as a kind of ether in which all things float, or conceiving it abstractly as a characteristic that they have in common, we must think of it [space] as the universal power enabling them to be connected... I catch space at its source, and now think the relationships which underlie this word, realizing that they live only through the medium of a subject who traces out and sustains them; and pass from spatialized to spatializing space (p. 284). Not only does this deal a blow to Kant and Descartes's dividing line between *cogito* and world, it shifts the emphasis of existential philosophy off the *cogito* and onto relational dynamics—crucially, not sociological relatedness but rather the fundamental interrelations of our perceptual processes, where spatiality and subjectivity are forces in eternal cahoots, see Maurice Merleau-Ponty, *Phenomenology of Perception* (trans. C. Smith; New York: Routledge, 2002 [1964]); Komarine Romdenh-Romluc, *Merleau-Ponty and Phenomenology of Perception* (New York: Routledge, 2011), pp.162-63.

> What does produce mean here? In my attempt to explain that, I would ini-
> tiate a justification of my principles of reading. A justification, as we shall
> see, entirely negative, outlining by exclusion a space of reading that I shall
> not fill here: a task of reading.[41]

To say that Rousseau writes *in* a language, or that I read *in* another, is not simply an idiomatic turn of phrase but an affirmation of the situatedness of both writing and reading, it is a statement that recognizes reading as a double inhabitation: 'I am *within* the history of psychoanalysis just as I am *within* Rousseau's text', as Derrida puts it.[42]

All text is shot through with this politics of internality. Not only does the very idea of textual communication assume a navigable 'gap' between reader and text, reading also involves the spatial structuration of the page (columns, paragraphs, footnotes) and the vectorizing power of the sentence, which carries us from left to right (or right to left, or top to bottom) across that page. Moreover, reading assumes one's involvement *in* a language and *in* a culture while one is reading. And, not least, reading involves the reader's inhabitation of the imagined spaces that texts prompt their readers to produce (Middle Earth, the Hundred Acre Wood, biblical Israel). Derrida's work does not suggest that these varied 'locations'—in a language, on a fictive landmass, halfway through a paragraph—are comparable or equivalent spaces but *that they are simultaneous*. All these readerly locations are multiplications of the same 'signifying structure': to read is to inhabit. Within is the only position from which reading is possible, culturally, phenomenologically and cognitively. Text constitutes an inside with no outside. *Il n'y a pas de hors-texte.*[43] For Derrida's purposes, this proposition that 'there is nothing outside the text' designates text, and Rousseau's text particularly, as an 'indefinitely multiplied structure—*en abyme* [in an abyss]' (an idea we shall circle back to later).

Derrida's provocation on text notwithstanding, some kind of spatial epistemology would seem to be required before we can go much further in trying to reimaging what it might look like to 'map' the Song of Songs.

41. Derrida, *Of Grammatology*, p. 158.
42. Derrida, *Of Grammatology*, p. 158.
43. Derrida, *Of Grammatology*, p. 163. Derrida's work on Rousseau similarly traces the textual 'abyss'—the famous 'supplements'—looking at the duplicating strategies that make Rousseau's texts a description of textuality itself. In literary critical parlance, *en abyme* comes to operate as a term that describes any part of a text that reproduces the entire structure of that text. André Gide introduced the term in 1892, in an article citing paintings by Memlin in which a mirror *in* the painting reflects the whole of the scene, and to scale (we shall see something similar at work in the process of 'reading' Dali's paintings below). See André Gide, 'Pleiade', in *Journal 1889–1939* (Paris: Gallimard, 1951), p. 41. For an excellent treatment of the term in the late twentieth-century see Craig Owens, 'Photography "*en abyme*"', *October* 5 (1978), pp. 73-88.

Derrida can highlight just how embroiled space and text are, and so broaden out how we imagine what an approach to spatiality, textuality and their interfaces might involve, but as a cartographer he really does not go the whole way. Who can we read along with if not Soja or Lefebvre?

Worlds of Meaning in Benjamin's Labyrinth

> Benjamin recalls a 'violent' desire, which seized him in Paris, in the Café des Deux Magots, to schematize in diagrammatic form his own life. The result was what he calls a 'labyrinth' of 'originary relations' inscribed on a sheet of paper he was to lose a year or two thereafter, but which continued to haunt him.[44]

Walter Benjamin is famous for penning a number of texts. Two of the most influential are probably the map of his own life, drawn in a Parisian café and promptly lost soon after, and his great and unfinished opus, *Das Passagen-Werk*. *Das Passagen-Werk*, or *The Arcades Project* in its English incarnation, is not an ordinary book. It is just as labyrinthine as the apocryphal map.[45] Published some time after Benjamin's death in 1940, it consists not of a single thesis *per se*, but of fragments of notes and citations, all gathered and carefully ordered into thematic 'Konvolutes'. These fragments, observations, citations, preliminary critiques and half-formed thoughts—which Benjamin edited and added to right up until the end of his life—essentially deal with the cultural milieu of nineteenth-century Paris: the museum, the spa, the collector, iron construction, exhibitions, prostitution, catacombs, the café mirror. Benjamin's controlling concern, however, is on the Parisian arcade, those great glassy features of the Parisian streetscene that fell into obscurity as a result of Haussmann's redevelopment of the city at the end of the nineteenth century. Benjamin considered these architectural forms the most significant of the age and he linked them with 'a number of phenomena characteristic of that century's major and minor preoccupations'.[46] The ruined arcades were, for Benjamin, a spatialization of a lost Paris, while Paris itself was nothing less than the capital city of the nineteenth century.

In both its message and its mode, *Das Passagen-Werk* might well be considered the opposite to, or perhaps the very inverse of, Lefebvre's *La*

---

44. Jeffrey Mehlman, *Walter Benjamin for Children: An Essay on his Radio Years* (Chicago, IL: University of Chicago Press, 1993), p. 63.

45. Published in English as *The Arcades Project* in 1982; Walter Benjamin, *The Arcades Project* (trans. and ed. Howard Eiland and Kevin McLaughlin; Cambridge, MA: Harvard University Press, 2002 [1927–1940]). Benjamin recalls the aformentions 'violent desire' in Walter Benjamin and Peter Demetz (ed.), *Reflections, Essays, Aphorisms, Autobiographical Writings* (trans. Edmund Jephcott; New York: Shocken, 1978), p. 5.

46. Howard Eiland and Kevin McLaughlin, 'Introduction', *The Arcades Project*, p. ix.

production de l'espace.[47] While Lefebvre is concerned with the headlines of history, its dominant modes of production, and with the reconstruction of a coherent past, Benjamin is extremely suspicious of the historical project, a project which he saw as an attempt to justify capitalism by means of the myth of human progress: 'The continuum of history is that of the oppressor', he wrote.[48] By this, Benjamin means that history is a modern invention, a product of a fetish for orderly progression. It is not merely that the contents of historical research are ideologically tainted, says Benjamin, but that the very substance of the historical project is part of the discourse of oppression and shot through with attempts to control. The museum or the textbook are not windows onto the past, they are garrisons or pillboxes, attempts to colonize the past on behalf of the present. Benjamin was far more interested in the innocuous, the sensual and the everyday spaces of society, reveling in what Ernst Bloch once called an uncanny 'feel for the peripheral' that had the effect of disrupting the controlling, retroactive discourses of capitalism and history. Importantly, Benjamin's work did not aim to do away with history, but to redeploy it, to renegotiate its use as a critical venture.[49] The innocuous detail became Benjamin's means in this renegotiation. As Ansom Rabinbach notes of Benjamin's work:

> Benjamin's eye for detail, for the discordant or emblematic is unsurpassed. His works are pictorial histories without photographs. He often talked about his interest in 'perception as a reading in the configurations of surfaces'. This reading is that of the physiognomer. His 'micrological-philological sensibility' (Bloch) is always trained on the 'imperfect and incomplete' in the conviction that cultural phenomena (visual, spatial gestural, linguistic) are always loaded with the promise of revealing their origin. In this sense the physiognomer considered the world to be a 'script to be read'.[50]

The beauty of Benjamin's work, however, is that Benjamin does not stop with the idea of the spatial world as a script. As Rabinbach goes on to point

47. Despite their common Marxist underpinning, situating Benjamin's thoughts on the same Marxist map as Lefebvre is a complicated and probably ultimately impossible affair. On mapping Benjamin's approaches to history alongside Marx's, see Christian Lenhardt, 'Anamnestic Solidarity: The Proletariat and its Manes', *Telos* 25 (1975), pp. 133-54. For more on Benjamin's approach to the project of history, see Walter Benjamin, 'Theses on the Philosophy of History', in *Illuminations* (trans. Harry Zohn; New York: Schoeken, 1969). See also Ansom Rabinbach, 'Critique and Commentary/ Alchemy and Chemistry: Some Remarks on Walter Benjamin and this Special Issue', *NGC* 17 (1979), pp. 3-14.

48. Walter Benjamin, 'Problem der Tradition I', in Rolf Tiedemann and Herman Schweppenhäuser (eds.), *Gesammelte Schriften* (Franfurt am Main: Suhrkamp, 1974), p. 1236.

49. Ernst Bloch, 'Erinnerungen', in Theodore Adorno and Rolf Tinnermann (eds), Über Walter Benjamin (Frankfurt am Main, Suhrkamp 1968), p. 17.

50. Rabinbach, 'Critique and Commentary/Alchemy and Chemistry', p. 8.

out, Benjamin's is a 'mimetic and not a synthetic idea of reading'. Indeed, the more one reads of Benjamin's work, the more one feels as though Benjamin's concern for language is due to its experiential quality. The world is a script, but scripts are also worlds.[51] Rabinbach goes on, 'Benjamin's writing is perhaps the most visual and corporal philosophical prose we possess. He calls forth something we all desire, but can no longer retrieve: the ability to "speak in pictures"'.[52]

This duality, the ability to see the world as a text and to usher his readers into a world of writing, is key to understanding Benjamin's contribution to dialectical thinking. His goal was to unsettle his readers, alerting them to the potentiality and alterity of the world around them. Benjamin took spaces

51. What is suggested by my approach here, then, is a tacit alliance between Walter Benjamin and Jacques Derrida. This marriage is not so peculiar as one might initially think; work has already been done on the ways in which Benjamin anticipates and models Derrida's work, and the ways in which Derrida himself draws from Benjaminian modes of discussion in his writings on deconstruction. The most notable volume on this subject is that of Carol Jacobs, *The Dissimulating Harmony* (Baltimore, MD; Johns Hopkins University Press, 1978). Since the work of this thesis itself will demonstrate the potential for walking a line between these two thinkers, I shall forgo another lengthy technical discussion; it would be largely unnecessary in the present context (not to mention tedious for the reader). It is worth briefly mentioning, however, that while Benjamin's approach to language seems to have been more inclined toward logocentrism than Derrida's, Benjamin did recognize the limitations, the 'impurity', of all linguistic systems outside of transcendental relationships—'post-Adamic' languages, so to speak. Indeed, as Roland Boer has pointed out, Benjamin's adroit textual criticism becomes highly speculative (and a little ham-fisted, actually) when it comes to the biblical texts upon which he makes his logocentric claims. It seems possible, then, that Benjamin's attitude towards language need not be taken wholesale with the rest of his cultural critiques, as though the one does not function without the other. In fact, Benjamin's somewhat strange/strained relationship with the biblical texts becomes suggestive of openings for deconstructive criticism in his work (and which are exploited in projects like Carol Jacobs's volume). The confusing nature of Benjamin's approach to language, moreover, is indicative of a need for biblical scholars to engage more closely with Benjamin's work, and without having him necessarily sewn up before putting pen to paper. The whole point of his analyses, after all, was to facilitate the discordant shocks that produce illumination. For an example of skepticism on Benjamin's amenability to the inherent openness of linguistic systems see Irving Wohlfarth's (somewhat scathing) rejoinder to Carol Jacobs's aforementioned volume: 'Walter Benjamin's Image of Interpretation', *NGC*, 17, pp. 70-98. For an exposé of the somewhat shaky biblical foundations of Benjamin's notions of pure language, see Roland Boer, 'The Bowels of History, or the Perpetuation of Biblical Myth in Walter Benjamin', *Journal of Narrative Theory* 32 (2002), pp. 371-90. For Benjamin's work on Adamic language and the like, see Walter Benjamin, *The Origin of German Tragic Drama* (trans. John Osborne; London: Verso, 1998 [1928]); and Benjamin, *Selected Writings*, 1913–1926 (2 vols.; trans. Rodney Livingstone; Cambridge, MA: Belknap Press, 1996).

52. Rabinbach, 'Critique and Commentary/Alchemy and Chemistry', p. 11.

(among other things) and wrenched them from the realm of the known in order to situate them in new, and often seemingly incongruent, intellectual contexts. By making sense of the apparently discordant results of these syntheses, Benjamin authors space afresh, challenging traditional, capitalist-authorized modes of spatial encoding. My favorite example is his equation of the self-weighing machines (which one used to find at the thresholds of shopping centers) with the threshold to the Oracle at Delphi; both spaces, he reasons, are phenomenologically identical, a cultural *déjà vu*: they are the *gnothi seauton*, the 'know thyself', of the age. Benjamin thus bends the idea of historical progression by means of literary and poetic equation. Greece and Paris twist, fold, meet and fuse: divisions in space and time, and between history, space, and text, buckle and are forced to speak afresh. The profound implications of Benjamin's flashes of decontextualization are designed to undermine space as the realm of the already known, disrupting assumptions and so rousing people from the cultural myths under which we all labour. If a Lefebvran approach to space prizes historical situation, and seeks meaning by recourse to over-arching metanarratives, Benjamin reminds us of the potency of the incomplete vision of place, of the fragmentary and the partial, and the unique opportunities for connection, for interpretation and for reading that these sites have to offer. Benjamin inspires us to re-inhabit spaces by means of irreverent connections.

Benjamin's approach to the analysis of space has several key things to offer us in a rethinking of biblical spatial analysis and my reading/mapping of the Song. First, Benjamin frees us from the prescriptive modality that we have grown used to in Lefebvre and Soja's work. Benjamin does not offer us a three-step plan, but he does gives license for a critical poetics of space that is properly poetic. Benjamin offers, in other words, a heuristic starting point for my attempts to re-inhabit the Song of Songs and thus critically re-engage with its textual fabric. Second, Benjamin's recognition of the actuality and the potentiality of space, of space as a real concrete project and as a contrived ideological illusion, allows us to consider the spatiality of text and the textuality of space in the same stroke. We can approach textual cities as we might approach so-called actual cities, and we can do so with a sensitivity to the fact that space can be read, and that text is a sensory, inhabitable medium too. Indeed, it seems to be Benjamin's faith in the ability of analysis to awaken the unrealized potential of spaces—concrete and textual alike—that drove his *Arcades Project,* itself a kind of subterranean textual labyrinth that rather exactly describes in its form the kind of Paris espoused in its content.

Benjamin is not only a particularly fitting antidote to the prescriptive legacies of Lefebvre, he also embraces an attitude toward spatiality that is fitting for the Song as a fragmentary and ambiguous text, the various parts of which resist historical placement and which deal with the subjective, the emotional and the tension between the everyday and the downright mythic. Of course, what is also attractive about Benjamin is his hope that his work might shock his readers from the interpretative habits that form around what is familiar. For Benjamin this meant rousing the masses from the myths of history and of fashion and of the commodity. As I have already mentioned, there are a good many 'habits' in our interpretations of the Song too: that gardens are good, say, or that cities are sinister, that the lovers 'describe' each other's bodies, that the Song's poetic realm is dreamlike. I am interested in whether a study that runs according to a more Benjaminian set of concerns can undermine and subvert the traditional expectations of the Song's textual world; can what Benjamin did for the West's great city of love be attempted for the cannon's own great love poem?

Benjamin's is not a universal theory of space so much as a mode of approach to the text as a spatial structure, and so my own attempts to re-inhabit the Song, and thus to recontextualize our intellectual approaches to the spaces of the text, will need to draw on other voices as well. That is, Benjamin does not supply us with a ready-made or rigid methodological schema—those tend not to work out well for the Song of Songs anyway—but the variegated quality of his work can serve to hold in place a formation of varied and specialized theoretical approaches to space. This move is not to plug the gaps in Benjamin's work so much as to enact the kind of physiognomies that he instances for us. Addressing textual worlds as real, inhabitable spaces gives us some freedom to take the already fractured textuality of the Song and consider its numerous spaces in light of their differing, specialized intellectual contexts, and to read along with theory for the 'shocks' produced. Urban contexts can be considered in the light of urban theories of space; correlations between gendered positions and spatial ones can be considered in reference to gender theories about space; gardens can be read with specialist works on garden-theory in mind, and so on. This is not to say spatial reading is left to become scattergun. Benjamin and his work can guide and shape what kinds of voices enter the fray, and since so many types of discourse have adopted Benjamin's approach, several methodological marriages rather suggest themselves. In the end it is Benjamin's power to re-imagine and his ability to find within the emblem the whole world contained that so neatly describes the Song's textual and sexual politics, and which, by extension, can situate a range of methodological approaches to the poem.

How is this going to work in practice? The next chapter, 'Undreaming the Song's World' starts my enquiry by asking after the kind of broad textual world imagined by the Song of Songs. This chapter is not concerned with the analysis of specific spaces—individual scenes and settings—but focuses instead on the general space of the text, the spatial logic by which the Song functions as a whole. Scholars most often use the terminology of dreaming to describe this world and, taking my cue directly from Benjamin, I endeavor to wake scholarly analysis from this dream rhetoric and to think about the Song's world in properly spatio-textual terms. To this end I employ Benjamin's work on the Phantascope—a kind of magic lantern, and arguably the most persistent explanatory image in his *Arcades Project*—as a replacement for the dream. I argue that the Song's spatial structure fits the trope of ideological illusion better than that of the dream and that its spatiality is one of projection, of a negotiation between performance and secret. The structure of its poetic world thus facilitates the text's (con)fusion of the positions of lover and loved with those of reader and text.

This broader overview of the Song's discursive systemicity demands that we give more detailed attention to how power, desire and space function in individual settings. Chapter 2, 'Locked Gardens and the City as Labyrinth', addresses these issues, performing a close reading of the two most prominent spaces of the Song's landscape, the city and the garden. Beginning with the garden, I use contemporary theorists on the subject—Yi Fu Tuan, Robert Riley, and James Elkins particularly—to question the garden's Arcadian and feminist credentials.

When it comes to the city, of course, Benjamin again becomes useful. So prolific was Benjamin on the subject of the city, in fact, that whole schools of urban theory are indebted to his work, and I take up some of the most literarily sensitive of these schools—particularly the writings of James Donald and Steve Pile—to read Song's city with the concerns of Benjaminian urban theorists in mind. Apropos my foregoing phantasmagoric claims, these two analyses lead us to the question of whether or not the garden and the city represent properly distinct spaces at all, or if, in the end, they function as reimaginings of each other. Are the garden and the city all that different, or are they disquieting re-imaginings of the same thing—just, in fact, as the 'sites' of reader and Song become mutual positions by means of the textual phantasmagoria.

My fourth chapter circles back to two ideas that quietly inform these first two discussions on the poem, namely that of gender and that of the archetypal spatial symbol, the threshold. Here I think about the ways in which spatial positions and gendered positions become coterminous in the Song. The chapter contrasts Luce Irigaray's approach to the gendering of spaces with that of Gillian Rose, with two passages in the Song that revolve around thresholds working as base texts: the episode of the latticed window of Song of Songs 3 and the encounter at the door in Song of Songs 5. I argue that the contrast between my two (equally fitting) readings of gendered space allows for a deconstruction of gendered identity in the Song by means of a deconstruction of the text's spatial dividing lines. While a quote of Benjamin's provided the initial inspiration for this discussion—preserved as the chapter's epigraph—it is Derrida's work on the hymen that is most useful in thinking about the implications of this deconstructive move; what other textual categories break down in the wake of our rendering null the threshold and its power to divide? And how do these relate to the issues of inhabitation, and the situatedness of reading that Derrida has (in Benjaminian fashion, actually) raised for us already?

No discussion on spatiality would be complete without treatment of the body, an inhabited space in its own right and the locus around which external space is experienced and organized. My final chapter tackles the bodies in the Song, paying special attention to the so-called *wasf* passages, and the itemized (so-called) descriptions of the female lover. In this instance, however, it is the surreal that proves most useful in understanding the interplay of bodily and cartographic space in the Song, and I employ a reading of the Song's bodies alongside readings of Dali and of Deleuze and Guattari to connect this last discussion into the heuristic Benjaminan concerns of the book as a whole. In the emblem of the body we encounter those same textual and spatial dynamics that I have been arguing are at work in the rest of the Song of Songs. We encounter the body as a textual constitution, and as a constitution that reflects and represents the project of writing itself, whose presence is hard to ground precisely because of the text's confusing of textuality with sexuality.

Truly, the Song is a kind of labyrinth, full of blind corners and seeming repetitions; it constantly doubles back, and swings us around in circles. What emerges in this book, then, is not a flat two-dimensional assessment of the Song's spatiality, or, indeed, a strictly linear A–B argument about the nature of the language or the settings of the Song. Instead, my aim is to place the varied and variegated ways of conceiving of space in the Song—phenomenological, literary, theoretic, ideological—as parts in a simultaneous network of potential connections (one could connect these various chapters in various different ways, in fact, mapping different lines-of-flight between them). What I am striving for in this volume, then, is a kind of map after all—not the kind I had originally envisaged, but a conceptual system of simultaneous relationships that expresses the numerous facets of space in the Song.

As readers will no doubt note, the curious thing in these discussions is the duplications and internalizations of the same spatial politics time and time again: projection, concealment and the deconstruction of the lines betwixt and between. The networks and imaginative planes that we must inhabit as readers can, with some help from the re-contextualizing forces of Benjamin *et al.*, shock us into radical reinterpretations of the love poem. These flashes of re-reading also illuminate the labyrinthine qualities of language itself. Benjamin raises the possibility that the spatiality of the labyrinthine Song and the spatiality of textuality might be one and the same structure. And for that reason perhaps a labyrinthine monograph is a welcome phenomenon.

Advice for the Traveller

Finally, a number of caveats are in order—advice, if you will, for the traveler-cum-reader. Because my focus is on the text as a spatial system, and because of my preoccupation with foregrounding the world conjured up in the Song, I will circumvent certain concerns that have tended to occupy scholarly treatment of the poem. Specifically, the dating of the text, the notion of overall poetic structure, and what we imagine the Song to *mean*.[53] There are good reasons for these omissions. The thorny issue of dating is of very little relevance to my discussion;[54] my sense of the text as a phantasmagorical structure undermines, to an extent, the very idea of hard and fast structural divisions in the poem (as discussed in Chapter 2), and, as will be clear throughout what follows, I am uncomfortable with the notion of fixed textual meanings anyway. I am more interested in reading for the instability of meaning itself, and the ways in which the text enshrines its own openness and self-referentiality. That said, in terms of an overall approach to the Song, I subscribe to the so-called literal readings of the text that take it as a largely non-religious poem about the ins and outs of sensual, sexual, human, male-female love. I also treat the poem as a single literary entity,[55] with the understanding that the

53. The options tend to be: a drama, so Delitzsch, *Proverbs, Ecclesiastes and the Song of Solomon* (trans. James Martin; Grand Rapids, MI: Eerdmans, 1980 [1872]); or an allegory, so André Robert and Robert Tournay, *Le Cantique des Cantiques* (Paris: J. Gabalda, 1963); or a cultic rite, Theophile J. Meek, 'The Song of Songs: Introduction and Exegesis', *IB* 5 (1956), pp. 91-148, or secular love poetry: Falk (see discussion above at n. 3); Jill Munro, *Spikenard and Saffron: A Study in the Poetic Language in the Song of Songs* (Sheffield: Sheffield Academic Press, 1995); Richard Soulen, 'The *wasfs* of the Song of Songs and Hermeneutic', in A Brenner (ed.), *A Feminist Companion to the Song of Songs* (Sheffield: JSOT Press, 1993), pp. 214-24.

54. For discussion on this point see J. Cheryl Exum, *Song of Songs: A Commentary* (Louisville, KY: Westminster/John Knox Press, 2005), pp. 63-70; Michael Fox, *The Song of Songs and the Ancient Egyptian Love Songs* (Madison, WI: University of Wisconsin Press, 1985), pp. 186-90; Othmar Keel, *The Song of Songs* (trans. Frederick J. Gaiser; Minneapolis, MN: Fortress Press, 1994), p. 4; Roland Murphy, *The Song of Songs* (Minneapolis, MN: Fortress Press, 1990), pp. 3-7; Marvin H. Pope, *Song of Songs* (New York: Doubleday, 1977), pp. 22-33. For more recent discussions that use linguistic and philological analysis of the poem to date the text see, Elie Assis, *Flashes of Fire: A Literary Analysis of the Song of Songs* (The Library of Hebrew Bible/Old Testament Studies, 503; London: T. & T. Clark, 2009); and Scott Noegel and Gary Rendsburg, *Solomon's Vineyard: Literary and Linguistic Studies in the Song of Songs* (Atlanta, GA: SBL, 2009).

55. While it is the case that some scholars see the Song's frequent, and often apparently abrupt, shifts in voice, scene and mood as evidence that the Song is a collection of lyrics rather than a unified work, the problems with this position are now well known. First, commentators cannot agree on how many poems an anthological Song of Songs

whole text refers to the same two lovers throughout, I have resisted the urge to name these lovers; as Fiona Black writes, the 'lack of identity is important...it means a certain unanimity and universality for the lovers' experience'.[56] This openness of the text to change, or to reconfiguration, is an underlining feature of the poem, and one that I am keen to accentuate rather than to erase.

In several senses, then, and as will be clear to anyone familiar with the literature, I take my overall cue on the Song from Exum's 2005 commentary. Indeed, in key parts of the discussion that follows my work attempts to use critical theory to develop the kind of literary approach her volume models, with spatiality working as a critical mode of (re-)reading the text. It is worth signaling at the start that in this sense my work is indebted to her forgoing scholarship, not simply in terms of its factual content but in terms of its feel, its timbre and its cadences.

If Exum's work has provided the tone for my approach to the Song as a literary text, another voice has been instrumental in helping me form a more cynical approach than some readers of the Song may be used to. Fiona Black's excellent, warm and witty warnings that the Song has a tendency to enrapture its readers—to make them weak at the knees and thus secure its own good press—has been of increasing interest to me as this project has progressed.[57] I have done my best, then, to resist the text's own amorous advances and keep a level head. I have made the attempt in the hope that, at the very least, I can thereby experiment with some new

would represent. Moreover, there are no superscriptions within the Song—as we have in the Psalms, say—that would signal the different poems as such; the superscription we do have (1.1) refers to the Song as a single superlative lyric; the Song's frequent scene changes involve too much repetition, too much redeployment of identical tropes, images and phrases to make them obvious as separate texts. And, as Exum persuasively argues, 'the Song offers no clue that the male and female speaking voices belong to different men and women—indeed, some see the consistency of character portrayal as a sign of unity'. See Exum, *Song of Songs*, p. 34. All that said, the discursive line between the idea of the unitary Song and the anthological Song is an eminently deconstructable one. If the Song is an anthology it is one readers tend to read together into a single poem. This has already been adroitly discussed in Fiona C. Black and J. Cheryl Exum, 'Semiotics in Stained Glass: Edward Burne-Jones's Song of Songs', in J. Cheryl Exum and Stephen D. Moore (eds.), *Biblical Studies/Cultural Studies: The Third Sheffield Colloquium* (Sheffield: Sheffield Academic Press, 1998), pp. 315-42. Similarly, though, if we read the text as a single poem, it seems to be about lovers compiling a collection of poetic texts for each other (all they do is talk, after all). So perhaps the division does not hold as well as scholarship wants it to. We shall come back to this idea in Chapter 2.

56. Fiona Black, *The Artifice of Love: Grotesque Bodies and the Song of Songs* (London: T. & T. Clark, 2009), p. 7.

57. Black, *The Artifice of Love*, p. 9.

attitudes towards reading the poem (Chapter 3 in particular is an effort on this score).

With all this in mind, I want to turn to look more closely at Benjamin's work on the Phantasmagoria. From there my own responses to an afternoon of failed cartography will, I trust, make much more sense.

Chapter 2

UNDREAMING THE SONG'S WORLD:
ON INHABITING A PHANTASM

Properly speaking, a phantasmagoria is an exhibition of optical illusions, a shifting series of images or a succession of imaginary figures. Phantasmagoria and phantasm are also names for the particular set of optical illusions produced by a Phantascope, an early cinematic device of a kin with the magic lantern. In this chapter my aim is to use the varied motif of the phantasmagoria as a critical model for understanding the underlying architecture of spatial relationships in the Song. The hope is that such a model might disrupt the rhetoric of dreaming that has tended to condition mainstream readings of the Song's imaginary landscape, and open the poem up to other kinds of spatial discourse.

As will become clear, my phantasmic reading strategy borrows heavily from Walter Benjamin and his own appropriations of the phantascope, but before we come to a detailed synopsis of Benjamin's technical phantasmagoria it is probably worth signalling the broad political and ideological import of the idea itself. Why bother with it at all? The general sense of the phantasm as an intellectual tool, its critical promise, its affective seductions and its political dangers are best summarized by another writer, but one who shares Benjamin's love for the fragmentary and the self-referential: Borges.

> 'The greatest magician (Novalis has memorably written) would be the one who would cast over himself a spell so complete that he would take his own phantasmagorias as autonomous appearances. Would not this be our case?' I conjecture that this is so. We (the undivided divinity operating within us) have dreamt the world. We have dreamt it as firm, mysterious, visible, ubiquitous in space, and durable in time; but in its architecture we have allowed tenuous and eternal crevices of unreason which tell us it is false.[1]

Here Borges describes the potential hoodwinking power of the phantasmic apparition. The phantasm does not merely enchant, it erases its own producedness to seduce its onlookers, even if those onlookers are, structurally

---

1.   Jorge Luis Borges, 'Avatars of the Tortoise', in *Labyrinths: Selected Stories and Other Writings* (London: Penguin, 2000 [1964]), p. 243.

speaking, an integral part of the ruse. It is my contention in this chapter that the Song's lovers find themselves in a similarly tangled position to Novalis's arch mage. The biblical lovers are forever buying into their own conjuring tricks, subject to worlds they create through their interactions with each other. Crucially though, this is what constitutes the process of reading the poem too. The Song is a spell we gleefully cast over ourselves as readers, and one by which we create ideological worlds to suit our own needs. Perhaps, then, the biblical text betrays something not just about the nature of loving but about the nature of reading and of textual enspacing itself.

Holey Ground

The 'poetic world' of the text is constantly alluded to in Song scholarship, but usually only in passing. André LaCoque admits of the Song, for instance: 'the more I entered into it myself the more I became enthralled'.[2] Cheryl Exum also wishes to 'enter into its idyllic world of eroticism'.[3] David Carr is scholar turned tour-guide in his recent essay on the poem, which he subtitles 'A Walk through the Song of Songs'. For Robert Alter, the poem is the 'imaginative realization of a world of un-inhibited self-delighting play'.[4] For Francis Landy, the text allows passage 'into the world of the Song, as [one of] the circle of friends listening to the Beloved'.[5] For Albert Cook, the Song's world is an everywhere (it 'achieves the condition of Eden... Eden is everywhere').[6] The list goes on. Fiona Black—in response to Exum and LaCoque particularly—writes that the mysteries of the text can easily be put aside because, really, 'it is entry into the Song's world that readers seek'.[7] But what kind of world is it, exactly, that we clamour to gain entry to?

The Song's poetic landscape is one of the most breathtaking spectacles in Hebrew literature, it consists of vibrant vistas, exotic hinterlands, and lavish royal enclosures. But the biblical wonderland is an infamously unstable and

2. André LaCoque, *Romance, She Wrote: A Hermeneutical Essay on Song of Songs* (Harrisburg, PA: Trinity Press International, 1998), p. ix.

3. J. Cheryl Exum, 'Developing Strategies of Feminist Criticism/Developing Strategies for Commentating the Song of Songs', in David J.A. Clines and Stephen D. Moore (eds.), *Auguries: The Jubilee Volume of the Sheffield Department of Biblical Studies* (Sheffield: Sheffield Academic Press, 1998), pp. 206-49.

4. Robert Alter, 'The Garden of Metaphor', in Harold Bloom (ed.), *Song of Songs* (New York: Chelsea House, 1988), p. 139.

5. Francis Landy, *Paradoxes of Paradise: Identity and Difference in the Song of Songs* (Classics Series; Sheffield: Sheffield Phoenix Press, 2nd edn, 2011), p. 26. All further references to *Paradoxes of Paradise* are to this, the second revised edition, unless otherwise stated.

6. Albert, Cook, *The Root of the Thing: A Study of Job and the Song of Songs* (Bloomington, IN: University Press, 1968), p. 60.

7. Black, *Artifice of Love*, p. 14.

ambiguous territory too and, as one delves deeper into its various nooks and crannies, it becomes, like Alice's pale imitation, curiouser and curiouser. For as the lovers move effortlessly between guises, the Song's landscape reorders itself, reconfigures, or collapses completely.

This feature of the text is often noted in the literature too, again usually in passing. Ariel and Chana Bloch affirm, for example, the presence of a 'dizzying fluidity' in the Song's poetic environment designed to play havoc with the reader's senses.[8] Jill Munro notes that the text's scenes 'shift and fuse with oneiric ease…[as] one environment quickly gives way to another'.[9] Harold Fisch calls this phenomenon a 'heightened dreamy atmosphere', an 'iridescent movement', and a 'shifting kaleidoscope'. It establishes a bizarre sense of continuity through the 'dreamlike' deferral of sensory coherence.[10] Michael Fox believes the fluid environment is apt for a literary work that deals with the heady and distortative world of romance.[11] Roland Murphy is a touch more sober: the Song's quirky spatiality reflects its 'relish [for] the subjective dimensions of nature'.[12] Cheryl Exum uses the free flow of images to critique the tendency among some commentators of historicizing the Song. The notion of splicing reality from flight of fancy is, says Exum, distinctly problematic; the text's 'lack of temporal or spatial continuity' makes even the simplest division between these types of 'reality' more or less meaningless.[13]

One has only to flick through a few pages of the Song to see what these scholars mean. In the first chapter alone, the woman's implied surroundings include vineyards (v. 6) and pastureland (vv. 7-8), a foreign battlefield (v. 9), the exotic En-Gedi (v. 14), and a house-cum-forest (v. 17). In fact,

---

8. Ariel Bloch and Chana Bloch, *The Song of Songs: A New Translation with an Introduction and Commentary* (Berkeley, CA: University of California Press, 1995), p. 15.

9. Jill Munro, *Spikenard and Saffron: The Imagery of the Song of Songs* (Sheffield: Sheffield Academic Press, 1995), p. 124.

10. Harold Fisch, 'Song of Songs: The Allegorical Imperative', in *Poetry with a Purpose* (Bloomington, IN: Indiana University Press, 1988), pp. 80-103 (88-89).

11. Fox is here applying E.H. Falk's observations regarding romance in the French Novel to ancient literature; Michael V. Fox, *The Song of Songs and the Ancient Egyptian Love Songs* (Madison, WI: University of Wisconsin Press, 1985), p. 226. Perhaps, though, the Song of Songs shares more with the surrealist movement than with Balzac and Zola.

12. Roland Murphy, *A Commentary on the Book of Canticles or the Song of Songs* (Minneapolis, MN: Fortress Press, 1990), p. 69.

13. Exum, *Song of Songs*, pp. 45-47, 190. Kathryn Harding sums it up superbly when she writes that Song is a text in which 'narrative logic is suspended and the boundaries between wishes, fantasies, dreams and what could be called poetic reality are blurred and unstable'; Kathryn Harding, '"I sought him but I did not find him": The Elusive Lover in the Song of Songs', *BibInt* 16 (2008), pp. 43-59 (49).

in the space of just two verses the female's body visits the royal chamber (v. 4), enjoys the briefest of interludes as a black beauty and a tent of Qedar, and becomes comparable to the royal enclosure itself (1.5, 'like the curtains of Solomon').

These kinds of spatial shift do not simply work at the level of the individual line. They mark the broader shifts of the poem too: between chaps. 2 and 3 a carefully described springtime panorama is consumed by a city. This metropolis, in turn, gives way to a wilderness setting (3.6-11), which is itself engulfed by the exuberant descriptions of the woman's body in 4.1-7. The garden becomes a city between chaps. 4 and 5, the city becomes a garden between chaps. 5 and 6, and so on. In some of these transitions the characters move consciously between the scenes ('my lover has gone down to his garden', 6.2), but there is never any impression of an intervening space; imagining a location simply causes it to come into being around the lovers. Some of the Song's strange cities and countries may appear solid and settled, then, but they fold-up, deflate, or fade away with little warning. Naturally, for the would-be tour-guide this is a troublesome reality to chart.

In the face of these spatial diffusions, biblical scholarship has tended to resort to the very inverse of the phantasm: the language of dreams.[14] All

14. The other main way that scholars have found to cope with the Song's diffuse nature is to carve it up into sections, pericopes, tricola, chiasms, and all manner of other neat literary strictures. The hope, it seems, is to give readers some poetic footholds in an otherwise disorienting landscape. This formalistic approach to the text requires less attention here than the dream rhetoric I am about to discuss. This is because, first, the imposition of structural divisions onto the Song is a far more self-conscious interpretative maneuver than the deployment of the dream. It is also now reasonably clear that the project of demonstrating a definitive poetic structure in the Song has failed. Structural arguments, designed to give us some mastery over the text, have grown, multiplied, and cross-pollinated over the years to the point, now, where the body of work designed to explicate the Song has become more unwieldy than the difficult text itself.

Roland Murphy suggests that the Song has ten sections (with divisions falling at 1.2, 1.7, 2.8, 3.1, 3.6, 4.1, 5.2, 6.4, 6.13 and 8.5); Murphy, *Song of Songs*, pp. 8-9. William Shea sees only six (1.2, 2.3, 3.1, 5.1, 7.10, 8.6); Shea, 'The Chiastic Structure of the Song of Songs', *ZAW 92* (1980), pp. 378-96. G. Lloyd Carr went down to only five sections (1.2, 2.8, 3.6, 5.2, 8.5); Carr, *The Song of Solomon: An Introduction and Commentary* (Leicester: InterVarsity Press, 1984). Richard Davidson pushes up to fourteen (1.2, 2.8, 3.1, 3.6, 4.1, 4.8, 4.16, 5.1, 5.2, 5.9, 6.4, 6.13, 7.10, 8.3); Davidson, 'The Literary Structure of the Song of Songs *Redivivus*', *Journal of the Adventist Theology Society* 14 (2003), pp. 44-65. Timothea Elliott discerns six sections (1.2, 2.8, 3.6, 5.2, 6.4, 8.5); Elliott, *The Literary Unity of the Canticle* (Frankfurt: Peter Lang, 1989).

As Exum points out, Elliott uses these sections to demonstrate the Song's literary unity, while Diane Bergant has the same six sections working as part of a poetic collection (Bergant, *Song of Songs* [Collegeville, PA: Liturgical Press, 2001]). These six sections are, quite naturally, a different six from Shea's, just as Dorsey's seven sections (1.2, 2.8, 3.1, 3.6, 5.2, 7.11, 8.5) differ from Krinetzki's seven (1.2, 2.8, 3.6, 5.2, 6.4, 6.13,

the trouble is explained, apparently, by designating the Song as oneiric, as a dream text—or, at the very least, a dream*like* text. Dream rhetoric has thereby become a way of describing and, I would suggest, of mastering the awkward nature of the Song's poetic landscape, while leaving untroubled the elaborate system of smoke and mirrors on which the text's spatiality is built.[15]

Rude Awakenings, or, The D-Wor(l)d

It was in the works of Johann Leonard von Hug, circa 1813, that the idea of the Song as an extended dream sequence first appeared. Hug assumes 5.2, 'I slept but my heart was awake', to be the interpretative key for the whole poem, and reads the Song as one long, complex dream sequence. The text's sustained spatial disarray is, apparently, indisputable proof of this conclusion.[16] Hug's attempts at dream interpretation—a political reading of the Song involving a seventh-century Hezekiah—failed to gain much consensus. Nevertheless, Hug instituted a broader dream rhetoric in Song scholarship that has been hard to escape.[17]

The idea that the Song's is a dreamt world was discussed again by Solomon B. Freehof in 1949, and on the same terms: '[O]nce the book is read thus [as a dream] its very disorder makes sense'. More recently, Harold Fisch has argued for the Song as a dream text in his essay 'Allegorical

8.5), see David A. Dorsey, 'Literary Structuring in the Song of Songs', *JSOT* 46 (1990), pp. 81-96 and Leo Krinetzki, *Das Hohe Lied, Kommentar zu Gestalt und Kerygma eines alttestamentlichen Liebesliedes* (Düsseldorf: Patmos-Verlag, 1963). See also Yair Zakovitch, *Das Hohelied* (Freiburg: Herder, 2004), pp. 74-76.

As Francis Landy has indicated, the central problem with this is not that there are insufficient pairings, parallels and linguistic relationships in the text but rather that there are far too many (Francis Landy, 'Review of Timothea Elliot, *The Literary Unity of the Canticle*', *Biblica* 72 [1991], pp. 570-72 [571]). Formalist analysis simply turns the text into a hydra; attempts to delineate any given section—whether through motif, parallel, or inclusio—simply become suggestive of three more parings that would violate the proposed boundary. Cutting up these sections simply gives rise to more. If dream rhetoric has exerted a measure of control over the space of the poetic world, the formalist approach has attempted to a similar measure of control by working to define the space of the page. The poetic structure divides and excises in order to define the difficult text, and thus the reader's progress through it. Dream rhetoric tames a diffuse poetic world; structuration tries to give the reader an anchor within it.

15. As an interpretative strategy it thus sits alongside the kind of approach adopted by Falk, as discussed in my last chapter, mastering the Song by means of categorizing it.

16. Johann Leonard von Hug, *Das Hohe Lied in einer noch unversuchten Deutung* (Freyburg and Constanz: Herder, 1813); *Schutzschrift für seine Deutung des Hohen Liedes, und derselben weitere Erläuterungen* (Freyburg and Contanz: Herder, 1816).

17. Solomon B. Freehof, 'The Song of Songs: A General Suggestion', *Jewish Quarterly Review* 39 (1949), pp. 397-402. See the discussion in Marvin Pope, *Song of Songs*, pp. 132-35.

Imperative'. Fisch insists that the Song works by means of a dream syntax, an assertion that he, like Freehof and Hug, bases on the poem's diffuse and incoherent world: '[T]he whole poem is dominated by a heightened dreamy atmosphere', he writes. 'The poem seems to be a jumble of different lyrics and snatches of story. *But this is precisely the incoherence of the dream.*'[18] For each of these writers, the label 'dreamlike' is based upon the indeterminacy of the text, and, at the same time, proven by that same indeterminacy; the dream assumes and explains itself in the scholarship (and *what* the 'dream' label is supposed to tell us about the Song that 'poem' cannot is never quite made clear).[19]

Other scholars see only certain sections of the Song as dream sequences, namely 3.1-5 and 5.2-8—the parts of the text where beds are mentioned (so, Delitzsch, Krinetzki, Wurthwein, Rudolph, Gordis, Zakovitch and Assis). This conclusion is now generally accepted as a problematic one, however, since these passages (1) have no western Semitic dream vocabulary whatsoever, (2) are some of the most coherent sections of the entire book, and (3) contain no 'waking' that would define the 'dream' as such (except in 5.2, before the 'dreaming' has actually begun). Still others affirm that while there are neither actual dreams nor sleepwalking episodes in chaps. 3 and 5, these sections are 'dreamlike' or informed by dreams (Fox, Garrett, Keel, Murphy, Mariaselvam, Munro).[20] This is a very similar position to others still, who see a kind of somnolence at work in 3.1-5 and 5.2-8, that is, a quasi almost-sleep in which the female's conscious and subconscious desires wander dozily across the city, hand in hand (so Pope, Bergant, Bloch and Bloch, Carr, Hess).[21] It is not clear how replacing the dream

18. Freehof, 'The Song of Songs: A General Suggestion', p. 401, emphasis mine.

19. Fisch suggests that the 'dream' deals a deathblow to the pursuit of a 'literal meaning' in the text. I would suggest, however, that to label something a biblical 'dream' is to beg for an interpretative Daniel or Joseph to enter the discursive fray; see Harold Fisch, 'Song of Songs: The Allegorical Imperative', p. 89.

20. Michael Fox, *Song of Songs*, p. 119; Duane Garrett, *Song of Songs* (Nashville, TN: Thomas Nelson, 2004), p. 206. Othmar Keel affirms at one point in his commentary that poetry 'uses artistic means to create a reality of its own' but later circles back to infer, in reference to 5.2, that a kind of dream syntax has informed the Song's production; its 'conventions [are] fed as much by events in the real world as by daydreams or dreams during sleep'. Dreams are a part of its milieu, then; see Othmar Keel, *The Song of Songs: A Continental Commentary* (trans. Frederick J. Gaiser; Minneapolis, MN: Fortress Press, 1994), pp. 120, 188. See also, Jill Munro, *Spikenard and Saffron*, pp. 120-22; Falk, *Love's Lyrics Redeemed*, pp. 32-33. For further discussion on the problems inherent in these kinds of position see, Exum, *Song of Songs*, p. 45. Abraham Mariaselvam, *The Song of Songs and Ancient Tamil Love Poems: Poetry and Symbolism* (Analecta Biblica, 118; Rome: Pontifical Biblical Institute, 1988). For the opposite view see Zakovitch, *Hohelied*, pp. 164-66, 210-13.

21. Pope, *Song of Songs*, p. 511; Bergant, *Song of Songs*, p. 60; Bloch and Bloch,

text with the dreamlike text or the somnolent text has any demonstrable effect on one's reading of these chapters.[22]

The unavoidable implication of these dreamlike positions is that since 3.1-5 and 5.2-8 are typical of the Song—a fact that all sides of the debate are keen to point out—the whole book becomes a little dreamy by association. Affirmation of a 'dreamlike' chapter turns into a tacit affirmation of a whole oneiric book when those chapters are as standard and central as chaps. 3 and 5 are in the Song. This view is exemplified by Jill Munro's monograph. Unable to discern dream from reality in Song of Songs 3 and 5, Munro ends up treating the whole composition as a 'dreamlike' text—an interpretative move that is based, again, on 'temporal and spatial sequences which begin abruptly and have indeterminate endings'.[23] Ironically, this was precisely Freehof's argument in favour of the dream text in the first place.[24] Fisch's argument in favour of the dream runs similarly:

> Though there are only three [Fisch adds 2.8-14 to the standard two] iden-
> tifiable dream sequences, these are very centrally located and the mood
> and imagery of these scenes merge with the rest of the poem. There is no
> clear division between the waking and dreaming portions of the poem,
> no announcement by the lady that she is now quite wide awake and that
> we are to take her account of events from now on in a different, more
> everyday sense. The whole poem is dominated by a heightened dreamy
> atmosphere.[25]

Scholarly debate on the issue of the dreamt text has served mainly, then, to turn an arbitrary designation into an arbitrary description. The dream has, over the page inches, morphed into the dreamlike. This shows up the odd attachment Song scholarship has developed for dream rhetoric itself; we tinker with the details of our oneiric labels, we even countenance the very logic we are attempting to overturn, but very seldom do we step out of this imposed language entirely.

Perhaps one reason we have kept dream rhetoric around is that it provides a handy mechanism by means of which almost anything in the text can be explained.[26] Like the allegorical readings to which it is doubtless

Song of Songs, pp. 15, 180, 182; G.L. Carr, *Song of Solomon*, p. 130; Hess, *Song of Songs*, p. 102. Some Bible versions have begun to follow suit; the JPS, for example, adds a footnote at 5.2 reading 'i.e. in a dream'.

22. A point that Elie Assis makes, in fact, though he does so in defense of the dream; see Elie Assis, *Flashes of Fire*, p. 96.

23. Munro, *Spikenard and Saffron*, p. 120.

24. Freehof, 'The Song of Songs: A General Suggestion', p. 400.

25. Fisch, 'Allegorical Imperative', p. 89.

26. A good example would be Jill Munro's explanation that the alliterative sequence of ר, ה and ח in Song 3.4 is a reflection of the Song's oneiric nature; see Munro, *Spikenard and Saffron*, p. 71.

related,[27] dream rhetoric provides a way of reducing the sexual exuberance of the Song to socially acceptable levels. As Delitzsch succinctly puts it: 'How could this night-search [in Song of Songs 3], with all the strength of love, be consistent with the modesty of a maiden? It is thus a dream which she relates.'[28] Pope raises the same issue in gentle critique of the Song's 'dramatic interpreters': 'anything can happen in a dream and even the most chaste of maidens may have erotic escapades in dreamland'.[29] The dream covers a multitude of sins, it seems. The dream has even been used to write the violence out of chap. 5 ('they beat me, they bruised me, they lifted my veil...', 5.7) by psychologizing the confrontation. Müller, for instance, sees the violence in 5.7 as a psychic repercussion of the woman's guilty conscience over the sexual encounter earlier in the chapter (vv. 2-3).[30] Similarly, Pardes and Polaski see the violence as part of a guilty dream in which repressed desires are punished.[31] If we are to surmise that the couple's exploits are not real sex, are we also to surmise that the beating is not 'real' violence? Presumably it is not 'male' violence either since the silly girl's imagination has brought it on herself.

More recently, some commentators have begun to question the validity of discussing 'dreams' and 'reality' in poetry at all. As Tremper Longman writes, 'once we remember that this is poetry and not the account of an actual event, then the issue becomes less pressing'.[32] Exum pushes this same sentiment further:

> What is confusing here is the language of 'dream' and 'reality'. Where in the text, one wonders, would dreaming end and reality begin? Murphy...exemplifies a prevailing tendency among commentators to treat literary creations as if they were real people, and not personae created by the poet. The Song's lovers have no relationship, there is no episode, apart from what is on the page before us, or in the reader's consciousness.[33]

---

27. For a lengthy discussion of this relationship, see Pope, *Song of Songs*, p. 511.

28. Franz Delitzsch, *Commentary on The Song of Songs and Ecclesiastes* (trans. G. Easton; Grand Rapids, MI: Eerdmans, 1970), p. 58.

29. Pope, *Song of Songs*, p. 419.

30. Hans-Peter Müller, *Vergleich und Metapher im Hohenlied* (Göttingen: Vandenhoeck & Ruprecht, 1984), p. 27.

31. Ilana Pardes, *Countertraditions in the Bible: A Feminist Approach* (Cambridge, MA: Harvard University Press, 1992), pp. 136-39; Donald Polaski, '"What Will Ye See in the Shulammite?" Women, Power and Panopticism in the Song of Songs', *Biblnt* 5 (1997), pp. 64-81 (78-79). See also, Elie Assis, *Flashes of Fire*, pp. 151-52. Garrett believes that the violence is somehow indicative of 'anxiety' over the loss of virginity, whatever that means; see Garrett, *Song of Songs*, pp. 409-12.

32. Tremper Longman III, *Song of Songs* (New International Commentary of the Old Testament; Grand Rapids, MI: Eerdmans, 2001), p. 128.

33. Exum, *Song of Songs*, p. 45.

Dream rhetoric has not served to elucidate the Song so much as push its difficult, racy, or troubling aspects into the background. Yet the particular problem of oneiric interpretation is that while it hides sex and violence with one hand it tames the exuberant text into everyday experience with the other. For the two processes that Exum touches upon above—making the Song of Songs a dream and looking for an historical reality that underpins it—are related interpretative moves. Or, rather, they are moves that occupy different ends of the same rationalizing spectrum. Like historicizing the Song's content (which wilderness is this in 3.6? What kind of woman would have lived alone as in 5.2?), fixing the term 'dreamlike' boldly above the poem has the effect of taming it by making its fluidity culturally intelligible. Dream rhetoric closes down the text's diffuse field of reality by supplying a rubric under which the fanciful and fantastic can be rendered logical and sensible. To name the Song a 'dream', in other words, is a critical move that wedges the text, however awkwardly, somewhere within our lived experience. The wild and difficult poem becomes part of the furniture. As Theodor Adorno once wrote, if you transpose an image 'into consciousness as a "dream" you not only take the magic out of the concept and render it sociable, but you also deprive it of that objective liberating power which could legitimize it'.[34]

Sharing the 'Bath of Madness'

Those who have poured scorn on the very question of dream versus reality in the poem have pushed toward what I want to grapple with here. That is, the issue of poetry—indeed, of literature more generally—representing something beyond the confines of logical and intelligible experience. Poetry is a space in which human experience can be perceived differently, from odd and perverse angles. But in returning again and again to the notion of the dreamlike as a way of characterizing the strange poetic outlook that we find in the Song, scholars continue to evoke the dream, so valorizing the dreaminess of the text without fully rousing readers to its produced-ness. The result is a kind of critical somnolence. The dream scenarios argued for by some, as well as the dreamlike rhetoric of those who know better, tend to keep scholarship half snoozing under the text's spell. The odd thing for such an oft-used term is that dream tells us *so little* about the text. Read the dreamlike Song as such and one cannot help remaining within the dreamt world it offers at first glance. I may marvel at its dream scenes but I watch the performance from the inside, often forgetting (in the manner of a dream) that I have been kept in the audience and denied a peek through the stage

---

34. Theodore Adorno, 'Letters to Walter Benjamin', in Fredric Jameson (ed.), *Aesthetics and Politics* (London: Verso, 1977 [1935]), p. 111.

door. Really, as a critical reader, I want to be watching the show from the wings, or from the tottering scaffolds of the lampies, indeed from anywhere but the stalls or, God-forbid, from the royal box of allegory (or is that dream interpretation?). Dream rhetoric, subtle though it may sometimes be, runs the risk of denying scholars access to what lies behind love's producedness in the Song by explaining the text away too quickly: 'dreamlike!' Dreams are spaces with no outsides.[35] But as a critical reader it is very much the 'outsides' I am interested in. Without them odd and perverse angles on the text are impossible.

One could take the surrealist movement as an analogue. Guy Debord's *The Naked City* is a surrealist map of Paris. It consists of disconnected 'zones of ambience' that float on a white background. Lines of emotional connection and repulsion link the fragmented Parisian districts and indicate Debord's own sense of the city as he moves around in it. The map was designed to outline Paris as a loose collection of 'psychogeographical hubs', to re-collect the city as an experienced place rather than as a measured one. The anonymously produced *Surrealist Map of the World* (1929) displays a similarly 'distorted' image, this time of the whole globe. An unruly equator snakes across the centre in uneven peaks and troughs and the continents have been re-arranged; some nations are missing entirely. The aim of these surrealist cartographies was to contest the basis on which maps are made. By consciously shifting their priorities they sought to foreground the decisions that lie at the heart of a supposedly empirical practice.[36] To approach Debord's map as a 'dreamt' Paris would thus be an entirely inappropriate interpretative action *because Debord's map aims to demonstrate that every one of our Parises is a dream.* To reduce his cartography to dream rhetoric, as to reduce André Breton's *Nadja* to a dreamt body, would be to fail to appreciate the power of the work ('which could legitimize it', as Adorno says). Debord's call, as Breton's, is to wake us from the fanciful notion of the wakeful itself. To push Debord's Paris into the arms of Morpheus is to lose Debord's work, therefore, and an infinite collection of Parises along with it.

Henri Lefebvre's own sense that his work cannot be put to use in the literary analysis of specific texts has already been examined in Chapter 1. That sentiment notwithstanding, his comments on the critical-cum-spatial possibilities aroused by 'art' are especially fitting here:

> What is the fantasy of art? To lead out of what is present, out of what is close, out of representations of space into what is further off, into nature, into symbols, into representational spaces. Gaudi did for architecture what

35. 'Arcades are houses or passages having no outside—like the dream', Walter Benjamin, *The Arcades Project*, p. 406 (L1a,1).
36. David Pinder, 'Urban Encounters: Dérives from Surrealism', in E. Adamowicz (ed.), *Surrealism: Crossings/Frontiers* (Oxford: Oxford University Press, 2006), p. 44.

Lautréamont did for poetry: he put it through the bath of madness. He pushed the Baroque as far as it would go, but he did not do so on the basis of accepted doctrines or categorizations. As a locus of a risible consecration, one which makes a mockery of the sacred, the Sagrada Familia causes modern space and the archaic space of nature to corrupt one another. The flouting of established spatial codes and the eruption of a natural and cosmic fertility generate an extraordinary and dizzying 'infinitization' of meaning. Somewhere short of accepted symbolisms, but beyond everyday meanings, a sanctifying power comes into play which is neither that of the state, nor that of the Church, nor that of the artist, nor that of theological divinity, but rather that of a naturalness boldly identified with divine transcendence. The Sagrada Familia embodies a modernized heresy which disorders representational space where palms and fronds are expressions of the divine. The outcome is a virtual eroticization, one based on the enshrinement of a cruel, sexual-mystical pleasure which is the opposite, but also the reverse, of joy. What is obscene is modern 'reality', and here it is so designated by the staging—and by Gaudi as stage-manager.[37]

It seems to me that to approach the Sagrada Familia as a 'dream' cathedral would be to commit a horrendous crime of reduction against a work designed to blow apart modernity's own attempts to reduce. One can detect a critique of space itself within Gaudi's cathedral; one can dive headlong from its precipices into an 'infinitization of meaning'; one can see the religious establishment's claims on space answered with a 'virtual eroticization'; one can find a sexual-mystical heresy rendered in bricks and mortar. Or, one can have a 'dream cathedral'. But one cannot, I think, have both. Approaching the staging of staged-ness as a mere dream robs the concretized 'heresy' of its critical power.

Obviously, the Song is not a prophetic foreshadowing of the surrealist movement. But is its spatial effect all that different? The text is certainly not wrapped up in the same self-consciously political and existential concerns that Debord, or Gaudi, or Dali, or Breton, were. But the text's privileging of subjective experience and emotional response over causality, temporality and spatiality ends up having a similar effect to their surrealist projects. The same tension between person and world, between the 'realistic' and the 'rendered', is thrown up by the Songscape, simply because of the poem's intense focus on people as subjective, and thus changeable, engines of reality. This leaves us with a foldable world in which the 'wakeful' and 'sober' become troublesome concepts. The more general, and now famous, challenges that the Song raises for biblical readers—unprecedented erotic content, unorthodox biblical gender portrayals, a lack of overt divine preoccupations—raise familiar challenges: what is the fantasy of the *Song*? 'To lead out of what is present, out of what is close, out of representations of space into what is further off...'

37. Lefebvre, *The Production of Space*, pp. 231-32.

I want to engage with this 'staging' of the Song, acknowledging the obvious fact that, as a literary construct—whether completed with glacial slowness over centuries or scribbled in a single spring afternoon (it really matters not, as I shall touch on in due course)—the Song's poetic landscape is not the vague manifestation of a nameless subconscious, as dream rhetoric so unfortunately implies. It is a 'product', and an odd 'product' at that. I want to deal with space in the Song, then, but I do not want to historicize it. I intend to engage with its fluid atmosphere but I do not wish to succumb to its spell. I want to find a way of mapping its basic poetic architecture without reaching for the droperidol. How?

Benjamin's Critical Phantoscope

Designed in the nineteenth-century by the Belgian inventor-cum-doctor-cum-aeronaut Etienne-Gaspard Robertson, the Phantoscope was built to summon ghosts and ghouls. By merely throwing onto a hot burner a copy of *Réveil du peuple*, papers from the revolutionary court and some vials of long-cold blood, Robertson could use his device to raise the spirits of the revolutionary mob for a paying audience. The Phantasmagorian could call a red-capped Marat. He could summon Virgil and Voltaire. The Phantoscope could even bring forth the ghost of a long lost lover—in which case, quite delightfully, the sorcerer's more macabre ingredients would be replaced by a handful of dried butterflies.[38]

Strictly speaking, the Phantoscope is a kind magic lantern, an early cinematic device, and as a form of evening entertainment it was both spectacularly popular and spectacularly lucrative. This was due in part to Robertson's keen sense of showmanship. Abandoned Gothic convents—draped in black, peppered with bric-à-brac, and daubed with hieroglyphs—were used to stage these diabolical escapades while the ghosts themselves were backlit, allowing Robertson considerable freedom to animate the images without breaking the theatrical spell. The spectres appeared on a theatrical scrim, often in colour, and danced, gradually, imperceptibly, melding into another apparition, and then another, and so on. Robertson sometimes projected his ghouls directly onto smoke to enhance the effect (it is said that the slow-vanishing Cheshire Cat and the baby-turned-pig in Lewis Carroll's *Alice in Wonderland* were directly inspired by Robertson's cinematography).[39] Lunging at the audience and able even to 'press against' some of its more delicate members, Robertson's phantoms could bring their

---

38. Margaret Cohen, 'Walter Benjamin's Phantasmagoria', *NGC* 48 (1989), pp. 87-107 (88).

39. Marina Warner, *Phantasmagoria: Spirit Visions, Metaphors, and Media into the Twenty-first Century* (Oxford: Oxford University Press, 2006), pp. 147, 153.

master's performance to a terrifying climax by literally running spectators
out of the room.[40] Such was the emotional investiture in the show that the
French police once closed it down for fear that Robertson's backlighting
projector might actually bring Louis XVI back to life.[41] As Margaret Cohen
has pointed out, Robertson was not merely playing with the public's sense
of spirituality and history, he was, sociologically speaking, exorcizing the
French revolutionary demons that lingered in Parisian cultural memory.[42]

As I mentioned at the outset, my interest in the Phantoscope stems from
the use Walter Benjamin found for it as a model for mapping the processes
of ideological production.[43] For Benjamin, the Phantasmagoria became a
way of understanding the producedness of ideology, which Benjamin figured as an essentially phantasmagoric enterprise, consisting as a stream
of unstable ideological images that blur seamlessly into one another. Like
Robertson's backlit pictures, these images cover up the very fact of their
production and, through these self-obscuring operations, elicit a suspension
of disbelief that keeps the illusion going. These three ideas (1) of the merging of imagery-in-procession (2) of the self-effacement of production and
(3) of emotional investiture are key ones in Benjamin's conception of space,
the modernist project of history, and ideological production itself.[44]

> [T]he new economically and technologically based creations that we owe
> to the nineteenth century enter the universe of a phantasmagoria. These cre-
> ations undergo this 'illumination' not only in a theoretical manner, by an
> ideological transposition, but also in the immediacy of their perceptible pres-
> ence. They are manifest as phantasmagorias. Thus appear the arcades…thus
> appear the world exhibitions…also included in this order of phenomena is
> the experience of the flâneur, who abandons himself [*sic*] to the phantasma-
> gorias of the marketplace. Corresponding to these phantasmagorias of the
> market, where people appear only as types, are the phantasmagorias of the

40. Warner, *Phantasmagoria*, p. 147.

41. Terry Eagleton, 'Phantasmagoria: Spectral Technology and the Metaphorics of
Modern Reverie', *Critical Inquiry* 15 (1988), pp. 26-61 (35).

42. Margaret Cohen, 'Walter Benjamin's Phantasmagoria', *NGC* 48 (1989), pp. 87-
107 (91).

43. Benjamin's opus remains unfinished, as I have already mentioned. The phantasm
is obviously an important part of Benjamin's analysis, but the precise role of the phantasmagoria in his work is the subject of discussion. I am particularly persuaded by the work
of Cohen, who sees the dream and the phantasm as distinct in Benjamin's work. While
some (Steve Pile, for instance; see below) take the dream and the phantasm as synonymous in the *Arcades Project*, Cohen persuasively demonstrates that this is so only in
Benjamin's earliest summations of his work. In time he began to see the phantasm as a
different kind of structure, one that her formulated as a counterpoint to Marx's camera
obscura, and which he intended to disrupt the idea of the dream *qua* dream.

44. Steve Pile, *Real Cities: Modernity, Space and the Phantasmagorias of City Life*
(London: Sage, 2005), pp. 19-21.

interior, which are constituted by man's [*sic*] imperious need to leave the imprint of his private individual existence on the rooms he inhabits. As for the phantasmagoria of civilization itself, it found its champion in Haussmann and its manifest expression in his transformation of Paris.[45]

The Parisian arcade, the commodity-packed world exhibition, the teeming marketplace, the experiences of flâneurs (like Debord, with his fractured map), the domestic lounge: each is a phantasmagoric procession of images. Benjamin requires us to look beneath the polished surface of things to realize their nature as constructs, as cultural impositions. Each is a manifestation of modernist ideology, and a reflection of modernity itself; Haussmann's Paris is no more than an ideological séance without the copy of *Réveil du peuple*. As such, the phantasmagoric, as Steve Pile explains, 'encompasses an appreciation of the general condition of modernity in which people sleepwalk their way through their lives, unable to wake up to their [true] desires'.[46]

There are useful connections between Robertson's and Benjamin's phantasmagorias. Robertson's phantasmagoria images are projected onto a screen in mesmerizing succession. By concealing the producedness of the images, Robertson caused the audience to suspend their disbelief and invest their own fear in the spectral projections. If his Parisian audiences found something scary in a projected image, it was because they had thrown their own fears up onto the scrim. Robertson's phantasmagoria relied, then, on a *double* projection: the lamplight projects from behind the scrim and the audience projects from in front of it. Benjamin sees ideology as phantasmagoric on these same (spatial) terms. Modernism projects mesmerizing 'images' into the world. The arbitrary producedness of the marketplace, the arcade, the bourgeois living room, the shopping channel, the city, is concealed. Society suspends its disbelief, investing belief (and finance) into these phantasms. If a modern passer-by sees something they desire on a billboard, it is because they have thrown their own desire up onto it, as though it were a theatrical scrim. Modernism relies on a double projection too; ideology projects from 'behind' culture; psychic investiture is projected from inside it. Cutting through the theatrical scrim upon which these images were culturally projected, and seeking to show the producedness of ideology itself, Benjamin's hope seems to have been to use the phantasmagoria as a means of critical illumination, as, in other words, a means by which he could wake people from the fanciful theatrics of the 'real'. He wanted to break the dream.[47]

Fittingly, then, I want to use the phantasmagoria to disrupt the assumption of the dream in our reading of the Song's world. Firstly, by demonstrating

45. Benjamin, '1939 Exposé', in *The Arcades Project*, pp. 14-15.
46. Pile, *Real Cities*, p. 19.
47. See Pile, *Real Cities*, p. 19-21.

that the repeated spatial incongruity in the Song is neither as obvious nor as ubiquitous as the commentary tradition suggests. And secondly, by using the spatiality of projection, as suggested by the phantasmagoria's technical manifestation, to sketch out the kind of spatial relationships that underlie the Song.

On the Scrim: Fluid Continuity in the Song

'By-the-bye, what became of the baby?', said the Cat. 'I'd nearly forgotten to ask.'
'It turned into a pig', Alice quietly said, just as if it had come back in a natural way… 'and I wish you wouldn't keep appearing and vanishing so suddenly: you make one quite giddy.'
    'All right', said the Cat; and this time it vanished quite slowly, beginning with the end of the tail, and ending with the grin, which remained some time after the rest of it had gone.[48]

The Song is not a simple literary world. But neither is it random. The Song's is a deviant space, certainly, but, along with Wonderland, its complexity arises because its logic is not strictly causal. The Song's procession of spaces is, oftentimes, phantasmic: a parade of illusions that merge together, images that slowly fade in and out of focus.

As an initial example of the Song's phantasmagoric parade, let me take a segment that I mentioned earlier to illustrate the text's spatial fluidity. There I pointed out that in the space of two short verses, 1.4-5, the female lover flits effortlessly between numerous settings and bodily spatialities: royal chamber, exotic camping equipment, blackened beauty, and Solomon's curtains:

Draw me after you, let us run!
The king has brought me to his chambers.
We will revel and be glad in you,
    we will savor your embraces more than wine.
How right they are to adore you!
I am black and beautiful, daughters of Jerusalem,
    as Qedar's tents, as Solomon's curtains.

These movements between images are actually quite carefully crafted. The woman who is black and beautiful maps neatly onto the tent of Qedar—from an Arabic root meaning 'dark'—because, historically, the people of Qedar made their tents of black goatskins.[49] The movement represents a thoughtful, though lateral, progression. These black canvasses then shift

---

48. Lewis Carroll, *Alice's Adventures in Wonderland* and *Through the Looking-glass* (London: Vintage, 2007 [1865]), pp. 78-79.
    49. See Exum, *Song of Songs*, p. 104.

into Solominic curtains, maintaining the theme of canvas coverings, and so the text returns full circle to the same kind of intimate royal space that v. 4 begins with: a kingly enclosure. The blackness of the woman's body returns in the next verse. This time her body is blackened by sunburn, which in turn transmogrifies into the brothers' 'anger':

> Pay no heed that I am black,
>   that the sun has ogled me.
> My mother's sons were angry with me.
> They made me the vineyards' keeper.
> My own vineyard I have not kept.

When William Phipps writes that the Song's poet 'showed little concern for the sequence of ideas in arranging the stanzas', he is perhaps mistaken.[50]

What I want to call attention to here is that in some of the most significant transitions in the Song the liquidity of the poem's landscape is achieved not at the expense of spatial continuity but rather by means of spatial continuity. In the Song later verses often cannibalize the spatial configurations that have directly preceded them. Here the female body remains at the centre of the text. It is subject to a variety of transformations but the body itself remains the focus of the text. These transformations follow a kind of logical pattern, even if that logic is a florid and poetic one. The cannibalizing does not occur in a strict and programmatic way, of course—this is a loose technique rather than a poetic rule—but it does characterize several of the key scene changes in the poem.

Landy terms this kind of continuum of images a 'divine flow'. Whereas Landy's discussion of the poem's fluidity of images is focussed on literary structuration (he detects a broad, fluid chiasmus of contrasting images at work in the poem), I would like to look at the spatial structuration that underwrites this 'flow'.[51] The Song's phantasmagoric shifts are most obvious when one focuses on the spatial formations in the text, particularly, and most poignantly, in the so-called dream passages of chaps. 3 and 5.

Song of Songs 3 is generally taken to consist of two scenes, one in the city (vv. 1-5), one on the edge of the wilderness (vv. 6-11).[52]

---

50. William Phipps, 'The Plight of the Song of Songs', in Harold Bloom (ed.), *Song of Songs*, p. 5.

51. Landy, *Paradoxes of Paradise*, pp. 46-54.

52. Suggestions as to the precise identity of the wilderness topography invoked by 3.6 include the wilderness to the southwest of Palestine (Hess and Gordis), an arid stretch to the east of Jerusalem (Delitzsch, Keel, and Goulder), and even the Theban desert (Gerleman); see Richard S. Hess, *Song of Songs* (Grand Rapids, MI: Backer Academic, 2005); Robert Gordis, *The Song of Songs and Lamentations: A Study, Modern Translation and Commentary* (Texts and Studies of the Jewish Theological Seminary of America; New York: Ktav, 1974), p. 20; Delitzsch, *Song of Songs*, p. 61; Keel, *Song of Songs*,

Nightly,[53] on my bed,
I sought my soul's beloved,
I sought him but I did not find him.[54]
I will rise now, I will go around the city,
   through its streets and its squares,
I will seek my soul's beloved.
The watchmen found me
   as they went on rounds of the city.
'My soul's beloved—have you seen him?'[55]
Barely had I passed them
   when I found my soul's beloved.
I held him and would not let him go
   until I had brought him to my mother's house,
   and to the chamber of she who conceived me (3.1-5).

Who is this[56] coming up out of the wilderness

p. 126; Michael D. Goulder, *The Song of Fourteen Songs* (Sheffield: JSOT Press, 1986), p. 28. For discussion on Gerleman's position, see Fox, *Song of Songs*, p. 120. It is important to remember that the Hebrew term מדבר does not at all signify the arid expanse that modern readers might associate with the term 'desert'. Pope runs through a variety of understandings of the use of מדבר in his commentary. As well as meaning the deserted wilderness proper he asserts the usage of מדבר in denoting meadowland just outside the city, an open unused area immediately external to the city gate, an unsettled semi-arable plain on the periphery of pastoral lands, and, indeed, the netherworld as a 'between' or non-space (for which Pope draws on the mythological stories of Baal and Dumazi); Pope, *Song of Songs*, p. 424. Carr points out that the מדבר can also refer to the outer steppe where flocks could graze; see G. Lloyd Carr, *Song of Solomon*, p. 108. Attempts to pinpoint the wilderness that the lovers are cavorting on the rim of, as though it were a real-world location, simply undermine the tenor of the writing. As Bergant stresses, the wilderness setting is most useful to readers as a poetic emblem for the rough far horizon and marks a 'stark divergence from the lush vernal settings' of the earlier parts of the Song (Bergant, *Song of Songs*, p. 38).

53. I retain the plural here, nights, to indicate repeated action.

54. The Septuagint adds 'I called him but he did not answer'; some manuscripts add the phrase at the end of v. 2. Exum suggests the addition may be the result of the use of this phrase in the parallel account in 5.6; see Exum, *Song of Songs*, p. 122.

55. Literally: 'my soul's beloved—have you seen'. I have taken Exum's translation here, which retains the emphasis suggested by the Hebrew word order, see Exum, *Song of Songs*, p. 122. For a different take on the verse see Keel, *Song of Songs*, p. 119.

56. There is considerable discussion in the commentary literature on the nature of this phrase, and on the connection between the female protagonist and the litter of vv. 7-10. Is she watching the palanquin, or riding in it? Does this question refer to her? Does she speak it? The confusion stems wholly from the Hebrew phraseology of 'Who is this...?' in v. 6. 'This' (זאת) is the feminine singular demonstrative and so anticipates a reply that is feminine in form. However, the dénouement of the episode is praise of the *male* lover in kingly guise (v. 11). So how does one square the two images? The fact that the litter in v. 7 is a feminine noun goes some way to answering this problem, but, then again, the use of מי (who) suggests that a person is at the centre of the speaker's attention rather

> like columns[57] of smoke,
> fuming[58] myrrh and frankincense
> from all the merchant's powders?
> Look! It's Solomon's litter.
> Sixty warriors encircle it
> from the warriors of Israel.
> All of them sword-seized[59]
> and skilled in warfare.
> Each with his sword at his side
> against the terrors of the night.
> King Solomon made himself a palanquin
> from the wood of Lebanon.
> He made its posts of silver,
> its covering of gold,
> its interior inlaid with love.[60]

than an object (where one would expect the impersonal מה, 'what'). As Pope points out, in Akkadian 'who' and 'what' are interchangeable anyway and some slippage might be expected in closely related languages (Pope, *Song of Songs*, pp. 423-24). It seems, then, that either the text imagines the female to be *in* the palanquin through the use the phrase '*who* is *she*' in v. 6, or else v. 6 refers to the palanquin itself as a personified female object. So, the litter might be associated with the female gender because it has a female occupant (though this does not *automatically* follow), or, equally, the litter might be personified as a female entity *despite* its male occupant. In actual fact, the male '*king*' *inside* the 'female' enclave conjures up a suggestive picture that would certainly not be out of place in the Song. Indeed, if we reject the amended reading of the MT in v. 10 on the basis that it has no versional support and that the resultant plural form of 'love' is entirely without parallel, the palanquin is further feminized by virtue of the fact that the Daughters of Jerusalem are said to have had a hand in its construction. It is a womanly box.

57. Murphy and Pope render columns as a singular, column, by reading the Hebrew plural as a generic plural; Pope, *Song of Songs*, p. 426; Murphy, *Song of Songs*, pp. 148-49. They thus bring the MT into agreement with the Vulgate, which has a singular here. There really seems no need to do so; something can look like many pillars of smoke from a distance, as Exum stresses (*Song of Songs*, p. 139).

58. This is a *pual* participle of the root קטר, which in the *piel* form is used to describe the offering of a sacrifice, to describe making the animal go up in smoke. As Pope notes, the passive form of the factitive stem here is unique, and numerous scholars have suggested that perfumed would be appropriate here (Pope, *Song of Songs*, p. 426). I have opted for 'fumed' since it seems to adequately indicate the gaseous nature of the word without sacrificing any of the violence attached to its normal usage, as I fear 'perfumed', or Exum and Pope's 'redolent', does (Exum, *Song of Songs*, p. 139).

59. This passive participle is often taken to mean 'skilled' or 'trained' in warfare (Exum, *Song of Songs*, p. 139; Pope, *Song of Songs*, p. 435). The root means literally to grasp or take hold of, and the full Hebrew construction here—'seized of the sword'—is more suggestive of the weapon than the English term 'trained' allows. My (admittedly exuberant) compound attempts to retain the primacy of the weapon here, and thus retains a 'grip' on the rather phallic tenor of the text.

60. I opt to stay with the MT here, rather than correct אהבה to אבנים. Not only is there evidence that scenes of lovemaking were laid as mosaics into litters of this kind (see

While these two scenes in chap. 3 are very different,[61] they make use of the same basic spatial configuration. Between vv. 6-11 we are presented with the royal sedan chair, or palanquin, an emblem often associated with sexual encounter in the ancient world.[62] This opulent litter is concentric and enclosed (it has a wooden base, silver posts and a golden covering) and is encircled by sixty mighty men with swords strapped to their thighs. We are told in v. 8 that the sword-seized sentinels are present to defend against the 'terrors of the night'. The basic floor plan of the wilderness scene, then, is built on a central enclosure that is surrounded at its outer edge by an armed, male circle. The city-scene immediately preceding the palanquin-scene bears a striking resemblance. The city also focuses on a central enclosure, designed, apparently, to hide the lovers (even from the reader, as, indeed, the palanquin does—which the league of page inches devoted to identifying the occupant of the royal litter aptly demonstrates). This city, like the palanquin, is delineated at its outer edge by a male circle. The implicit function of these nocturnal, circling sentinels is identical to the desert guards, who defend against 'terrors of the night' in v. 8. The two scenes use the same Hebrew root (סבב) to describe their respective encirclings, underscoring the similarity.[63] In other words, the same underlying world from v. 1-5 seems to have been re-coded in the text between vv. 7-11, thus the oft noted lack of spatial continuity may well be a misnomer, at least in chap. 3. There is not a lack of continuity in the text, but rather a mismatch between its continuous and discontinuous elements. Given the Song's reliance on imagination and subjective perception,

n. 62 below), but the idea of lovemaking as a kind of interlocking works well here as a poetic image. Of course, strictly speaking, 'love' cannot be tessellated, but neither can the dust kicked up by a few soldiers create columns visible from a distance, nor indeed would silver posts be of practical construction; if the Song of Songs cannot display whimsy, what text can?

61. Many commentators see no link between these two episodes, inserting a section-break at v. 6. Michael Fox divorces 3.1-6 from vv. 7-11 entirely, separating even the question posed in v. 7 and the answer given in v. 7; Fox, *Song of Songs*, p. 122. Pope sees the two sections as connected by the question and answer game but by no more; Pope, *Song of Songs*, pp. 414-25. Murphy, Carr, Bergant, Davidson and Krinetzki all place section divisions at 3.6 (see n. 14 above). Longman says that '3.6-11 clearly stands out as a separate poetic unit' (*Song of Songs*, p. 131). Exum, however, sees these two scenes (along with the previous one) as a triad of connected stories that the woman tells, linked by themes and key words; Exum, *Song of Songs*, pp. 37-41.

62. See Keel, *Song of Songs*, pp. 130-34, where he offers Hellenistic, Ugaritic, Samarian and Egyptian examples of this phenomenon, including a Talmudic inscription that suggests Jezebel had erotic scenes installed into the frigid Ahab's transport so as to 'heat' him for lovemaking.

63. The repeated use of סבב begs the question of how, exactly, we are to interpret the movements of the woman and the city watch. Do they move around the metropolis is actual circles? See the discussion on pp. 97-98 below.

one could read this shift in imagery not as a poetic movement into new surroundings but as a poetic terraforming of the old ones.[64]

A similar process is at work in the transition between the Song's fourth
and fifth chapters. In Song of Songs 4.12, the male lover turns the female
into a locked garden and a sealed fountain. As chap. 4 goes on, these two
images merge; she is a garden fountain in the garden and, at the same time,
she is the garden itself ('come O south wind! Blow upon my garden', v.
16). Some commentaries (and all the formalist literary structures applied to
the Song)[65] place a section boundary after 5.1 on the basis that this locked
garden/body imagery seems to give way in 5.2 to a city scene (this city-
scene runs to around 6.2 and forms the second so-called dream sequence).[66]

> I come to my garden, my sister, my bride.
> I pluck my myrrh with my spice,
> I eat my honeycomb with my honey,
> I drink my wine with my milk.
> Eat friends. Be drunk with love.
> I slept, but my heart was awake.
> Listen! My lover is knocking!
> 'Open to me...'

As we have already seen, the notion of dream scenes itself rather
relies—sometime explicitly, sometimes less so—on this new (dream) scene
operating as a discrete entity. But the practical needs to divide the poem notwithstanding, there are profound links between these two sections. Sleeping
is, after all, a universal response to both heavy drinking and fervent lovemaking and both are mentioned in the prior lyric (v. 1). While the beginning
of v. 2 marks a subtle temporal change (the morning after the night before?),

---

64. As I have said, there is a great deal of discussion on where the lovers are situated between vv. 6-11; is the man or the woman in the palanquin? Are they riding in it
together? Who is the speaker in v. 6? It seems, though, that if the litter is imagined to
conceal the man, it carries the themes of male concealment over from 5.4; if the litter is
understood to contain the woman, it brings resonance between the female house/cham-
ber/bed (5.1,4) and this more ornate female enclosure. If both lovers are in the litter, the
palanquin becomes the twin of the concealing trysting place in 5.4. Indeed, the facts that
one can draw spatial-thematic parallels so readily between the two episodes and that the
chapter itself is so reluctant to answer these kinds of questions perhaps indicates that the
text is so unwilling to close down the links between the two sections.

65. See n. 15 above.

66. Even commentators who tend to stress the poetic continuity of the Song have
characterized these two verses in terms of contrasts. Take Landy, for instance: 'The
centre is the space, the silence, between consummation in the garden in 5.1 and the
beloved's awakening in 5.2; a point that cannot be spoken in the poem, and is marked by
profound contrast'; Landy, *Paradoxes of Paradise*, p. 47; Exum stresses the poetic continuity here, and the blurring of temporal lines between wishing and fulfillment; Exum,
Song of Songs, pp. 182-84. I wish to add a spatial element to that observation.

the stative participle—'I slept'—simply continues the dynamic list that precedes it.[67] The series: plucking, eating, drinking, sleeping forms a neat and coherent progression. Thus, it is only when the sound of the lover 'knocking' is combined with male's words in the second part of 5.2 ('Open to me') that readers realize the lovers are no longer together and that the garden-world of 5.1 has silently succumbed to some kind of construction project.

The new, urban scenario forms gradually in chap. 5.[68] Between vv. 2-6 the woman's space slowly takes shape as a domestic environment in which sleeping, bathing, and personal safety are possible; there is a securely fastened entrance and the male lover seeks admittance, poking his 'hand' into her 'keyhole'.[69] 'At which', intones the breathless woman in 5.4, 'my insides thrilled!'[70] The interesting feature of this verse, of course, is that it once again places the female *in* a space and makes her body identical with that space. The whole configuration of chap. 5, then, raises the question of whether very much has changed, spatially, between 4.12 and 5.6. While the controlling *imagery* has changed in the text—from garden to city—the underlying spatiality that structures chap. 4 rolls into chap. 5. The description of a locked garden/lover (4.12–5.1) has made way for a locked house/lover. The focus of the text is still a fairly unelaborated enclosed space (containing clean water). This space is still locked and bolted. It is still inhabited by the female. It must again stand in for the female body as the double entendres build up.[71] The domestic space unfolds as a loose replication of the garden and the configuration of the lovers' world forms a form point of relative continuity as the poem moves into a new symbolic world. If these sections are to be read as entirely different, why reuse the same notions—of locking, of enclosure, of the female-as-container? Why has the basic spatial supposition of the text, the supposition of entry, exclusion and access, not changed too? Like the blurring of context at 5.1-2, the use of space between 4.12–5.6 engineers a fine balance of continuity and discontinuity through a kind of reimagining.[72]

Is this also how one is to understand some of the constant minor changes in the earlier parts of the poem? Consider, for instance, the section that runs between 1.12 and 3.1. In 1.12 the royal couch becomes a green daybed

---

67. Exum, *Song of Songs*, pp. 186-87; Pope, *Song of Songs*, pp. 503-10.

68. Readers do not have enough data to assume the apparent barrier is a door, or even that it forms part of a house, right away.

69. These are well-attested euphemisms for penis and vagina respectively.

70. I borrow here from Exum's translation, *Song of Songs*, p. 183.

71. And, indeed, contains a cleansing supply of water, 4.13-15, 5.3.

72. The male who seeks entry to the locked garden of chap. 4 now seeks the opening of a locked house. The dewy-haired man is not simply knocking from the street in 5.2; in a manner of speaking, he is seeking admittance from the last section of the poem. The elemental male has been left behind while the dominant poetic theme changes around both him and the spatial configuration of the scene.

(v. 16) in a verdant forest abode (v. 17). The daybed then becomes a lone apple bower in a forest (v. 3). By 2.5 the forest is replaced by a wine house,[73] in which there is (a bed of?) raisins.[74] The wine house is replaced by a latticed room, which is itself overtaken by a rocky crevice in 2.8-14. The confined trysting place reappears with a bed, in various guises, throughout these stanzas, while the imagery it is decked in changes, thematically, around it. Michael Fox notes this constant adaptation of the same basic trysting enclave when he muses that the royal chamber, the verdant house and the wine house might all be identical spaces recreated by the creative speech of the lovers.[75] Though Fox goes no further in elucidation of this point, he alludes to the fundamental similarity of these various spatialities. These thematic transitions are even carefully ordered, taking readers

73. Keel believes the 'banqueting hall' to be a private residence, replete with banner, that opened for revelry during the harvest (*Song of Songs*, pp. 84-85). Exum and Murphy take the wine house as a fusion of mutual dwelling and mutual intoxication, two abstract ideas about love earthed in a single spatiality; see Exum, *Song of Songs*, p. 115; Murphy, *Song of Songs*, p. 136.

74. The first verb in 2.5 is the Piel form of סמך and means, literally, lean, prop or support (Pope, *Song of Songs*, p. 378). The verse thus plays with the ideas of feeding the woman fruit and of the male bracing her up against a pile of it as part of the throes of passion. This second sense, of the wine house containing an edible 'bed', grows as the verse goes on, since the verb רפד from the second part of 2.5 (NRSV's 'refresh me with apples'), might be translated as underlay, spread or support; Pope suggests 'brace' (p. 380). As Exum points out, the vocabulary here is so rare that it is difficult to come to a definitive sense of the verse; in Job 17.13 the רפד is used of spreading a bed and later in the Song (3.10) the nominal form of the root refers to a covering, but there is no literal bed here at 2.5. Exum further objects to the bed on the grounds that raisins would make for an unlikely divan, Exum, *Song of Songs*, pp. 115-16. However, if the lovers are in a wine house (the uncertainty of that phrase notwithstanding), where one might find piles of dried grapes, or even a floor covered in a thin layer of discarded fruit, it does not seem too far fetched that an appropriate fantasy might involve being 'braced' up against some produce for an impassioned, if unhygienic, encounter with one's beloved. Such an abundance would fit with the plentiful, fecund landscape that features in the rest of the Song. A barn connected with wine making and an impromptu fruity surface for sex seem, particularly in the economy of the fantastical Song, then, reasonably congruent images. In this vein, Bloch and Bloch, Garrett and Fox all understand the text to refer to a fruity bed here. Fox writes: 'Put me to bed among fruit clusters, spread me my bed among apricots' (*Song of Songs*, p. 84). At the very least, the sense of being fed fruit as a romantic act and the idea of fruit providing a surface for lovemaking seem to rub up against each other in the uncertain verse by virtue of the text's (purposefully?) oblique vocabulary. An objection to the impracticality of a fruity bed in this context seems no more valid than turning down a roll in a haystack on the basis that hay gets really quite itchy after a while. For a detailed treatment of the various uses for סמך, see *DCH* 6, pp. 168-69.

75. Fox makes the royal chamber, the verdant house of 1.16-17 and the wine house identical as a 'bower...in the field or orchard', a single enclosed meeting spot reimagined again and again (*Song of Songs*, p. 108).

from wild forests, to lone fruit-bearing (apple) trees, to the produce of cultivable land (wine and raisins), to the refrain directed at urban inhabitants (the daughters of Jerusalem, 2.7). The poet moves the boudoir from wild spaces toward progressively more civilized ones; it shapeshifts on the way, of course, but it anchors the other imagery on a fairly coherent vector: out from civilization and back again.[76] If the lovers are allowed to become universal sweethearts, it is only because their unmade bed is allowed to become the universe.

It is reasonably clear why a poet might use these kinds of re-imaginings to fashion the lovers' a trysting place that both contains and reaches out to the whole cosmos; when meeting, the lovers' immediate surroundings become an Everywhere. There is only Here and it must serve as every sphere under the sun. John Donne expresses a similar sentiment in his love poem, 'The Sun Rising':

> Thou, Sun, art half as happy as we,
> in that the world's contracted thus;
> thine age asks ease, and since thy duties be
> to warm the world, that's done in warming us.
> shine here to us, and thou art everywhere;
>   this bed thy center is, these walls thy sphere.

Donne expresses the power of the lovers' imagination, linked with the intimacy of the bed itself, to transform and to transport. In the Song the lovers' bedroom becomes a royal chamber with a kingly bed (1.12), then a forest abode with a green daybed (1.16); now it is a shady bower surrounded by wild forests (2.3); now it is a fruity house erected in the vineyards (2.4) with a bed made of raisins (v. 5); now it is a latticed house (2.9); now a little crevice in the rock (2.14); now it is the dynastic bed in a town-house; it is a city surrounded by watchmen (3.1-5); now the bed is a royal palanquin and the watchmen are turned into a circle of royal guards; 'she's all states, and all princes I'.[77]

The idea of the phantasmagoria is doubly useful. First, the term itself acts as a fitting replacement for the semantics of the 'dream'. The phantasmagoria acknowledges the diffuse, even morphic, qualities of the Song's world without resorting to mythic, magic, or oneiric terminology. Behind the phantasms, the text remains technical. At the same time the idea of the phantasmagoria acknowledges how hard the poem's images work to create the semblance of

---

76. The value system changes with the location of the lovers. Wild woods may have been in vogue in 1.16 but they are the objects of derisory comparison two short verses later. The lovers, alas, have moved on; the text's notions of spatial value have moved with them.

77. My sentiment here runs from, and feeds back into, Exum's sense of the universality of the lovers. See Exum, *Song of Songs*, p. 8.

magic. Moreover, the technical manifestation of the phantasmagoria—as a phasing series of blending images—better describes the Song's spatial transitions. The Song does not simply switch between spatial images; rather, it melds them. The Song reuses floor plans, overlaying new 'themes' on them to affect scene changes. The Song frequently creates a sense of fluidity, not at the expense of spatial continuity but by means of spatial continuity. Somewhat ironically, this careful staging of morphic imagery is most keenly observed in and around the so-called dream sequences, the sequences that are so often touted as explanations for the text's unruly spatiality. The second way in which the phantasmagoria is useful in approaching the Song is the subject of the next part of my discussion.

Behind the Scrim: The Song's 'Space of Two'

In order to be a love poem the Song of Songs must, by definition, be a spatial poem. This assertion may seem to be an odd leap of logic, but as I touched upon in Chapter 1, relationality (there I called it systemicity) requires and implies spatiality. Lovers without distance, without bodies or boundaries—and so without the capacity for either discourse or intercourse—are not really lovers at all. We can move spatial discussion of the text beyond mere scene setting by acknowledging that space is what makes lovers possible. And since the text is structured as a dialogue, with characters speaking, hearing and yearning aloud, the multivocal form of the text re-enforces this implied spatiality; it is implied that there is room to speak into, distance to speak across. One must assume a kind of literary space before the Song's settings, or the concepts addressed in them, can be imagined at all.[78]

---

78. One obvious objection to critical spatiality would be that spatial theory has claims on far too much. *Everything* is situated in space, so *every* phenomenon is liable to fall under the purview of spatial analysis. Is spatial analysis not an approach that fails to provide any kind of meaningful intellectual taxonomy, then? A statue falls over: it is spatial; a man looks out of the window: spatial; smoke rises: spatial; sexual penetration: spatial. This allegation of unbridled applicability is, of course, quite accurate. The key issue is how one approaches this idea of the universality of space. If, as has often been the case in biblical spatial studies, spatiality is merely the triumphant conclusion of analysis, then this objection probably has some merit. But if we come at the objection from the other direction (so to speak), and acknowledge instead that space *must necessarily always be pre-thought* in whatever it is one is writing about or relating to, then space offers us a way of getting at the fundamental 'assumeds' that lie beneath the social and communicative processes all around us. Space is the universal 'already-given'; as Calvino's self-consciously failed attempt at nonspace creation indicates, we must produce space before we can produce anything else. Foucault famously wrote that 'power is everywhere, not because it embraces everything, but because it comes from everywhere…one is always *inside* power' (*The History of Sexuality*. I. *The Will to Knowledge* [London: Penguin, 1976], p. 93, emphasis mine). Similarly, space is not a meaningless category because it

Doing without this kind of constituent space is unthinkable. Italo Calvino demonstrates just how necessary constituent space is to a narrative in his risible rendition of a creation myth, 'All at One Point'.[79] In 'All at One Point' Calvino describes the unlikely 'community' that lived before the dawn of time within the pre-cosmic point, the dense particle in which all matter was compressed prior to the universe's expansion. Calvino's narrator—the non-human Qfwfq—recalls the striking Mrs Ph(i)Nk$_0$ a woman whose ample bosom and orange dressing gown aroused a variety of emotions in her point-bound 'neighbours' (of which there were a fair few; the point is *all* the universe compressed, after all). Because of the fundamental spacelessness of the pre-cosmic point, however, these feelings get quite complicated:

> The fact that she [Mrs Ph(i)Nk$_0$] went to bed with her friend Mr De XuaeauX was well known. But in a point, if there's a bed, it takes up the whole point, so it isn't a question of *going* to bed, but of *being* there, because anybody in the point is also in the bed. Consequently, it was inevitable that she should be in bed also with each of us. If she had been another person, there's no telling all the things that would have been said about her… [t]he happiness I derived from her was the joy of being punctiform in her, and of protecting her, punctiform, in me; it was at the same time vicious contemplation (thanks to the promiscuity of the punctiform convergence of all of us in her) and also chastity (given her punctiform impenetrability)…and all of this, which was true for me, was true also for each of the others.[80]

The inevitable, and quite purposeful, failure of Calvino's logic is designed to highlight the fundamental reliance of relationality upon spatiality. In an environment without space all one's notions of penetration, protection, connection, chastity, promiscuity, alliance, allegiance, joy and jealousy, as well as the boundaries of the bedroom, become meaningless. Everything is necessarily punctiform 'in' everything else. In order for two individuals to be two, there must be spatiality between them, defining and separating them. This 'betwixt' is a powerful and omnipresent field, it is the precondition of connection, and thus of relatedness itself. Calvino's self-consciously ridiculous scenario is intended to make just this point and, for my purposes, helps illuminate Merleau-Ponty's rather more opaque formulation of the same idea:

applies to everything. Rather, it applies to everything because it is the pre-thought-of of thinking itself.

79. Italo Calvino, *Cosmicomics* (trans. William Weaver; London: Penguin, 2011 [1976]), pp. 46-47, italics original. Each of Calvino's *Cosmicomics* takes a factual scientific premise and turns it into a mythological account. In so doing he plays with the ideas both of mythology and of factuality.

80. Calvino, *Cosmicomics*, pp. 46-47.

> This means instead of imaging it [space] as a kind of ether in which all things
> float, or conceiving it abstractly as a characteristic that they have in common,
> we must think of it [space] as the universal power enabling them to be con-
> nected...I catch space at its source, and now think the relationships which
> underlie this word.[81]

In thinking about space in the Song one must delve deeper than a discussion of liquid setting. There is a spatiality to the poem that comes about
prior to these fluid environments, a poetic architecture that emerges from its
very subject matter: the space of two. To talk only of a procession of scenes
is too simple an approach, because, when one looks back over the Song, one
sees that a powerful absence surrounds and pervades the whole work. This
absence is not simply the intermittent absence of one or other of the lovers
from the scene but a blank space that makes up the very structure of the
Song itself: the space 'betwixt' in which the voices must speak, the space
'behind' the characters' words, the space through which the lovers communicate, both with each other and with us. This is the space that allows there
to *be* lovers. This 'space of two', the space from which dialogue springs
forth, is never elucidated, never described.[82] But this space-between is necessarily implied. The alternative is meaningless punctiformity.

Getting a sense of this implied spatiality in the text is easiest at the beginning of the Song (1.2), where the gap between space-as-spoken and spaces-
of-speaking is first opened up:

> Let him kiss me with the kisses of his mouth,
>   for your love-making is sweeter that wine.

In the first brief snippet of the poem the female lover calls out to her
beloved. Where *is* this aroused woman[83] exactly? A major point of Exum's
commentary is that as readers of the Song we only ever have what is on the
page before us.[84] By that reckoning the Song's female protagonist is not, of
course, actually *anywhere*; her words of desire are oddly disembodied and
lack context. Crucially, though, this is not to say these words are devoid
of spatiality. There is actually a great deal of spatial production going on

---

81. Maurice Merleau-Ponty, *Phenomenology of Perception* (trans. C. Smith; London:
Routledge, 2002 [1964]), p. 284.

82. Cognitive linguistics would see the Song in terms of text worlds and sub-worlds.
The Song is a text world, but all of its content is a sub-world, a secondary literary
creation of the characters *within* the poem. See Paul Werth, *Text Worlds: Representing
Conceptual Space in Discourse* (London: Longman, 1999), and Gilles Fauconnier, *Mappings in Thought and Language* (Cambridge: Cambridge University Press, 1997).

83. It is worth mentioning, of course, that on a first reading the only factor that suggests a woman speaks these opening words is a heteronormative bias on the part of the
reader.

84. Exum, *Song of Songs*, p. 45.

in this first short call. One might go so far as to say that all the text's spatial requirements are forged here. Readers are presented with self and with other, with a sense of distance (implied through absence), with bodily anteriority and bodily interiority, and, actually, with a world of subordinate possibility: 'let' or 'there will be'.[85] The whirl of poetic imagery that follows this verse phases in and out of various states of fancy dress but these images deck out the underlying shape that is articulated in this first exchange. The shape itself is never imprisoned in a contextual paradigm, however. Or, as Murphy puts the problem (spatially as it happens): 'the life setting escapes us'.[86]

If the disjunctions between spatial production and spatial contextualization were not sufficient to alert one to the blankness of the Song's constituent space, commentators' varied attempts to fill it certainly are. Krinetzki, for example, believes that the female's opening words are uttered in the newlyweds' house, based on the mention of a 'royal chamber' in v. 4.[87] Delitzsch imagines the women of Jerusalem singing this line around Solomon's dinner table.[88] For Würthwein, 1.2 takes place in the lovers' shared home.[89] Gordis assumes a vague courtly backdrop.[90] Daphne Arbel argues that 1.2 is an 'inner monologue', or an 'inner fantasy'.[91] Bloch and Bloch similarly suggest that the female's address 'belongs to their fantasy world'.[92] These last two positions seem, again, to invoke something akin to the power of the dream to bring the Song into a coherent (or, as Bloch and Bloch put it here, a 'plausible') overall framework. When Bernard of Clairvaux 'hopes with every fibre of his being' that the Christ will 'kiss him with the kisses of his lips', he seems to be filling in the blank backdrop of the text with his very own world: the divine voice is crooning straight into the pulpit.[93] Suffice it to say, the shared abode, the Cistercian abbey, and the marital bed are not settings demanded by the text itself. In the same vein, Delitzsch's dinner-party is more dependent on his idea of a royal/rural love triangle than on the

85. Or else, 'he will' since it is rendered in the imperfect. But the jussive is normally assigned to it.

86. Murphy, *Song of Songs*, p. 127.

87. Krinetzki, *Das Hohe Lied*, p. 85.

88. Delitzsch, *Song of Songs*, p. 19.

89. Ernst Würthwein, 'Das Hohelied', in Otto Eissfeldt (ed.), *Die Fünf Megilloth* (Tübingen: J.C.B Mohr), pp. 25-71 (27).

90. Gordis, *Song of Songs*, p. 45.

91. Daphna Arbel, 'My Vineyard, My Very Own, is for Myself', in Athalya Brenner and Carole R. Fontaine (eds.), *A Feminist Companion to the Bible (Second Series)* (Sheffield: Sheffield Academic Press, 2000), p. 93.

92. Bloch, *Song of Songs*, p. 137.

93. Bernard of Clairvaux, *Sermons on the Song of Songs*, I (Kalamazoo: Cistercian Publications, 1976), pp. 8-9.

poem. And, as Duane Garrett has pointed out, the lovers cannot *begin* in the royal chamber, because v. 4 has them ending up there.[94] This is an important observation insofar as it highlights the fact that we have a *destination* in v. 4, but no original locus in the text. There is no 'original' setting to which a reader's orderly sensibilities can appeal, only a void obscured by a flurry of movement: 'Draw me after you, let us run!' Of course there is no chamber in the text of v. 4 either, there is only speech that projects a chamber.

The array of potential locations that some scholars have provided for the poem's opening demonstrates, perhaps, just how successful the Song is in concealing its projectedness behind its whirlwind romance. It also indicates just how strong the readerly desire for situation can be. It is this lack of an original parent context that gives the text such freedom to shift and change its scenes at will. As Albert Cook puts it, 'every one of the (Song's) shifts of statement brings in its train a shift of evoked scene'.[95] The inverse also holds true: shifts in evoked scene rely on the lovers' ability to shift statement willy-nilly. The blankness of the Song's background makes these constant shifts possible, freeing words from context and using them to re-create, or re-condition, the fabric of the very space they imply.[96]

Robertson's phantasmagoria was simultaneously a projection and a concealment: images were projected onto the scrim; the scrim concealed the

94. Garrett, *Song of Songs*, pp. 127-29.

95. Cook, *The Root of The Thing*, p. 101.

96. The end of the poem is, if anything, even more spatially ambiguous than the beginning. Song 8.13-14 is a final conversational exchange between the male and female lovers. The singular feminine suffix on 'you' and 'your' suggests that the woman is the addressee in v. 13. In v. 14, the woman replies to the man, telling him to 'take flight' over the suggestive 'mountains of spices'. The woman's command here (reminiscent of her charge in 2.17) is inherently spatial: it consists of an order to flee and a destination. However, there is neither an obvious reason to take flight, nor a locus to take flight *from*. The destination is no clearer. Are these mountains a distant place of refuge, or the location of a rendezvous? Or are they close by, are they nothing other than the undulating body of the woman herself, whose breasts have doubled as mountains at several points already in the Song? Verse 14 is a highly spatial command, but it becomes spatially ambiguous precisely because of the blankness of the setting. Faced with the absence of text after 8.14 (the end of the book), one realizes just how unanchored the words are. That is, without anything to follow them, stand-in locations cannot be cobbled together for 8.14 as they have been for 1.2. On this point, Landy sketches the gap that opens up between the poet and the poem at 8.13-14, calling attention to the idea that the end of the text becomes the moment when the performance 'in' the text and the text itself merge, becoming self-referential. To put it more exactly, Landy argues that the text becomes aware in these two verses of its own vocality, drawing attention to the fact that the whole space of love and rendezvous has been rendered by the power of speech that has been internalized 'in' the text itself. The exclusion of the author at the Song's close highlights this difference between spaces-of-speaking and space-as-spoken. See Landy, *Paradoxes of Paradise*, p. 196.

production of those images. The phantasmagoria thus both describes and highlights the importance of certain modalities of space: the space between the projector and the scrim, and the space between the scrim and the audience. These modalities are what gave Robertson the power to create an experiential environment that transcended the transactions between lamp/scrim and scrim/audience. These transactions in—or, more cynically, manipulations of—space are reminiscent of the Song's creation of and reliance upon poetic silence. On one level, the Song of Songs consists of an unstable world of phasing images: the settings, stories and bodies that it poetically projects for our enjoyment. But, like the phantasmagorian's ghosts, this seamless blur of images relies on a backstage that we, as readers, never see. The Song too is 'backlit'. It creates a series of images but hides—through omission—where they come from. Like the phantasmagorian, the poet thus secretes the mechanics of the artistry behind the magic produced by it. This very concealment is what allows the Song to play with imagery so freely, in fact. Without the blank constituent space of the Song, the phasing, changing, phantasmic shifts of the poem would be impossible for the poet to stage—a parent space, an original context, would be forever in the way. The Song's 'space of two' is a blank-world in which new worlds can be easily rendered. The Song's textuality relies on the staging of the staged, the representation of the representational.

Space, then, is another name for the silence of the Song of Songs; it is the 'opening' that makes discourse and intercourse possible there. As Foucault observes,

> Silence itself—the things one declines to say, or is forbidden to name, the discretion that is required between different speakers—is less the absolute limit of discourse, the other side from which it is separated by a strict boundary, than an element that functions alongside the things said, with them and in relation to them within over-all strategies. There is no binary division to be made between what one says and what one does not say; we must try to determine the different ways of not saying such things, how those who can and those who cannot speak are distributed, which type of discourse is authorized, or which form of discretion is required in either case. There is not one but many silences, and they are an integral part of the strategies that underlie and permeate discourses.[97]

The Song of Songs comes to be about love, not just because of what it shows us about love, but because of what it conceals. The biblical text projects a parade of diffuse, phantasmagoric images, and yet in doing so it works hard to conceal the bodies, the lovers, the author, the narrator—the sites that are the very precondition of its existence. The text implies an awful lot more than it delivers, and yet what it delivers relies on all that hiddenness. Is the

---

97. Foucault, *The Will to Knowledge*, p. 27.

most valuable lesson the Song has to offer its readers that love is a tense negotiation between performance and secret?

Conjuring Tricks: Turning Sex into Discourse

So far, I have been occupied with mapping the two types of space that constitute the poetic world of the Song. First, the bewitching landscape that the lovers colourfully narrate, a sphere with its own maps and configurations and blueprints. Second, I have been concerned with the basic poetic architecture that underlies the text and makes these phantasmagoric projections possible, the 'space of two' across which the lovers converse but which is never coloured in for the reader. Those two spatialities have been instructive in different ways, in terms of looking afresh at the Song's world and the nature of the text itself. I wish now to look at the phantasmagoric nature of the text from the perspective of its implied reader. Might the merging, melding and projecting power of the Song's phantasms affect the spatiality of reading too?

Earlier, with some help from Calvino, I described the way in which space is the necessary precondition of relationality; the notion of 'the multiple' presumes the possibility of a 'betwixt'. Lovers will always have a complex interaction with space, then, for space must inevitably define and vex them as they make repeated attempts—physical, emotional, verbal—at a comingling that can never be fully achieved. It is important to realize that reading relies on space too, and for all the same reasons. The space that intervenes between the person and the page is no less necessary that the space between lovers, and no less intimate. As Blanchot points out,

> the work is a work only when it becomes the intimacy shared by someone who writes it and someone who reads it, a space violently opened up by the contest between the power to speak and the power to hear.[98]

Hearing, saying, writing, and reading have their own kind of shared intimacy. Love, text, speech, sex: all are attempts to appease the violence of the thresholds that run betwixt and between us. The curious feature of the Song is that it (con)fuses the spatiality between its lovers with the spatiality between it (as a text) and its readers.

The root problem that gives rise to the spatial questions I have been exploring here is that the whole text is rendered as direct speech. The reader only ever *overhears* the Song's love affair. The poem's dialogic character is often praised for giving a stamp of realism, or a certain experiential *je ne sais quoi*. In employing dialogue, the poet 'chooses to show

---

98. Maurice Blanchot, *The Space of Literature* (Lincoln, NE: University of Nebraska Press, 1989), p. 137.

us how lovers behave', says Michael Fox.[99] Exum tell us likewise that, 'the poem presents its readers with a vision of love, not in the abstract but in the concrete, through showing us what lovers do *or, more precisely, by telling us what they say*'.[100] Exum's final modification is a crucial one. Strictly speaking, we are not shown what lovers do anywhere in the poem, only what they announce. All the biblical lovers do is talk. This gives rise to the sense of malleable spatiality 'betwixt' the pair that I have already discussed at length, as I have said, but it also serves to conflate the idea of love with the practice of poetry.

To approach this from a different angle, Exum rightly recognizes that the poet has deftly effaced him or herself from the text by throwing the authorial voice entirely into the mouths of the lovers themselves.[101] But what if we do not to accede to the ruse? If we actively recognize that the poet has invested poetic power in the characters, we then have to come to terms with the inescapable fact that in the Song of Songs to be a lover is to be a poet. To be a lover in the Song is to be a composer of literature. Or else it is to be a respondent to literature. The Song is a text within which text is produced and consumed. The idea of a lover who is *not* a poet is an anathema to the basic structure of the Song itself, by which I mean that one loves in the Song by means of wordsmithery, and one is loved by means of receiving words. The Song's vision of love is, in fact, something akin to an editorial process.[102] The Song is a text in which the characters do nothing but compose literature for each other, after all. In other words, while the Song can indeed be seen as an anthology turned into a relationship by the organizing power of the reader, one can also recognize that its romantic relationship consists entirely of poetic compositions.

99. Fox, *Song of Songs*, p. 217.
100. Exum, *Song of Songs*, p. 4, emphasis mine.
101. Exum, *Song of Songs*, p. 4.
102. On one level, the Song's preoccupation with lovers as text-producers speaks fairly directly to the ongoing debate regarding the compositional nature of the Song: is the text an anthological collection of poetry or a unitary literary work? Dianne Bergant suggests that the issue of the Song's literary unity may not necessarily be as clear-cut as the simple exclusionary pair of collection/unity. Even if the Song is an anthology, its collection and ordering displays considerable artistry. 'Though the poems may have originated as discrete pieces', she explains, 'as they appear in this collection they create a kind of coherent plot of longing, searching, finding, losing, longing, etc.' (*Song of Songs*, p. xv). The anthology becomes, in practice, a developed single-piece by means of the editor's particular collation of the material. Exum and Black go further, arguing that to be reader is to be a 'producer' of meaning, and that the collation of disparate fragments of poetry into a 'coherent' whole is a natural response to reading the Song, see Black and Exum, 'Semiotics in Stained Glass', pp. 315-42 The notion of the anthological Song is, they insist, a moot one.

As a result we might say that the Song neatly represents a sliding together of textuality and sexuality. The Song transforms sex into discourse, not simply because it is a discourse about love, but because it is a discourse about sexual discourse. The Song poses a product of its own protagonists, a feat it achieves by putting its entire content in the mouths of its own characters. Thus, readers do not see or hear of love in the Song so much as read of it being heard of and spoken of. What we take to be the ins and outs of love in the text are actually the ins and outs of the transformation of love into poetry.[103] The Song internalizes its own textuality (it is a text within a text), it turns itself into a product of its own production, and it poses as its own necessary precondition.[104]

Turning Readers into Phantasmagorians

So, what of the act of reading this poem inside the poem? By reading the Song we become participants in the same spatiality that we read about; we participate in a 'space of two' characterized by poetic initiation and poetic reception. We engage with the Song on the same terms that the lovers engage with each other. The space between lovers becomes coterminous with the space between the Song and its readers. As I have discussed, the lovers within the Song's world transform one scene space into another—city into palanquin, say, or garden into town-house, or black body into scorched vineyard. But these same blurrings of space are what constitute the textuality of the Song as a whole. The poetic architecture of the book allows for an overlapping of the space between lovers with the space between person and page. These spaces of poetic interaction merge, blur and mingle like the phantasmagoric scenes themselves. The text does not simply contain moments of phantasmagoric melding, then; the act of reading itself becomes a phantasmic blurring of landscapes. The text internalizes

---

103. This feature of the Song is, of course, a natural effect of the poet having 'deftly effaced' him or herself from the text by avoiding any third-person narration, as Exum points out (*Song of Songs*, p. 123). We could argue that this feature characterizes many poems, and especially love poems, which tend to be written in the first person. That said, not all love poetry internalizes its own discourse. Byron's 'She Walks in Beauty Like the Night', for example, or Philip Larkin's 'Love Song in Age' both involve narration and as such they might be called discourses about love, rather than discourses about discourses about love. In any case, the fact that the Song's form tells us something about the discursive nature of poetry itself (and the poetic underpinnings of all discourse), and the fact that close reading of the Song's poetic spatiality can make comment on the genre more generally, makes these comments more, not less, pertinent, and thus worth rehearsing here.

104. We shall come back to this idea of the created corpus posing as its own precondition below, in Chapter 5.

its own textuality, its own discursive spatiality Like the encircled bedroom that both haunts and prefigures the lovers' spoken worlds, the text's space-of-loving both haunts and prefigures its space-of-reading.[105]

Fiona Black has addressed the correlation between the lovers of the Song and the Song and its readers in *The Artifice of Love*. Using the image of the grotesque body, and particularly the œuvre of Rabelais as discussed by Bakhtin, Black exposes the lovers' bodies as sites of ambiguity and multiplicity in the text. Recalling the work of Barthes, who famously equates the physical body with the literary corpus,[106] Black's discussion culminates by exploring the ways in which the Song itself, as a text, operates as a grotesque 'body'. Like its metamorphic characters, the Song entices and frustrates its readers/critics—its lovers—by inviting and resisting their interpretative advances. As Black shrewdly observes, 'to have a discussion about the lovers' relationship is to have a discussion about readers'.[107] In this way, Black attempts, among other things, to explain the sometimes unnerving attachment that critics and commentators have displayed toward the Song.

Space is actually an important, and tacitly acknowledged, feature in Black's analysis of the place of the body in the poem. Black uses de Certeau's analysis of the mystical subject as an instructive analogy of the subject-in-love. De Certeau's mystical subject is a seeker of the unknown and unknowable. The mystical subject is thus characterized by absence. This is not the absence that all desire implies, but an absence that comes from self-emptying, an absence that comes from losing all definition of self, an absence that defines the subject entirely by its response to an Other.[108]

---

105. Is it any wonder that allegoresis has ruled the interpretative tradition of the Song? Allegorical readings may themselves, in their individual details, be odd and sometimes gross impositions on the text (the idea that the two breasts of the female lover correspond to the Old and New Testaments springs particularly to mind in this regard), but is the Song not setting itself up as the reader's lover? By merging the spatiality of loving with the spatiality of reading, the Song invites the broader project of 'mistaking' the text for one's beloved. The world the poem invites us to evoke as readers is predicated on these very terms. While the oddness of the nitty-gritty of allegorical reading stands, allegorists may well be able to claim that the text was, as it were, begging for it. The 'space of two' is itself a kind of allegorical honey trap. Exum notes the Song's 'invitation to the reader' to participate in its world of love, seeing in the Song a particular series of strategies at work that involve the reader in its heady romance, Exum, *Song of Songs*, p. 7. It is possible, though, that this invitation is not limited to becoming part of the romance qua romance, but that the text, and the invitation, are open enough to be shaped by the reader's own structures of perception, by their own sense of what they should be loving, whether human, divine, or otherwise.

106. Black, *Artifice of Love*, pp. 207-17.

107. Black, *Artifice of Love*, p. 187.

108. Black, *Artifice of Love*, p. 182.

Lovers in the Song of Songs become desiring subjects in much the same way, argues Black. Defined by seeking alone, these paramours become hidden—emptied even—by their own desire for the unknowable other; the lover is 'a respondent who speaks from her own experience of that which she cannot fully experience or articulate'. As Black explains:

> In the process of absenting the self, then, the mystic/lover has a need to 'found the place from which he or she speaks'. This means both creating the new subject—the 'I'—who will speak, but also, eventually, a space from whence to speak, 'an imaginary mode', a 'field for the development of discourse'. The 'I' momentarily takes the place of the other (inarticulable), and, as a consequence, develops an equally substitutory locale from whence to speak.[109]

By this, Black means that the Song's lovers cast themselves 'out' of themselves by speaking of the other. They 'found', in the body of their beloved, a new place to speak that is beyond themselves. In doing so they re-create themselves as a respondent. They also create a field for the development of discourse, a 'space of two' across which they communicate.[110]

What is the 'substitutory locale' of the biblical lovers?, asks Black. Is it the natural world, is it the mountains of spices, is it the mother's house? Black's conclusion is that the body itself forms the Song's fictional space, but not the body of the lover-subject. Rather, the Song's substitutory locale is the body of the beloved other. The lovers speak back to themselves, as it were, from the place of their lovers' body, which comes into being as they articulate it. Embodiment does certainly intersect all the other phasing, shifting phantasmagoric scenes in the text, but these bodies are rendered absent, unknowable, by the very processes Black describes. The issue, of course, is that the self-emptying, or self-concealing, goes a layer further to the invisible poet. If the female lover empties herself and finds, in her formulation of her lover's frame, a new space from whence to speak, then the poet too founds a locus for poetic articulation in the personae of the lovers. In the lovers the poet invests the power to speak, emptying the poem of the poet in the process. In other words, the whole Song opens up as a 'field for the development of discourse', an 'imaginary mode', a fictious space between the poet and the characters, who are sites for speaking from.[111] By the same logic, the Song's audience, the reader, does the same—finding in the text a place for his or her own articulations. The fusing together of textual spatiality and intimate spatiality exploits the fluidity of the categories of author/character/reader in the Song. The text is one vast substitutory locale, not situated 'in' bodies but rather situated as the between that

---

109. Black, *Artifice of Love*, p. 183.
110. Black, *Artifice of Love*, p. 183.
111. Black, *Artifice of Love*, p. 183.

makes bodies, that is, established positions of signification—reader, narrator, textual corpus—possible. The Song exists as a gap betwixt, a space of two created by and inviting of projections—all manner of them, interlaced, overlapping and humming with potential energy: a phantasmagoric space, a Pandæmonium.

What Robertson's phantasmagoria achieved was remarkable, not because the phantoscope represented any great technological leaps but because it affected such intense emotional investiture from the public. As I pointed out earlier, the great feature of the phantasmagorian's lantern was not its ability to scare but its ability to make the audience project their own neuroses onto the theatrical scrim. The phantasmagorian's scrim, I argued, is thus to be considered a double surface with projections colouring it from both sides. The Song of Songs is also a space that enables double projections. It too works through complex mechanisms of projection and concealment, and with manipulations of space designed to blur what we see into a hypnotic parade and to draw us into emotional investiture by conflating our interactions with the text with the interactions between the lovers themselves. For Robertson's Parisian audience, the phantasmagoria worked hard to exorcize the cultural demons left over from the French Revolution. However, in trying to show up the demonic as technological, Robertson ended up displaying the diabolical nature of technology itself. Does the Song have a similarly double function? In displaying a discursive romance, does it end up showing us the romance inherent to discourse and to text more particularly?

Turning the Page, Making the Bed

A recap is in order. The Song's is a distortative and heady world. Its scenes merge and meld. But the application of dream rhetoric to the Song serves only to describe this fluidity, socializing the Song and effacing its producedness at the expense of analysing it. In actual fact, a closer look at the spatiality of the so-called dream sequences reveals a more conspicuously produced text-world than one might think. The continual modulations in the lovers' environs cause the entire cosmos to become crammed into the space between them, and cause this 'bedroom' to reach out, to widen into a universe of possibilities. The text has an architecture more fundamental than its setting, however. The Song is a space of speaking and hearing, and it (con)fuses interpersonal space with communicative space to the point that our own reading-space becomes confused with the phantasmic blur of its lovers. The nature of the Song as a discourse of discourses enables the lovers to transform their environment with their words; sex is transformed into discourse, discourse is transformed into landscape, landscape (as we shall see in the next chapter) becomes a concretization, a spatial reflection, of sexuality.

Earlier, I likened this power of the lovers to transform and transport themselves to the power John Donne imbued his literary lovers with in 'The Sun Rising'. 'She's all states, and all princes I' croons the male lover in Donne's text, and, as the trysting place becomes the axis of the sun itself, this lovers' bed becomes a space of cosmic distillation. In elucidating the relationship between lovers and readers and between space and discourse here, it is worth now bringing in Georges Perec's comparable comments on the bed as a transformative and transportative space at the centre of a changeable and highly produced landscape.[112]

> *The Bed*
>   'For a long time I went to bed in writing' –Parcel Mroust[113]
>
> *1*
> We generally utilize the page in the larger of its two dimensions. The same goes for the bed. The bed (or, if you prefer, the page) is a rectangular space, longer than it is wide, in which, or on which, we normally lie longways…the bed is an instrument conceived for the nocturnal repose of one or two persons, but no more.
>
> *2*
> '*Lit=île*' –Michel Leiris[114]
>
> It was lying facedown on my bed that I read *Twenty Years After*, *The Mysterious Island* and *Jerry on the Island*. The bed became a trapper's cabin, or a lifeboat on the raging ocean, or a baobab tree threatened by fire, a tent erected in the desert, or a propitious crevice that my enemies passed within inches of, unavailingly.[115]
>
> I travel a great deal at the bottom of my bed. For survival, I carried sugar lumps I went and stole from the kitchen and hid under my bolster (they scratched…). Fear—terror even—was always present, despite the protection of the blankets and pillow.
>
> Bed: where unformulated dangers threatened, the place of contraries, the space of the solitary body encumbered by its ephemeral harems, the foreclosed space of desire, the improbable place where I had my roots, the space of dreams and of an Oedipal nostalgia:

112. Perec's text is designed to feel scattered and piecemeal, though it works through the suggestive nature of the concept of the page-cum-bed extremely thoughtfully. I have therefore attempted, as far as is possible, to retain the formatting in this (somewhat lengthy) quotation.

113. Georges Perec, *Species of Spaces and Other Pieces* (trans. John Sturrock; London: Penguin, 1997 [1974]), p. 16. As Sturrock points out in his notes on this part of the text, this is 'a play on the first sentence of Proust's great novel, *A le recherché du temps perdu*, which reads: 'For a long time I went to bed early'.

114. Bed=Island. Perec, *Species of Spaces*, p. 17. Though, of course, *lit* also means 'to read'.

115. Perec, *Species of Spaces*, pp. 16-17.

'Happy is he who can sleep without fear and without remorse
In the paternal bed, massive, venerable,
Where all his kinfolk were born and where they died'.
                                        —Jose Maria de Heredia, *Trophées*

Perec very carefully undoes the distinctions between page and bed here. The two blank oblongs, each inhabited in the same dimension (lengthways), converge in their ability to transport imaginatively their occupant, is to recode space by means of fantasy (read: desire). Each field, page and bed, is a 'foreclosed space of desire'. The question Perec is prompting from us here is this: is Perec lying on the oblong of the bed, or on the oblong of the page? The answer, of course, is both. His powers of inhabitation are doubled; his fantasy, his desire, grounds him on the bed/page and scatters him across the furthest regions of the earth. The ancestral bed, as the common space of birth, sex, and death, coincides with the page as a space of desire, of movement, and of refuge. Reading, fantasizing, and travelling mingle together on the surface of the everyday oblongs, which cocoons and casts us adrift all at once.[116] Like the audience member at a phantasmagorian's show, held within a prop-strewn gothic convent and processing through Pandæ-monium at the same time.

All this is to say that if, for Black, the Song of Songs becomes a body, a *corpus,* for me, its page correlates with the lovers' 'bed': a blank space of discursive transportation. The biblical lovers are transported, and transformed, by the trysting space 'between them'—worlds mingle and collapse around them as a centre. The body of our text, laid out on the page like a lover upon a bed, uses the page, the blank space that makes text possible, to transport us as readers, and, moreover, to *transform* us into communicators-with-poetry, that is—in the Song's economy at least—into lovers. Perec's bed becomes a 'trapper's cabin' and 'a lifeboat on a raging ocean' as he reads. The bed is a 'baobab tree', 'a tent erected in the desert', and a 'propitious crevice' in the mountainside. Similarly, as the lovers' love, their bedroom becomes a royal chamber with a kingly bed (1.12), then a forest abode with a green day bed (1.16), a remote bower (2.3), a fruit-house erected in the vineyards (2.4), and so on. Yet as we read the page takes on a strange power too. We enter into a world that transforms around the fixed, central oblong of the page, the oblong on which the textual corpus is laid out for our enjoyment. The lovers' worlds slide together and mingle. The space of discourse *in* the text and our readerly space connect in the same way. Snuggling under the covers with the Bible, we are cocooned and transported by the bed-cum-page.

The sheer complexity of the textual space in the Song, as I have tried to sketch in this chapter, is the result of a clash of geometries, or rather a series

116. Perec, *Species of Spaces*, p. 17.

of clashing geometries that the term 'dream' does not begin to describe adequately. I have tried to draw attention to the discursive nature of the Song in order to point out that the roots of the dizzying variety of images in the song—spatial or otherwise—are due to its overriding vocality. In a sense, my main task in this chapter has thus been to tackle the silences, the gaps, that make the Song's discourse possible, the missing pieces of information that create geotextual fissures in the text. Blank spatiality is the scrim that makes the lovers' poetic sorcery possible, and it is possible, and necessary, to get beneath the skin (/scrim) of the textual corpus, and to figure it, like the phantasm, as part of the trope of ideological illusion.

This does not negate the importance of the worlds that the lovers speak into being around themselves. On the contrary, the ideological quality of the Song's poetic architecture magnifies it somewhat. In the magical world of the lovers—the world of Novalis/Borges's mage where the actor and the stage entirely merge—how does the ideology of the lover engineer its own environs, and is all as we might expect in these particular spaces? In the next chapter, we shall look at two of the Song's most iconic spaces with just these questions in mind. How does the Song's urban environment work in the midst of these spatial politics, and what significance do my observations have for the poem's most famous spaces, its idyllic gardens?

Chapter 3

LOCKED GARDENS AND THE CITY AS LABYRINTH

All utopias are depressing because they leave no room for chance, for difference, for the 'miscellaneous'. Everything has been set in order and order
reigns. Behind every utopia there is always some great taxonomic design: a
place for each thing and each thing in its place.

—George Perec[1]

The phantasmagoric nature of the Song makes close analysis of its scenes
quite difficult. Many, if not most, of the spaces that the lovers conjure around
themselves are too fleeting to apprehend properly. Two spaces, however, are
of particular importance in the text: the garden and the city. The garden is
the Song's most developed metaphor and operates as both a setting and as
an image of the woman herself. It has been the subject of some considerable
scholarly analysis. The cities, by contrast, are perhaps the most involved
scenes of the Song—they contain whole plot arcs and several backdrops—
though the volume of analyses of the city *as a city* is rather paltry in comparison. The city is usually discussed in scholarship only as a counter-image
to the garden, or else as an incidental context for certain actions (most notably the watchmen's beating of the female lover in 5.7). This chapter consists of a close reading of these two spaces, a kind of sceneography of the
Song's most iconic settings. In it I shall explore the phantasmagoric relation
of the garden and the city and so make some moves towards troubling the
sense that there is a city/garden contrast in the the Song at all. I also want
to argue that the spaces of garden and city do not simply *emerge from* the
Song's politics of effacement and performance, as traced in the last chapter,
but that the internal workings of these spaces rely on these same operations.

The Green Green Grass of Biblical Academe

Whatever else commentators on the Song may quibble about, one idea seems
to enjoy general and unquestioned acceptance: gardens are good. Read any
scholarly literature on the Song and one will find numerous discussions on

---

1. Perec, *Species of Spaces and Other Pieces*, p. 191; this extract is taken from
Penser/Classer.

the poem's garden(s) that portray them in a remarkably positive way, or else work on the assumption that the garden is an unimpeachable symbol of light and life. Gardens evoke humanity's innocent, primordial days; gardens are intimate, sexually suggestive; gardens teem with love; gardens are sumptuous, luxurious, and resplendent. By extension so too is the female lover, with whom the garden is closely associated in the poem (4.12, 5.1, 6.2-3). I am not sure the garden is necessarily as Arcadian and innocent a trope as all that, but the symbol's positive image seems to have taken root in scholarship. And spread.

'The rarity of the vegetation produced by this fantastic garden suggests the exceptional nature of the woman's beauty. She is an incomparable garden, graced with beauty that is rare and unmatched', Dianne Bergant tells us.[2] Othmar Keel stresses the ancient importance of the garden as a positive symbol: 'one of the greatest pleasures known to the ancient Near East was a garden…to sit under these trees in peace and to enjoy their fruits without disturbance was the highest form of happiness'. Keel also indicates that it was impossible in the ancient world to describe either 'the blessed primeval time' or 'the coming age of salvation' without the utopian image of the garden. Like Bergant, Keel reads the woman in the Song to be 'wonderful, mysterious and exotic' by virtue of her association with this image.[3] Keel's is quite some garden then, but others are still more enthusiastic. Munro's fondness for *al fresco* living is far more pronounced, rose-tinted even:

> If the garden of Eden story is about dislocation and exile, and if it asks questions for which there are no easy answers, the Song on the other hand simply sings of love, and in so doing initiates a process of restoration and return. It is not that the world is repaired and that suffering ceases to exist—the element of menace is too powerfully present in the Song for that [does she mean the violent city?]—but simply that love transforms all things. Barriers, in the eyes of love, are thresholds, and divisions, distinctions. The garden, which in the Genesis story becomes an inaccessible place from which humanity is exiled, in the Song is rediscovered in the woman; it is in union or communion with her that her lover rediscovers the bliss of which the Eden story spoke. As a result, the world around them is also recreated; it too becomes a garden, a garden of love which the reader too may enter for a time.[4]

Munro's gardens are explicitly Edenic and, importantly, *healing*—not only for the textual lovers but for readers too, apparently. But idealized as Munro's treatment of the garden may be, she is actually taking her cue from others—namely, Phyllis Trible and Francis Landy whose works on the Song's garden tie it to paradise in the most explicit terms possible.

---

2. Bergant, *Song of Songs*, pp. 55-56.
3. Keel, *Song of Songs*, pp. 169-70.
4. Munro, *Spikenard and Saffron*, pp. 105-106.

Trible reads the Song's relationship as a reversal of humanity's Fall and exclusion from Eden. The lovers and their garden complete the story of Genesis 2–3, she argues, though she is (curiously) anxious to protect the image of the garden itself from any theological blame: 'Eden locates the tragedy of disobedience in Genesis 2–3. But the garden itself signals delight, not disaster, and that perspective reverberates in the Song of Songs.' She goes on to say of the Song's garden: 'person and place unite: the garden of eroticism is the woman. In this garden the sensuality of Eden expands and deepens'.[5] Landy pushes Trible's basic premise in a slightly different direction. He locates *two* different gardens—or two distinct versions of garden experience—in the text, one in 4.12-15, the other in 6.2. These two spaces focus on different lovers, and speak differently about the lovers' relationship and their senses of self. The Song's gardens do not 'complete' or 'answer' Genesis 2–3 in any intentional way, says Landy, but they do complement the biblical Paradise: 'the Song is not merely a commentary on the garden of Eden but a re-enactment, almost a hallucination of it'. 'The primordial couple in Eden lose their Paradise for the same reasons that the couple in the Song regain it', he says.[6] As far as Trible, Landy and Munro are concerned the Song's green precincts are not paradise, then; they are far better.

Other readings are less romantic but no less approving. In his infamous pornographic take on the Song, Roland Boer reads the much sought-after 'locked garden' (4.12) as nothing short of the point of climax itself—and not simply as a mediocre orgasm but as a messy, wet, 'festival of liquids': 'she lets loose, quickly and repeatedly, spraying, sprinkling her own cum over Beth's tongue and face'.[7] In Boer's titillating economy there is perhaps no greater status for a symbol.[8] Even Fiona Black, whose work is so careful

5. Phyllis Trible, *God and the Rhetoric of Sexuality* (Overtures to Biblical Theology, 2; Philadelphia: Fortress Press, 1978), pp. 154-56.

6. Landy, *Paradoxes of Paradise*, p. 172.

7. Roland Boer, *Knocking on Heaven's Door: The Bible and Popular Culture* (New York: Routledge, 1999), p. 68.

8. In a later article Boer treats the land a little differently; Roland Boer, 'Keeping it Literal: The Economy of the Song of Songs', *JHS* 7 (2007), pp. 1-14. In this essay, Boer discusses the world of the text as an economic arena with the help of metaphor analysis, ecocriticism, and Marxism. Boer argues that the Songscape is a fecund self-producing site in which commodities are spontaneously produced (and are subsequently allocated), rather than a site from which human agents forcibly extract commodities. Interestingly, Boer mentions the garden only twice in this discussion, both times to link it to a 'bucolic' Eden. The garden, though, might be said actively to resist Boer's reading of the Song's world. As we shall see, the garden's technological elements—its walls, its locks, its incongruent assortment of flora—do not suggest a self-producing Eden as strongly as they might, and I want to tease out those elements of the text here. Boer is keen to point out in his article that while the Song's is a literary and constructed world its writer(s) had to make use of the economic, ideological and social tools at their disposal

to rise above the gushing positivity that floods Song scholarship, is complimentary about the garden (as a fruity, edible space it sits rather nicely within
her grotesque reading, of course): 'Lush gardens are meant to be enjoyed,
even this *utopischer Phantasiegarten*, but they are also replete with exotic
plants that yield foods and spices, which means that their enjoyment may be
of a gustatory as well as a visual nature'.[9] The Song's gardens contain fun
and food, rest and relaxation, sex and satisfaction for all.

Spatialized goodness—whether in the form of a heaven, or Paradise, or
a divinely perfected world—is so closely associated with the image of the
garden that it seems difficult to separate the two ideas, and this seems to fuel
the kind of beaming horticultural fervour I have been describing. A perfect
human origin, a perfect historical climax, a perfect climax of an entirely different kind, a healing literary setting, a restorative feminist narrative, an idealized hallucination: the Song's garden boasts all manner of positive ideological
flora. It almost seems as though gardens are not good *per se*, but that we have
been trained to imagine the spatial manifestation of goodness as a garden, and
to search in gardens for our perfected, primordial or ecstatic selves. We know
that gardens are wonderful and we read on from there.

My intention here is to take apart this 'garden' term. Not simply by
means of reference to Egyptian or Assyrian horticultural practice—which
is the normal way to go about this kind of thing—but to go further back
into the logic of the spatial symbol itself, to think about the very fact of
imposing nurture upon nature. To say the Song's garden is a utopian fantasy is really only one side of the story. Gardens are the result of powerful
impositions of human will. Billed as a return to unfettered primordiality,
the garden is actually a product of human domination, a clearing away of
the raw in order to impose a theatrical theme-park version of 'creation', the
boundaries of which, ultimately, serve a political reality. Gardens function
only as spheres of enjoyment, relaxation and rest—and as viable settings for
the first humans and the Faithful, post-mortem—because people have gone
to great lengths to ensure that the garden is a space in which nothing really
matters. And in an androcentric economy what better space is there to conflate with the female body?

This perspective may seem like little more than unbridled cynicism, but
my unsympathetic 'reading' of the garden actually emerges from garden

(p. 14). It is with these same 'tools' of Boer's that I want to cultivate a different sort
of argument. I shall be making allusions to the economics of the garden space as I go
(namely, that it is a royal space, the very existence of which is predicated on an economics of exclusion), but a thoroughgoing technical Marxist reading of the garden (of the
type Boer might approve) is not possible here. I do aim, however, to raise some alternatives to kind of the economic and pastoral utopia he alludes to in his discussion.

   9. Black, *Artifice of Love*, p. 150.

theory, which has enjoyed a surprising proliferation since the late 1970s. Garden theorists are quick to note the social connections that run between space, power and gender in historical gardens, and I am keen to peruse the Song's fragrant enclosures with this kind of viewpoint in mind. This is not because the Song's gardens need vandalizing necessarily—though I am not ruling that out—but because the dynamics of power and domination that these spaces evoke have not simply been ignored by biblical critics, they have been buried and patio-ed over.

Painting the Roses Red: Gardens as Power

While garden theory could not boast as great a platform as urban theory, it is no insignificant programme. There is a whole host of publications on the garden, historically and theoretically informed work that deals with the garden as both a literary trope and as a social reality.[10] A handful of works, despite their age, remain central to the field and these are obvious resources to draw on here.

The first is an edited volume called *The Poetics of Gardens,* a book described by James Elkins in 2008 as still being 'arguably the most critically informed and carefully written recent work on gardens'.[11] The second is a collection of essays entitled *The Meaning of Gardens.* The particular essay I am interested in from that volume is Robert Riley's 'Flowers, Power and Sex', the relevance of which will no doubt be obvious from its title. Riley parses out gendered and sexual power dynamics in various gardens over the centuries.[12] The other major work(s) I want to draw on are two related essays by Yi-Fu Tuan, 'Gardens of Power and of Caprice' and 'Fountains and Plants'.[13] Tuan's essays are generally recognized to be the definitive statements on the garden as a mechanism of power. The goal of all these contributions is to displace

10. The journal *Studies in the History of Garden & Designed Landscapes*—formerly, and more pithily, the *Journal of Garden History*—alone boasts over a hundred years of scholarship on the subject.

11. Charles W. Moore, William J. Mitchell and William Turnbull (eds.), *The Poetics of Gardens* (Cambridge, MA: MIT Press, 1993); James Elkins, 'Writing Moods', in *Landscape Theory* (New York: Routledge, 2008), pp. 69-86 (79). For further background reading, generally along the same lines, see Robert B. Riley, 'From Sacred Grove to Disney World: The Search for Garden Meaning', *Landscape Journal* (1988), pp. 136-47; Anne Whiston Spirn, 'The Poetics of City and Nature: Towards a New Aesthetic for Urban Design', *Places: Forum of Design for the Public Realm* (1989), pp. 82-93.

12. Robert B. Riley, 'Flowers, Power and Sex', in Mark Francis and Randolph T. Hester Jr (eds.), *The Meaning of Gardens: Idea, Place and Action* (Cambridge, MA: MIT Press, 1995 [1990]), pp. 60-75.

13. Yi-Fu Tuan, *Dominance and Affection: The Making of Pets* (New Haven, CT: Yale University Press, 1984), pp. 18-36 and pp. 37-68 respectively.

what Riley calls the *Reader's Digest* view of the garden, in favour of a more critical, a more honest analysis: simply, that the garden is not a divine gift but a social artefact, and a potentially sinister one at that.

What, then, is the nature of this artefact?[14] First of all, gardens are not just symbols of power. They are, in Tuan's words, 'symbols of *surplus* power'.[15] Pleasure gardens are not necessary. Gardens are a gratuitous manipulation of the environment for personal pleasure and their creation and constant maintenance involves the expenditure of surplus resources. Historically, then, gardens have tended to be the provinces of kings, or, more latterly, have functioned as status symbols.[16] The connection that runs between luxury and power in the image of the garden—particularly the ancient garden—is all the more pronounced of course because the garden uses up those very resources that the untitled need to survive: arable land and water. Tuan points to the gardens of Chinese emperors in illustration of this point, and to Versailles, and to English medieval gardens, and to Nero's gardens, but we might just as readily point to the gigantic royal parks of the Assyrian kings: Tiglath-pileser I, Ashurnasirpal II, Sargon II, and Sennacherib, or to the oft noted gardens of wealthy Egyptians.[17] It is hard to imagine that these areas—and the water that sustained them—could not have been put to other, more nourishing, uses; in theory, every pleasure garden represents a family of serfs without a vegetable patch. As it was, these gardens—particularly the Mesopotamian examples—were advertized in other realms as symbols of royal power over the environment.[18]

14. In what follows, I will attempt to be as broad as possible—to deal with those most basic aspects of gardens, those features common to gardens of virtually every epoch and type—but tying some specific examples of gardens from the ancient Near East to Tuan's and Riley's work will, of course, help re-contextualize their argument (it will also pre-empt charges that I have applied theory entirely anachronistically). There are, of course, other kinds of theoretical approach to the garden to the ones I am employing here. There are, for example, theoretical models that stress the activity of gardening as a potentially subversive practice, as a mode of challenging political control and undermining certain kinds of prescriptive spatial schema. An excellent example of such work is George McKay, *Radical Gardening: Politics, Idealism and Rebellion in the Garden* (London: Frances Lincoln, 2011). In the case of the Song's garden, however, the imagery is far more difficult to tie to 'grass roots' concerns and, indeed, lends itself to mechanisms of political domination astonishingly readily. Work like McKay's is important, but there is so little in the Song's garden that ties it to rebellion and so much that speaks of socio-economic status and political power that the former, less sympathetic work on gardens seems a more prudent place to begin a critical discussion of the Song's greenery.

15. Tuan, 'Gardens of Power', p. 19, emphasis mine.

16. Riley, 'Flowers, Power and Sex', pp. 63-64.

17. Bruno Meissner, *Babylonien und Assyrien*, I (Heidelberg: Carl Winters, 1920), pp. 201-12.

18. Meissner, *Babylonian and Assyrien*, I, p. 201.

As Ahab and Jezebel's misadventure with Naboth's vineyard in 1 Kings 21 succinctly indicates, gardens, as utopian ventures, also tend to involve acts of demolition, dispossession and forced removal. 'Before anything can be made', Tuan writes, 'something must first be destroyed. We take for granted that in any artistic endeavor the finished product more than justifies the destruction that necessarily precedes it.'[19] Gardens are no different. Indeed, the most vividly idealized and ambitious projects imply the greatest violence; the more utopian the project the greater the need for a blank slate—and so a bigger wrecking ball. 'Whatever exists must first be removed. Feats of preparatory destruction, sometimes on a large scale, occur whenever and wherever landscape gardening has become a mania.'[20]

While we are thinking about the ways in which gardens impinge upon wider society, it is also worth remembering that the practice of gardening in one's *own* garden is a relatively recent phenomenon. Ashurnasirpal II did not, to the best of our knowledge, prune. The proud owners of the great gardens of antiquity tended to have lesser mortals to go about raking, weeding and painting the roses red. So, while gardens have tended to evoke in us ideas about rest, relaxation and escape from toil, they could be more accurately described as sites of some considerable labour, and ongoing labour at that since what makes a garden a garden is its sustained imposition against the forces of nature. The great trick of the utopian pleasure garden has been to render all this work, this constant and often backbreaking labour, virtually invisible. And yet the very idea of the garden—a *cultivated* wonderland—implies toil at its every plot, bed and floral border.

If the very fact of the cultivated paradise is wrapped up in power, so too are its inner workings. Most gardens are walled, or at the very least clearly demarcated from their surroundings. Carefully defining gardens' borders helps assure an antithetical relationship between gardens and both wider culture and wilder nature. As Riley says:

> [The garden is] a world apart not only from uncivilized nature but from the noise, filth, and stench of life…it was a world of special rules, relationships and status, excluding much human as well as animal life. The walled garden seems a persistent indicator of status, right down to modern times. Such gardens should automatically trigger our curiosity as to who is being excluded and why.[21]

Whether gardens are walled to keep out the riff-raff or merely to emphasize one's experience of encapsulation within a wholly different world from that of 'normal' life, exclusion and the power to prohibit seem to be presumed.

19. Tuan, 'Gardens of Power', p. 19.
20. Tuan, 'Gardens of Power', p. 20.
21. Riley, 'Flowers, Power and Sex', p. 63.

Within the confines of these walls, all gardens are a conspicuous 'blend-ing of nature and artifice'.[22] One way in which the artificial nature of the garden can be seen is in the cultivation of non-indigenous plants and flow-ers. The tendency to stock ancient gardens (as well as those at Kew; the practice has not died out) with all kinds of incongruous flora is well doc-umented. Queen Hatshepsut,[23] Tiglath-pileser I, Sennacherib and Cyrus all had plants and flowers from the far-flung reaches of their kingdoms planted in their royal parks and gardens.[24] By means of these additions— procured at great personal expense, no doubt—the garden came to oper-ate as a play-version of a wider domain, a kind of concretized fantasy of a conquered world. These, as Black (following Gerleman) mentioned, are *utopische Phantasiegärten*,[25] gardens specifically designed to showcase political control and domination. Naturally, the complex systems of irriga-tion that watered these plants were similarly declamatory. With whimsical disregard for the rules of nature, the gardeners and engineers channel, dam, and collect water; they build fountains, forcing it to defy even gravity.[26] As 'artificial worlds made from the stuff of the real', then, pleasure gardens are less cosmic repositories than cosmic parodies, contrived theme parks to the 'natural' that honour human vanity by expressing our ability to manipulate our surroundings.[27] They exuberantly express our desire, as Tacitus suc-cinctly put it, to 'outbid nature'.[28]

'One Man's Woman's Dominion is...'

Due, in part, to its fantastical nature, the garden is an obvious setting for play-times of all sorts, sex included. The natural world and its associated images have long been tied up with erotic goings-on, but the link seems especially well developed when it comes to the garden. And for good reason. Freud-ian analysis works just as well on the quintessential English lawn, with its hoops, croquet mallets, and balls, as it does in the wild forests of northern European fairy-tales, after all.[29] The most well known ancient examples are

22. Tuan, 'Gardens of Power', p. 21.
23. Tuan, 'Fountains and Plants', pp. 49-50.
24. Munro, *Spikenard and Saffron*, p. 103.
25. Black, *Artifice of Love*, p. 150; Gilles Gerleman, *Ruth, Das Hohelied* (Neukirchen–Vluyn: Neukirchener Verlag, 1965), p. 159.
26. Tuan, 'Fountains and Plants', pp. 39-41; Riley, 'Flowers, Power and Sex', pp. 61-62.
27. Riley, 'Flowers, Power and Sex', p. 63.
28. Tacitus, *The Annals of Imperial Rome* (trans. Michael Grant; Harmondsworth: Penguin, 1972), p. 364.
29. I wish this were my observation. It is in fact Riley's: 'Flowers, Power and Sex', p. 67.

to be found in Egyptian love poetry—of the kind that is so often linked to
the Song—which is a good deal more explicit than the average game of croquet. With stamens all aquiver, with rivers of fragrant liquid, with bursting
fruit, how could these vibrant, fecund spaces not be sexually suggestive? As
one Egyptian love poem goes, for instance:

> (Now) I've withdrawn with you to the trees of the Houses of———(?),
>   that I might gather the fronds of the Houses of———(?)
>   that I might take (them) for my fan.
> I'll see what it(?) does!
> I am headed to the 'Love Garden',
>   my bosom full of persea (branches),
>   my hair laden with balm.
> I am a [noble woman],
>   I am the Mistress of the Two Lands,
>   When I am [with you].[30]

Alongside this sexualizing of garden space, and perhaps even because of
it, gardens tend to be linked to what is often called (and patronizingly so—
thus it illustrates my point here) the 'fairer sex'. We can simply return to
the commentary literature on the Song that I briefly looked at above to see
the effects that this image has on the female body; Bergant: 'the rarity of
the vegetation produced by this fantastic garden suggests the exceptional
nature of the woman's beauty';[31] Keel: 'wonderful, mysterious and exotic';[32]
Munro: 'yet more significant is the erotic dimension lent to this sequence
by the organizing image of the garden. It describes, with great delicacy,
how she progressively opens herself to her lover and invites him to delight
in her.'[33] So, this woman is exotic, unusually beautiful, and an object of
delight. Are these associations necessarily positive though? As Riley points
out, it is not really a political victory to be associated with flowers: 'beautiful, frail and useless'.[34]

> The garden is an artificial place made from the real, an illusion of the world.
> What better place to give women (or prisoners) an illusion of power without
> actual power? What better place to keep them busy without their interfering
> in things that matter?[35]

If gardens are indeed make-believe worlds, fantasies that obscure their own
creative operations—as well as the work that sustains them—they are not

---

30. This is from a nineteenth dynasty papyrus, P. Harris, 500 Group A, no. 7, in Fox, *Song of Songs*, p. 15.
31. Bergant, *Song of Songs*, p. 56.
32. Keel, *Song of Songs*, p. 174.
33. Munro, *Spikenard and Saffron*, p. 106.
34. Riley, 'Flowers, Power and Sex', p. 67.
35. Riley, 'Flowers, Power and Sex', p. 69.

particularly emancipatory spaces for women to be connected to. Connecting the female *body* with the garden is worse; is the female body a fantasy wonderland to be demarcated from the political world that matters? Is the female body really only for evenings and weekends (or midday in the ancient world)?

Of course the most shocking implications of these connections involve the *artificial* nature of gardens. Gardens are beautiful because they tame and remodel 'wild nature' according to social mores and cultural tastes. Gardens are beautiful because they reflect the not inconsiderable reach of human agency. If the female's body is to be a garden, then its beauty emerges not so much from the growth of life—we could hike out anywhere to see *that*— but because, to paraphrase Riley, the charms of nature have been disciplined by the hand of art. The symbol assumes that women, like gardens, are 'produced' by men. Like the work that goes into gardens, this 'production' is often erased to render the 'artefact' natural. So, while the equation of the woman with the garden might well be suggestive of all manner of loveliness, there are other, more sinister, workings in the image as well. 'One man's woman's dominion is another woman's women's prison'.[36]

Given the numerous historical and cultural allusions in my discussion so far, I perhaps need to stress that my reading of the Song is not going to imply that the poetic garden was *real* in any historical sense, nor that it was tended to by teams of green-fingered Israelites in straw boaters. The Song's garden is not as tangible as that and I am not intent on making causal, historical connections between the issues I have been raising and the biblical text. What I am trying to tease out, however, is that the image of the garden, in whatever language we write it, carries with it and indeed *assumes* a series of carefully concealed operations that could be called, for want of a better word, violent: demolition, an (often) elitist division of labour, and, worse, an erasure of this labour from the scene. All gardens are symbols of domination, botanically and politically; they showcase one's ability to manipulate the basic elements that sustain us: water, land, plant life. As a symbol for the female body (often seen as another kind of repository of life), the garden does not simply imply (male) ownership and boundedness, but also the idea of women as 'products', as wild elements best 'enjoyed' once they have been worked upon, tamed, and subjected to cultivation. The garden-woman, moreover, is not part of a political reality; she is not a vegetable patch, for instance. She is a wonderland, and the inhabitant of a theme park that the 'real' concerns of life are not allowed to touch. In invoking the image of the garden, the Song necessarily invokes this 'violence' I have been tracing, however tacitly.

36. Riley, 'Flowers, Power and Sex', p. 69.

The Song's Garden Revisited

The garden is one of the most detailed images in the Song. It crops up as a setting in 6.2, when the male protagonist goes there to see the spring unfold, and again in 8.13, where it appears to situate the lovers' friends. The garden's main appearance is in 4.12, though, where the female lover is likened to a garden, which the male goes on to describe in some detail:

> A garden locked is my sister, my bride,
> A garden locked,[37] a spring sealed.
> Your water channels[38] are a pleasure garden[39]
>   of pomegranates with choice fruits.
> Hennas with nard,
> nard and saffron,
> cane and cinnamon,
>   with all trees of frankincense,
> myrrh and aloe,
>   with all the best spices.
> Spring of gardens,
> well of living waters,[40]
> flowing[41] from Lebanon.

37. There is some disagreement on the issue of the second 'garden' in v. 12. I have opted here to amend the MT's גל for גן, which is the reading of the LXX, Vulgate the Syriac and several Hebrew manuscripts. Those who have kept גל (Gordis, Meek, Ringreen, Pope) translate it 'fountain', or 'pool'. I am not sure what kind of physical mechanism those modern versions that have 'fountain' in this verse (NIV, NRSV, NJB, NEB) are imagining; the lovers' garden is not, after all, Versailles. That no one seems willing to elaborate upon it in the literature is itself interesting. The difficulty of picking between גל and גן based on their context is compounded by the ambiguity of the verse itself. If we read with the MT, the 'fountain' anticipates the water references of v. 13. If we read with the LXX *et al.*, the second 'garden' repeats the earlier part of the verse. In either case there is no new imagery (and no suddenly absent imagery) so its bearing on my discussion here is, ultimately, quite limited.

38. The term for Watercourses is a hapax but derives from a fairly common root meaning to stretch or to send out (שלח). As Exum writes, this seems to most likely mean 'shoots, branches, or channels of water (Exum, *Song of Songs*, p. 155). For more on the problems and possibilities of this term as an aquatic structure, see Fox, *Song of Songs*, p. 137.

39. My rather literal rendering of the verse here is designed to highlight the fact that the image of the watercourse collapses into the image of a pleasure garden in this verse. Here, as one metaphor lapses into another, we see another instance of the kind of phantasmagoric shifts I discussed in the last chapter. For a discussion of the other less idiomatic options for the translation of this verse see Exum, *Song of Songs*, p. 155.

40. The phrase 'living waters' means, essentially, running waters, flowing water (cf. Lev. 14.5-6, 50-52, 15.13, Num. 19.17).

41. This term is a participle, and while Exum takes it as a substantive, 'used synonymously for water, as in Exod. 15.8; Isa. 44.3; Ps. 78.16, 44; Prov. 5.15' (Exum, *Song of Songs*, p. 155), I take seriously the other possibility Exum raises for this verse, that the

  Awake, North Wind
    and come, South Wind!
  Blow upon my garden
    that its spices might pour forth![42]
  Let my lover enter his garden,
    and eat its choice fruits!

  I come to my garden, my sister, my bride;
  I gather[43] my myrrh with my spice,
  I eat my honeycomb with my honey,
  I drink my wine with my milk.

Let us take a more detailed look at this garden. Here it relates to the woman, obviously, but the poet slowly builds up the image as a kind of setting that requires some attention in spatial terms, at least initially. On this score three issues stand out, which I intend to take in order: the garden's fantastic assortment of flora, the provision of its water, and its secure perimeter. Other observations will fit around these three basic issues as the discussion unfolds. As might already be clear, this garden in this passage is reminiscent of the gardens-of-power I looked at in my last section—the resemblance between the Song's garden and the subject of Tuan's harsh critique is in fact quite remarkable. My intention here is to focus on the darker side of the Song's garden, to think through the spatial ideologies of the image without the rosy tint.

We start with the flora. The Song's garden boasts a fantastic array, and Murphy and Exum detail the varied and exotic origins of these plants. Pomegranates (רמונים) and henna (כפר) are Palestinian fare (though the latter could be obtained in Egypt too), while nard (נרד) has Indian origins.[44] Saffron (כרכם), likewise, hails from the Himalayan region—though a more local variety (the *crocus datives*) exists as well. The cane (קנה), myrrh (מר), and the trees of frankincense (עצי לבונה) on the other hand would have to be of Arabian origin. Cinnamon (קנמון) is native to Sri Lanka.[45] The Song's garden is, in short, a botanical impossibility. The species are simply not natural bedfellows.[46]

waters of the well in the previous line flow out of Lebanon. This retains the sense of the participle without co-opting it as a substantive.

42. The same verb appears here as in v. 15, where I translated the participle 'flowing'. Here the sense is more of an unleashing of the spices and their scent: pour fourth.

43. The verb for 'gather' here (ארה) has only one other occurrence in the Bible, Ps 80.12 [13], I have sided with Murphy's translation (Murphy, *Song of Songs*, p. 154). Exum choses 'pluck' (Exum, *Song of Songs*, p. 155), as does Pope (Pope, *Song of Songs*, p. 501).

44. Murphy, *Song of Songs*, p. 132.

45. Exum, *Song of Songs*, p. 179.

46. For more on this see Athalya Brenner, 'Aromatics and Perfumes in the Song of Songs', *JSOT* 25 (1983), pp. 75-81.

While it is true that no garden in the ancient world could have *naturally* produced this jungle, it is important to remember that the assemblage of incongruous plant specimens was a common feature of royal gardens, particularly in the Assyrian tradition—the very type of garden, in fact, that the Hebrew term פרדס, used of the Song's garden in 4.13, refers to. It is inconceivable that this varied plant-life could naturally spring up in a garden in the ancient Near East, but the image is of a royal and imperious garden, a garden in which the world's vegetative wonders have been intentionally brought together. The lovers' garden thus models itself on a very particular tradition, and one that is directly rooted in the processes of political control.

The textuality of this passage is something of a garden in and of itself of course. The Hebrew roots of these words are not *Hebrew* roots at all. They are foreign terms, making this parcel of text just as much of an international composite as the garden it describes. The term for 'pleasure garden' in 4.13 is a loanword;[47] 'saffron' is taken from Arabic. Indeed many of the words for the plants read in English just as they do in the Hebrew—'cinnamon' and 'nard'—because they are borrowed. These are not indigenous linguistic 'roots' just as the plants they describe are not indigenous flora. The lovers' garden is as much a garden of language as it is of plants. Which is to say that the passage is a treasure trove of linguistic borrowing (pillaging?) and replanting and exemplifies influence, control and the collapsing of the world in and through language.

If all gardens are a statement of human will and domination against the forces of nature, the garden that seeks to collapse and contain the world takes this trope up to ambitious new heights. Whatever romantic nooks and crannies our lovers' garden may hold, it is basically derived from a political sign. The garden presumes itself as a reterritorialization of the world, as a kind of theme park version of reality, a spatial celebration of one's own extended influence (and extravagance). Or, as I put it earlier, the garden functions as a kind of concretized fantasy of a conquered world. Ultimately, this is what Gerleman's *Phantasiegarten* is a fantasy *of*: the imposition of human will.

This is putting things in their starkest terms, of course. But Tuan's fundamental issue with gardens is their underlying identity as beautified and superfluous manipulations of the real world. Take these aspects out of the Song's garden and there is very little left, and that should have implications for the way we read the most pervasive image in the poem.

47. Where the term is loaned from is tricky to deduce. Traditionally, it has been attributed to Persia, though this is now contested. See Noegel and Rendsburg, *Solomon's Vineyard*, pp. 174-84; S.R. Driver, *An Introduction to the Literature of the Old Testament* (7th edn; Edinburgh, 1898), p. 449; Ian Young, 'Biblical Texts Cannot Be Dated Linguistically', *Hebrew Studies* 46 (2005), pp. 341-51; and, I. Young and R. Rezetko, with the assistance of Martin Ehrensvärd, *Linguistic Dating of Biblical Texts* (2 vols.; London: Equinox, 2008).

Let us take another example. The lovers' garden is sustained by an abundance of water. In v. 12 the male compares the woman to a locked garden and then to a locked or sealed spring. In the next verse when he connects the image of the garden to the image of the water, these two potentially independent metaphors appear to merge ('your watercourses are a pleasure garden') and we see, as Fox puts it, that 'the girl is represented by images of both the spring and the orchard it waters'.[48]

The term in v. 13 for these 'watercourses' (שְׁלָחַיִךְ) is a hapax but derives from a fairly common root meaning to stretch or to send out (שׁלח). The LXX has ἀποστολαί σου, while the Vulgate reads *emissiones tuae*. On the strength of these '*emissiones*', Boer, apparently unable to hold back, suggests translating the phrase 'your ejaculation of pomegranates'. Other readings give rise to translations that have a more arboreal flavour: 'shoots' or 'boughs'. These translations treat שְׁלֻחָה (cf. Isa. 16.8) as an analogous term without acknowledgment of the entirely different form of the two words. As Fox points out, there is actually a closer equivalent in Mishnaic Hebrew that refers to the irrigation channels that ancient labourers built to water their crops.[49] The term in v. 13, then, most likely refers to the channels that were built—'sent out'—to keep the garden alive.

As v. 15 makes clear, this 'living water' flows in from a great distance: 'Well of living waters, flowing from Lebanon'. Murphy suggests that the exotic nature of these waters works as a kind of cultural superlative in the text; Lebanon's water is the best, apparently: an ancient Evian.[50] The female lover is this water, and the garden into which it flows, and the technological means *by which* it flows.

These imported waters imply a great deal about the latent assumptions behind the garden image. This garden, an intentionally built artifice containing a great deal of rare and expensive flora, has been placed somewhere without water. Its water is brought in (through constructed watercourses?) all the way from Lebanon. Surely, even in the magical land of poetic fiction one does not imagine—in a text that goes so far as to *mention* artificial irrigation—that a spring in Lebanon would naturally open out in a (royal) Israelite garden. Or that a garden would be built around naturally occurring water courses. This is poetry not history of course, but what does this series of images tell us about the assumptions that lie behind the images on display? I cannot help being reminded here of the words of Louis XIV when he was questioned about the unpromising location of (a very dry) Versailles: '*C'est dans les choses*

---

48. Fox, *Song of Songs*, p. 137.

49. Fox, *Song of Songs*, p. 137. Fox argues that these channels and the fields they watered were metonymic, but there seems no real need to over-translate formal high verse based on the gradual concessions and contractions of farming terminology.

50. Murphy, *Song of Songs*, p. 157.

difficiles que nous faisons parasite notre vertu' (It is in overcoming difficult matters that we make apparent our power).[51] The garden is not centred upon water so much as it is centred upon its impressive manipulation. Two obvious questions thus arise. First, if control of water indicated power in seventeenth century France, how much more potent a symbol was it in the arid, agricultural lands of the ancient Near East? And second, what does the poem imagine the Lebanese get to drink?

We might infer from v. 12 that this water—that great, and indispensible ingredient of human life—is not for drinking anyway. The Lebanese Pellegrino is for watering plants. Or, in v. 13, for the pomegranates and choice fruits, which, like the water itself, are safely locked away from the riff-raff. Not only is the water (like the flora) imported, then, access to it is carefully regulated.

Locking, enclosure and the regulation of access are central to the image of the garden. The Hebrew noun for garden used in 4.12 and 5.1 (גַּן) is derived from a root (גנן) meaning to defend, enclose or protect (much like the English term, in fact).[52] This associates the garden with the marking off, even the protection of, a specific parcel of land. If the idea of the garden as a bounded space were not sufficiently clear from the term itself, the garden is 'locked', or bolted (נעל). Once more the Song's garden is defined as an imposition on the landscape; its boundaries, like its plant life, are culturally and technologically maintained. Often construed as a space of freedom, the garden is in fact predicated on a kind of surveillance: the garden is locked and only the authorized may enter.[53]

Suggestions as to the (sexual) significance of the 'locked' woman-cum-garden are various. The image is sometimes taken as a roundabout way of signalling the woman's virginity or 'modesty' (so Pope, following the Targum),[54] or as an image of thrilling inaccessibility (Keel) or her lack of sexual preparation (Assis), or of her relational exclusivity (Bloch and Bloch, Fox, and Exum).[55] The bolt, however, is a curious image on which to hang

---

51. The anecdote is mentioned by Tuan, 'Fountains and Plants', p. 44.

52. See A. van Erp-Houtepan, 'The Etymological Origin of the Garden', *Journal of Garden History* 6 (1986), pp. 237-31.

53. The blowing of the North and South winds in v. 16 might be read as an opening up of the Song's garden. But while the cardinal points may converge in this green and pleasant woman—making her yet another kind of cosmic repository—and while her fragrance wafts abroad (tantalizingly? flirtatiously?), this wind really serves to highlight the solitary man who is given actual *access*. Her garden flirts with openness and then denies it to all but the male. In this sense, then, the breeze could be seen to emphasize, not to reverse, the woman's enclosedness.

54. Pope, *Song of Songs*, pp. 488-89.

55. Keel, *Song of Songs*, p. 174; Assis, *Flashes of Fire*, pp. 136-37; Bloch, *Song of Songs*, p. 217; Fox, *Song of Songs*, p. 134; Exum, *Song of Songs*, p. 175.

ideas of commitment, images of utopia or promises of sexual fidelity. Locks and bolts do not imply a return to the blessed state of paradise so much as they imply a world of problems. Locks signify the pre-emptive defence of a space against expected incursions; in royal gardens locks keep out the commoners (more specifically, they protect the fruit-laden boughs of the king from—hungry?—ne'er-do-wells). Of course, the idea of exclusivity— of 'locking out' all others—is to be expected in the Song. It would not really be conceivable for the male to compare his lover, or her body, to a busy thoroughfare. But locking is a surprisingly negative image. It suggests that fidelity, if that indeed is what the image signifies, is not achieved through positive action or devoted fervour but by means of limitation and control. And who are readers to imagine has the key? If we take the sexual symbol- ism of the passage seriously and imagine the male 'key' to enter the female 'hole' (as the Song spells out itself in the city-scene of 5.2-8, actually), then might one be able to read the couple's fidelity as being a result of others being locked out? By extension the female garden comes to be a closely regulated space, the purity, beauty and status of which are only assured because of technological intervention. By using an image, not merely of fastening but of enforced boundary keeping, the lock implies either a resis- tance to alternative suitors, the need to keep the woman safe, or of the male enforcing her closed-ness. In other words, the effect of using an evocative symbol of enclosure as a cypher for fidelity has a variety of negative sub- texts that we could chose to read instead of the lighter, nicer ideas usually ascribed to it.

   If, on the other hand, it is the woman who has the power to lock and unlock her entrance, then this locking is less troublesome in terms of male/ female power dynamics. Yet, even on these terms, the garden loses some of its peace and serenity—its borders become the scene of an implied siege in which lusty young commoners are anxious to gorge themselves on the king's fruit (like the foxes in 2.15, in fact). The lock may keep the implicit threat of alternative suitors at bay, but it reinforces the garden's antitheti- cal relationship with the wider landscape. As such, as a space that derives its significance from an active resistance to the 'outside' world, the garden must always be either a space of domination or a potential site of abuse. That is not an especially romantic thought.[56]

   One thing we keep coming back to is the connection between the garden and socio-economic status. The Song's garden, as is especially clear from the terminology in v. 13, 'is associated with the royal paradigm', to borrow

---

56. In reality, of course, the opposition is not quite as stark as all that—my point, rather, is that there *is* a measure of sinister subtext that we can tease out, and that this darker edge, or undergrowth, of the garden image tends to have been neglected in scholarship.

Landy's phrase.[57] The commentary literature does not contest this connection; indeed, scholars seem to celebrate it. What often goes unarticulated in such discussions, though, is the effect of tying love to social rank, particularly when social rank is spatialized in such an obvious way. The lovers, at least in 4.12–5.1, are landed royals with access to their own pleasure garden and their fidelity is expressed by means of the exclusion of others from their luxury, theme-park mini-world. The Song presents its picture of sexual exclusivity here by manipulating (essentially economic) images of social exclusion.[58] The Song gives love status by reworking the implicit social inequality of the garden image into a division between the lovers (or those in love) and everybody else. As a poetic image that has been hailed by so many scholars as a liberating reversal of the problems, marginalizations and abuses inherent to the Eden story, the exclusive-royal-luxury-playground image is a curious thing for an apparently liberating text to be reliant upon. The Song's garden makes for an odd paradise indeed.

We might say that the garden is an artificially compiled site, an artificially sustained site, a controlled site and a site that implies the impressive—and entirely unnecessary—use of vital resources to display the application of human will over and against the wild forces of nature. Mine is obviously not the only way to read the confluence of vernal images in this passage, and really this three-part sketch of the Song's garden-as-setting is more a caricature than anything else. But, as my initial examples of scholarship on the Song's gardens indicate, most writing on this topic has an overblown quality. That is simply down to the nature of the text, I think, and is not helped by our cultural inclination to romanticize our gardens (as detailed in Elkin's work).[59] But my somewhat 'alternative' depiction of the Song's green space is important, since gardens—perhaps more than any other kind of space—have a tendency to naturalize the operations of power by which they are constituted.

Gardening as Vajazzling: The Horticulture of 'Her'

The issue of spatial power-mongering has particular relevance when we think about the gendering of this garden space. The linking of this image of the *locked* garden to the female in the Song is, as I have already mentioned, often assumed to be a reference to the woman's virginity, or else a reference

---

57. Landy, *Paradoxes of Paradise*, p. 179.
58. Lovers are symbolically royal in this part of the text; singles are peasantry.
59. The purpose of Elkin's essay is, in fact, to posit that there may be something peculiar about gardens themselves, given the 'reverie of gardens' that reigns in garden-theory but which, he says, 'is often dormant in our professional prose' (Elkins, *Landscape Theory*, p. 71).

to her sexual exclusivity. In either case, the image is taken to be a symbol that alludes to the female's sexualized body (and the male's access to it). Black, with help from Eslinger, Pope, Keel and others, has pushed the envelope of the bodily implications of this metaphor. The connection between the sexualized female body and the garden need not stop at the garden's bushy front door:

> The noun שְׁלָחַיִךְ (v. 13, 'your shoots'), located at the centre of the enclosed garden and pool, has been a source of some consternation for biblical critics. Though many have posited a range of meanings for the noun, as Pope observes, the possibility that it refers to a 'more intimate portion of the anatomy' has been suggested. Keel explains further that a parallel term in Job 33.18, שַׁחַת (pit) has encouraged the interpretation of שְׁלָחַיִךְ as a 'vertical excavation or shaft'. Transferred onto the body...the anatomical choice for שְׁלָחַיִךְ seems obvious. Keel also observes that the Arabic cognate *shalch* can mean vagina, and refers to various associations in Egyptian poetry of garden, canal, womb and vagina.[60]

Black extends this physiological interpretation—in which the garden is less bodily than genital—across the whole metaphor. She signals the sexual connotations of the verb of male 'entry' (בוא) into the garden in v. 15, discusses the potential of the MT's גל as an image of the womb, based on E.M. Good's interpretation of the term as 'cup', and argues (with Eslinger)[61] that the 'bolt' (נעל) of the bolted garden signifies 'the bulbospongiosus muscle as the locking or barring mechanism in the vulvic cavity'.[62] In terms of the garden's waters, Black reads with Boer in mind: 'the abundance of liquid suggests sexual fluids and their accompanying odours'.[63] The garden of love, which the woman both is and is in, and its waters—again, which both signify her and flow in and around her—are thus an extended, complex metaphor, a metaphor of the female body and that body's inhabitability.

We might take exception, then, to the comments of Munro—to take one example among many—that the woman is to be considered (necessarily) natural and innocent by virtue of the garden image:

> He comes to her as the source in Eden, as to the first garden where innocence, love and safety are joyfully restored...the natural world and the abundance of life visible there is recreated in her, for she, to him, is the personification of its beauty.[64]

---

60. Black, *Artifice of Love*, p. 147.

61. Eslinger himself argues that the image is a detailed anatomical sketch of the vulva, but that the text does not necessarily imply sexual congress; Lyle Eslinger, 'The Case of the Immodest Lady Wrestler in Deuteronomy XXV 11-12', *VT* (1981), pp. 269-81 (276).

62. Black, *Artifice of Love*, p. 149; Eslinger, 'The Case of the Immodest Lady Wrestler', p. 276.

63. Black, *Artifice of Love*, p. 148.

64. Munro, *Spikenard and Saffron*, p. 109.

While the association with the garden gives the woman (and her vulva) the potential to be exotic, opulent, luxurious, and exclusive, it has other implications too. This eroticized woman is a make-believe world, an impossible fantasy version of womanhood; her genitals are prized, but in economic rather than intimate terms. Her vagina (does the speaker really focus on anything more of her?) is a theme park, a place the king goes to play. She is locked, of course, but does this imply intimacy or that she is a discreet, bounded project of the male? Certainly, she is not naturally occurring. Her body, in fact, seems to be the result of substantial work; nature has been tamed, worked over, pruned, preened and seeded before the declaration of her beauty is made. Is the implicit colonialism of the composited garden, with its incongruous assortment of plants and flowers, an oddly transposed whimsy about male political reach, a statement of bodily control made in floral terms, or a fantasy of sex with Frankenstein's monster? The image surgically reconstructs her genitals as an impossibly international composite, after all. She is not wild and natural, but rather the archetypal symbol of the tamed, worked-upon project, a fixer-upper, a discrete segment of land kept away from the real world, and one that has taken considerable work to produce.

Comparing the female lover's genitals to this garden is closer to pining for her to get a Vajazzle than it is to selfless extolling of innate beauty. For any readers not aware of the practice, here is a quote from 'The Last Triangle'—an Essay by Meredith Dault, a member of a cultural studies department from Queen's University in Ontario, Canada, and one of the very few people, it seems, working on the politics of hair and preening in contemporary society (and its implications for feminism). Her work focuses on contemporary notions of gender performativity and body-control, particularly with the pubic region in mind. She writes:

> 'Vajazzling' is the practice of waxing away your pubic hair only to have it replaced by stick-on crystals in various patterns. Word is that this strange phenomenon is gathering something of a following (at least in North America), with fans apparently declaring that practice makes them feel like they have a sparkly secret hidden beneath their briefs.
>
> For anyone not up on their useless pop culture, Vajazzling first hit the big time when actress Jennifer Love Hewitt appeared on Lopez Tonight, an American talk show, to promote her new biography (January 2010). There she famously told Lopez and the audience about having a friend Vajazzle her 'precious lady' when she was trying to get over a nasty break-up. Love Hewitt made headlines by declaring that it 'shined like a disco ball', later declaring that all women should 'Vajazzle their va-jay-jays'.[65]

---

65. Meredith Dault, 'The Last Triangle: Sex, Money and the Politics of Pubic Hair' (Unpublished MA Thesis: University of Ontario, 2011), p. 24.

As Dault goes on to point out, Jennifer Lover Hewitt's language says something about attitudes toward the vulva in popular culture: it can only be talked about with cute euphemisms. The trend goes along, says Dault, with the sense many women have that their intimate regions are gross and dirty, and require special cultivation in order to make them socially acceptable and sexually ready. For Dault, the Vajazzle thus represents a commoditization of the female body, turning the correctly turned out pudenda into a kind of aspirational fashion accessory.

Of course what is most interesting about Jennifer Love Hewitt's charming turn of phrase for this study is the spatializing of her celebrity genitals: what does likening the area above her vagina to 'disco ball' do except turn her pants into a nightclub: a dark recreational space—crowned with a glitter ball—where people go for some bump and grind on evenings and at weekends? Her lady garden becomes a lady disco, a specially prepared area for people on the pull, clearly demarcated, sometimes exclusive (especially if you are Jennifer Love Hewitt one would imagine), guarded but very accessible. Sexual readiness, even sexual confidence—she is getting over a difficult break up, remember—comes from reimagining her body as a sexual space by turning that body into a kind of theme-park version of itself, a carefully controlled space, tamed, worked over, pruned, and preened. The disco-va-jay-jay is a representation, not of the natural female body or female control over that body, so much as an acceptance that the female body needs to be re-presented if it is to perform its vital spatial role: the attraction of weekend revellers into its internal spaces.

As bizarre an inclusion as the Vajazzle may at first seem, it is perhaps not too difficult to see why it works to translate the oddness, and potentially the unsavoury nature, of the garden image in the Song into appropriately jarring terms for us. Like the Vajazzle, the garden does not image the female body so much as project expectations of control, re-inscribing bodily space with facile cultural space, and, importantly, equating a *resistance* of natural bodily forms with female sexuality. Like the Vajazzle, the garden has a socio-economic tenor that effectively commodifies the woman's genitals, spatializing them in such a way as to make them not political, autonomous or genuine places, but theme-park spaces prepared for recreational pursuits.

Does the garden of the Song, then, necessarily imply beauty, exoticism and rarity? Does it not also form part of a particular mode of gender scripting, of prompting certain modes of female performativity that prize the female body as a site of cultivation? The equation of the woman in the Song with the royal garden not only figures the female sexual body as an impossible and idealized composite, it makes female genitals unready spaces that must be *fashioned* and *refashioned*, sites where culture must be made to hold off nature. What, in the end, is the difference between the garden of the Song, and Jennifer Love Hewitt's disco-bits? Not necessarily all that much.

We might sum up by returning to Riley's words from a little earlier:

> The garden is an artificial place made from the real, an illusion of the world. What better place to give women (or prisoners) an illusion of power without actual power? What better place to keep them busy without their interfering in things that matter?

It is tempting to say that Riley's words do not apply to the Song as a whole, that the woman is not left in the garden, that the scenes shift and move on and that the lovers meet outside its fecund confines, that they continue their love affair in the city streets and in the vineyards. In a sense this is true, of course. But as Francis Landy suggests, it is possible to see the garden as a metaphor not only for the female lover but also for the Song.

> The garden is essentially private, protected against the elements, against weeds and wildness. It is nature perfected by culture, enclosed also from the fields where humans cultivate for subsistence. It is an index of riches, of liberation from necessity. This is especially true of the magnificence and complexity of the garden in the Song, associated with the royal paradigm. However, in it culture returns to nature; it is a place of retreat and relaxation…[the garden is] a contained world…the garden is thus a metaphor for poetry, as an enclosed space within language that tries to encompass the world.[66]

Two main things stand out from Landy's comments on the garden and its potential as a metaphor for poetry itself. The first is that Landy's definition of what gardens are is really no different from the definition(s) I have been working with in my discussion here. My observations on the nature of the Song's garden are not particularly new, though I have attempted to push them in directions that are less sympathetic to the 'romantic' tenor of the poem. Second, more importantly, according to this definition, the Song's garden works very nicely as a symbol for poetry, and for the Song as a whole. It is 'an enclosed space within language', it is the result of some considerable artistry, and it is a space that draws on a wide geographical area for its literary technique and artistic form (as, of course, Fox and others have dealt with at length). It is a fantastic space, a fantasy space, and a space that has been

---

66. Landy, *Paradoxes of Paradise*, p. 179. In an essay on the nature of garden theory/history and its study, James Elkins gives a list of the better-trodden paths of analytic approach taken by his colleagues. Interestingly, Landy's summative treatment of the garden in the Song as quoted here combines all of them. Elkins' list runs like this: gardens are representations of history; gardens are representations of nature; gardens are representations of painting and fiction; gardens are the meeting places of various disciplines; gardens are sets of polarities; gardens are narratives of human life; gardens are open-ended sites of desire. So, the smattering of ancient examples (Egyptian, Mesopotamian) that I have been tying into Tuan and Riley's work notwithstanding, the applicability of contemporary garden-theory to the ancient, fictitious garden of the Song looks like a fairly legitimate move. Indeed, the literature on the Song would seem to invite it.

hedged off from the more usual, everyday concerns of biblical writers and readers. But if gardens often work as political mechanisms that compile and contain, and if they have often been associated with women as a means of imposing limits on women, what does that say about the Song-as-garden? Is the text that is so often trumpeted as an antidote to ancient patriarchy merely another abusive garden: a luxurious, opulent, fantasy space that has been carefully parcelled off from the serious business of theology, politics, kings, prophets, and Yahweh? 'One man's woman's domain is another woman's women's prison', after all. The garden is not an entirely utopian image, then. But what about the other pervasive spatial image in the Song? How does the city function as an ideological space, and how do its streets and squares relate to what we have seen of the darker side of the garden?

The City as Labyrinth: On Not-Reading the City

The city is the most developed 'setting' in the poem. Two whole narrative sections are devoted to it (3.1-5; 5.2–6.3), and in its streets the Song comes closest to having what could be loosely called a plot. Despite its prominence on the actual page, though, the city has tended not to draw the attention of critics and commentators to the degree that the garden has. The city is very seldom discussed *as a city* in the literature. The searching and finding themes that characterize the city sections of the Song have been analysed, certainly, as has the supposed dream language in which these sections are couched. And the episode of violence that unfolds in the city streets has, likewise, been given plenty of critical consideration. These issues, however, tend not to be considered in relation to the urban-ness of their context.[67] The walls and the fountains and the plants of 4.12–5.1 seem to give rise to wider discussions of 'gardens' and their significance as settings in the poem, but the lovers' encounter on the urban doorstep, the motif of the searching woman, and the violence of the men who encircle the city walls seem not to have given rise to a comparable sense of the city as a setting. More attention has been given to the fact of the woman's experience of the city as a kind of hallucination (as I examined in Chapter 2).

On those occasions when the Song's city has been discussed, the analysis has invariably served to contrast the city with the garden or the countryside. Writings on the Song's city seem to work on a particular understanding of what 'cityness' is in the text and then, with the idea of the glorious garden already in mind, draw very simplistic spatial distinctions between the two. So, in John Rogerson's work on the biblical city the Song's urban scene is described like this:

---

67. I suspect this is partly because most critics make a natural beeline for the Song's considerably more famous gardens. See, for instance, Landy, *Paradoxes of Paradise*, p. 197.

Something that may be implicit in this poem is the phenomenon of loneliness in the city…in that it is seen to portray a young woman living on her
own, as might well be the case in a modern city today…[t]he Song of Songs,
however else it can be read, is certainly a highly personal account of what
it means for a young woman to live in a city in Old Testament times. Conventions to which lives are expected to conform can be liberating or enslav-
ing, although there are graduated alternatives within these two extremes. The
Song of Songs portrays the countryside as liberating and the city as enslav-
ing, from the point of view of a young woman.[68]

Rogerson's reservations about the city emerge, it seems, from the violent
episode of 5.7, where the city-watch beat the Song's female protagonist.
While I would not want to minimize the brutality of this scene (and I shall
be devoting considerable attention to it in due course), it is worth pointing out that this forbidding city is also the site of some rather racy goings-
on. Only a few verses earlier (5.2-3) the poem describes the male 'hand'
entering the female 'hole' at the threshold of the urban dwelling. Doorstep-
sex, metaphorical or otherwise, does not suggest chronic loneliness, and yet
Rogerson is keen to use this very part of the text to paint the city as a stark
and violent environment for a lonely young woman (the Song makes no
comment on the woman's age or the size of her social circle, in fact). The
city is not merely a sphere of searching, it is a place that enables intimacy;
the city is where anonymity is possible and that can be a good thing, especially when one is in a (forbidden?) sexual relationship. Moreover, the idea
of a liberating 'countryside'—a decidedly *urban* word in that it tends to be
used by urban dwellers to describe the not-*urban*—is problematic on its
own terms; the 'countryside' can be wild, dangerous and incomprehensible;
they do things differently there.

Even Munro, who is normally so positive about the Song's varied scenes
and spaces, suggests that the Song's city is 'itself a kind of prison' due to
its walls and its watchmen.[69] What is particularly interesting about Munro's
observation on the forbidding city, however, is the very different way she
interprets exactly the same spatial features—walls and controlled access—
when they apply to the garden. The garden's carefully maintained perimeter does not symbolize control at all but rather the 'unity and community
of paradise.'[70] Is there a certain view of 'The City' that informs interpretation all too readily, one that is not necessarily about the urban so much as

68. John Rogerson and John Vincent, *The City in Biblical Perspective* (Biblical Challenges in the Contemporary World Series; Sheffield: Equinox, 2009), p. 30.
69. Albeit a prison that is redeemed in the Song's closing verses when the woman
states her independence in terms of architectural features. This move saves Munro's
overwhelmingly positive view of the Song's spaces, if a little belatedly; Munro, *Spikenard and Saffron*, p. 128.
70. Munro, *Spikenard and Saffron*, p. 138.

about spatial differentiation? This, certainly, is true of approaches like that of Yvonne Thöne's project (briefly reviewed in my Chapter 1), in which spaces are areas to be parsed out—countryside/city/gardens and public/private/intimate—or characterized through relationships of contrast, rather than ideologically qualified on their own terms.[71]

What if we start from a different point, though? What if we begin with a certain degree of uncertainty as to what a city actually is, and with a certain amount of caution about assuming too quickly that we know what constitutes cityness in the text? How is cityness constituted in the Song, particularly?

PhantasCity

There is an almost inexhaustible supply of intellectual work that I could draw on to address these questions. In this section, however, I have limited myself to one or two authors—and their muses and their disciples—who have been especially influential in the field, and who, importantly, have focused on the importance of *literary cities* in understanding how the 'urban' comes to be constituted as an ideological product. One such author is James Donald. In his seminal book, *Imagining the Modern City*, Donald assesses the links between the suppressed anxieties of modernist culture and its array of fictional urban spaces.[72] He identifies the city as a space characterized by the Freudian uncanny, or *Unheimlich*. Linking to this idea of the urban uncanny is Steve Pile's more recent volume, *Real Cities*. Pile looks at the kookier aspects of city life—the connections between our ideas about cities and our ideas about dreams, and about voodoo, and about vampires (Pile writes about cities as sites of aspiration, of control, and of the imperial predator).[73] Both theorists draw from Walter Benjamin and from Freud. It is with Benjamin that I begin:

> Attempt to develop Giedon's thesis. 'In the nineteenth century', he writes, 'construction plays the role of the subconscious'. Wouldn't it be better to say 'the role of bodily processes'—around which 'artistic' architectures gather, like dreams around the framework of physiological processes?[74]

This idea informs a great deal of writing on the contemporary city, specifically, that the City is not primarily a place, but an idea-become-artifact.[75] The

---

71. Thöne, *Liebe zwischen Stadt und Feld*.

72. James Donald, *Imagining the Modern City* (London: Athlone Press, 1999).

73. Steve Pile, *Real Cities: Modernity, Space and the Phantasmagorias of City Life* (London: Sage, 2005).

74. Walter Benjamin, *The Arcades Project*, p. 391 (K1a7).

75. This sense of the city has been recently developed into a strategy for reading the Bible's prophetic material in Mary E. Mills, *Urban Imagination in Biblical Prophecy* (London: T. & T. Clark, 2012). In this volume Mills develops Benjamin's approach to

City is the ossification of a cultural dream, a site where people's fluid inter-actions slowly harden into solid forms. The shopping mall, the cathedral and the sports stadium are kinds of callus, formed wherever bricks and mortar have been allowed to rub up against certain kinds of ideology. The basic facts of bricks and mortar, of civic apparatus, or of the relative distance between Macy's and the tram station are extensions of this metropolitan idea and they both reinforce and reinvent it. Once the metropolis is recognized as being an ideological structure in this way, with a body emerging from its own dreams, the city's cultural re-packaging—the city as depicted in film or in literature—becomes particularly significant. A society's representations of the urban tell us a great deal about the ideas that have been poured into the foundations of its innumerable physical constructions, or which come to be projected onto them. It would be difficult to figure a New York that did not draw at all from King Kong, or from the sit-com *Friends*, or from the very particular definition of urban community that arises from HBO's *Sex and the City*.

Steve Pile's work draws links between Walter Benjamin's ideas about phantasmagoria (as discussed in Chapter 2) and these kinds of modes of urban production. Pile's belief is that, in thinking about what is 'real' about cities, we need to think about the 'emotional work' that comprizes urban experience. Cultural forms of expression, he argues, may well be expressed in literature but not necessarily in an orderly or preordained way:

> Instead these structures should be thought to be fabricated, devious, contradic-tory, mobile, changing and changeable. To evoke the more febrile, secretive and ambivalent aspects of emotional life, I prefer the term 'phantasmagoria'.
>
> The term phantasmagoria implies many things. In some ways, it describes an experience of movement, of a procession of things before the eyes. In other ways it evokes the importance not only of what can be seen, of the experience of the immediate, but also of life beyond the immediately visible or tangible. It suggests a quality of life that is ghost-like…phantasmagoria is highly suggestive of the importance of particular kinds of emotional work for city life…phantasmagoria implies a peculiar mix of spaces and times: the ghost-like or dream-like procession of things in cities not only comes from all over the place (even from places that do not or never will exist), but it also evokes very different times (be they past, present or future; be they remembered or imagined).[76]

cities, including his observations on *flâneurie*, into a literary and ideological approach to the biblical city. She does so in close conversation with Steve Pile's appropriations of Benjamin. I am focusing my own reading of the city with the aid of Pile and another of Benjamin's acolytes, James Donald. This results in a slightly different focus from that of Mills (namely my preoccupation with opacity and transparency rather than blood, ghosts, dreams and so on), but a number of my observations are applicable to her sense of the city and vice versa, particularly the relation between gardens and cities Mills out-lines in her chapter 'Geography and Vision', pp. 193-215.

76. Pile, *Real Cities*, p. 3.

Cities are vibrant composites of the imagined-and-real, experienced, always, in the first person. The city contains a huge variety of dangers, desires, possibilities and threats. These kinds of qualities—just as visible in the Song as in the boroughs of London or Gotham, as we shall see—make cities phantasmagoric products. The City is already quite like the Song, then, insofar as it exists as a procession of images, in that it induces dreams that lend credence to its structures, in that it continues to thrive through facilitating the projection of people's fears and desires onto its surface.

James Donald has gone further than most in exploring the kinds of cultural relationships that inform ideas about the City. In *Imagining the Modern City*—and in the Essay 'Light in Dark Spaces' particularly, which is one of Pile's key intertexts—Donald looks at the links between culture and the fictional metropolis. Donald argues persuasively that whether cultural texts are staring up at us from the printed page or towering down from the silver screen, they do not simply record cities but actively constitute them around us. Text 'produces a city for the reading public', as he puts it, and Donald is interested in mapping the ways in which these urban narratives have 'disseminated certain perspectives, certain ways of seeing and so certain structures of the imagination'. As he explains:

> Among the more familiar are the opposition between rural utopia and urban nightmare; the Bildungsroman narrative of heroic self-creation in the great city; the Dickensian search for subterranean networks of community beneath the unreadable and irrational surface of a class-divided city; and the social complexity of the city recorded through its demotic idioms and slang by French novelists from Balzac to Zola.[77]

The cinematic cities Donald turns his attention to are also familiar ones. They range from the Freudian Gotham City—an in-fantile fantasy of origins and transgressed boundaries where men don tights to fight Jokers and Penguins—to the existentialism of *Blade Runner*'s hodgepodge L.A. In the New York of King Kong, Donald sees a commodified, fetishized primitive fighting a losing battle (from the Empire State building, no less) against the raging technology of capitalism. In Fritz Lang's *Metropolis*, the robot Maria 'conflates characteristic modern anxieties about sexuality, technology and the mob'.[78] These celluloid cities tell us something about the wider urban project of modernity, Donald argues. They describe the 'conflict with the claims of authority and the bonds of community, and also of the unfixing or the uncertainty of identity'. They flirt on the borders 'between human and technology, between human and nature, or between adult and infant'. Naturally, all of these urban texts do not exist in isolation from cities; they become actualized in and *as* them.

77. Donald, *Imagining the Modern City*, p. 127.
78. Donald, *Imagining the Modern City*, p. 89.

Really, then, it is Donald's example of urban *reading* that I want to seize upon here to explore the Song's city *as a city*. As Donald himself says, 'We do not just read the city, we negotiate the reality of cities by imagining "the city"'.[79] Donald's point is that the tensions that underlie the fictional cities of modernity betray a basic ambiguity in the collective psyche: our cities represent familiar spaces and foreign spaces simultaneously. Or, in other words, The City is always and inevitably a tension between opacity and transparency. Donald attributes this tension to the Enlightenment's fear of the dark and unknown (making the relevance of cinema-space as a, literally, *darkened* realm of potential En*light*enment all the more poignant). As will become clear, I think this notion of the urban as a tension between opacity and transparency underwrites the Song's urban spaces too.

Sex and the City

The female narrates her experiences of city living twice in the Song of Songs, once in 3.1-4 and again in 5.2–5.8:

Nightly,[80] on my bed, I sought my soul's beloved,
    I sought him but I did not find him.[81]
I will rise now, I will go around the city,
    through its streets and its plazas,
I will seek my soul's beloved.

The watchmen found me
    as they went on rounds[82] of the city.
'My soul's beloved—have you seen him?'[83]
Barely had I passed them
    when I found my soul's beloved.
I held him and would not let him go
    until I had brought him to my mother's house,
    and to the chamber of she who conceived me (3.1-4).

I slept but my heart was roused.
Listen![84] My lover is knocking![85]

79. Donald, *Imagining the Modern City*, p. 18.
80. Here the translation reflects the plural, 'in the nights', which indicates repeated action: night after night.
81. The Septuagint adds a further verse here: 'I called him but he did not answer me', which the MT has in the equivalent account in 5.6. There seems no particular reason to amend the MT here in 3.2.
82. Literally, circuits of the city (סבב).
83. As Exum writes, 'Literally "my soul's beloved have you seen?" with the object first for emphasis.' I have adopted Exum's translation here since it retains the Hebrew emphasis (*Song of Songs*, p. 122).
84. Exum's rendering of the Hebrew here, literally 'sound, voice', seems most faithful to the sense of the abrupt interruption of noise in the text (*Song of Songs*, p. 183).
85. The verb for knocks (דפק) is used in Gen. 33.13 for driving sheep. It is also used in

'Open to me, my sister, my friend,
    my dove, my perfect one;
for my head is wet with dew,
    my locks[86] with night sprinkles.'[87]

I had taken off my robe,
    how should I put it on?
I have washed my feet,
    am I to soil them?

My lover thrust his hand into the hole,
    at which my insides thrilled.[88]
I rose to open to my lover,
    and my hands dripped with myrrh,
my fingers with liquid myrrh,
    on the handles of the bolt.
I opened to my beloved,
    But my lover had turned[89] and gone.
My soul failed me because of him.

I sought him but did not find him;
    I called him, but he did not answer me.
The watchmen found me,
    those who go on rounds of the city.
They beat me, they bruised me,
    they took away my cloak,[90]
    those keepers of the walls.
I place you under oath, daughters of Jerusalem,[91]
    if you find my beloved, tell him this:

I am faint with love (5.2-8).

Judg. 19.22 of the Gibeonite mob as they batter the door of the Levite's lodgings. Pope, on the basis of the Song's sentimentality, suggests the term is less boisterous here. There remains a possibility, however, that a strenuous, violent knocking is implied.

86. The exact meaning of this term is uncertain (it appears only here and in v. 11 below). The sense of 'hair' is adduced by an equivalent term in Arabic meaning the hair over the forehead (Pope, *Song of Songs*, p. 512).

87. As sexually exuberant as Boer's translation is, it rather suits the text here in what is in what is arguably the most sexually suggestive portion of the Song of Songs ('Night Sprinkle(s): Pornography and the Song of Songs', p. 57).

88. Literally, 'my heart trembled because of him'. As Murphy puts it (Song of Songs, p. 165), the verb 'designates a physical and emotional response, either in pain (Isa. 16.11) or, as here, in joy (Jer. 31.20).

89. Exum highlights the *qal* form of the verb חמק here, and the fact that the passive participle is used in Song 7.1 [2] to refer to the woman's hips (*Song of Songs*, p. 185).

90. This word (רדיד) is a troublesome term in Hebrew; see the discussion below for my treatment of the term.

91. The Septuagint adds 'by the powers and forces of the field'.

There are important differences between these two accounts.[92] In chap. 3, the woman, in bed, bemoans the absence of her lover (v. 1). She rises and goes, literally, 'around' (סבב) the city's narrow streets (שׁוקים)[93] and squares (רחבות) in search of her lover. The text itself seems to make (linguistic) connections here between the woman's searches for her lover and the patrolling of the watchmen who come across her in the dark. In 3.2 the woman goes 'around' (אסובבה) the city, while the watchmen are described using the plural participle of the same Hebrew root (סבב); literally, 'the guards circling the city'. The repetition of the verb begs the question of whether we are supposed to imagine the woman and the city-watch moving around in actual circles, or whether the term denotes movement 'around' the city in a more general sense.

In other biblical texts the verb סבב tends to denote only circularity, meaning 'surround', 'turn around', 'circuit', 'encompass', etc. (see, for instance: Josh. 6.3-7; Num. 21.4; 1 Sam. 7.16; 1 Kgs 7.15; 2 Kgs 3.9; 2 Chron. 33.14; Job 40.22). The Targum of the Song directly exploits this sense of surround—in terms of the female's action, specifically—when it turns her city search into the nation of Israel 'surrounding' the tent of meeting. The Septuagint retains this sense too: it uses κυκλώσω, meaning, again, to 'encircle' or 'girdle round'. And, as Pope points out, behind both the Greek and the Hebrew is the Akkadian term *sāhir duri* 'one who goes around the wall', which is given in a lexical text as the equivalent of *ma-sar musi*, 'night watchman'.[94] Interestingly, Robert and Tourney have the following to say of the streets and squares that the woman visits on her search: 'les sont les larges espaces, les dégagements qui se trouvent principalement aux abords des portes. Ils forment contraste avec l'enchevêtrement des rues étroites.'[95] Their comments indicate that a spiralling, whirling passage around the edge of the entire conurbation may indeed work as a coherent reading of the whole passage in chap. 3; the woman moves between those areas at the city's doors, between spaces, that is, that lie only at its perimeter. Perhaps the woman's route around the city's 'ring-road' is why the keepers of the walls come across her so easily. This whole image—that of

92. As Exum and Black point out, though, the similarity of the two texts invites a whole set of readerly connections and narrative creations under the poet's license. See Black, and Exum, 'Semiotics in Stained Glass'. I will come back to the issue of the connections between the two texts *as two texts* in due course. For the moment, I am anxious to use them in tandem to build up a comprehensive picture of the textual city.

93. On narrowness see *DCH* 8, p. 310.

94. Pope, *Song of Songs*, p. 419.

95. רחבות and שׁוקים are large spaces, open areas that are mainly found around doors. They form a contrast with the tangle of narrow streets. Robert and Tournay draw this observation from Barrois's *Manuel d'archéologie biblique* (Cantique des Cantiques, p. 263).

the circular movement around a circular city—works nicely with the picture of the Song's city as painted by Jill Munro, 'a progressive narrowing of concentric circles'.[96]

In Song of Songs 3, the watchmen ignore the woman's request for information—at least, they offer her no answer at all—but she soon finds her lover and drags him (אחז, the terminology is identical to that of trapping animals from 2.15) home to the house of her mother (v. 4). The pair seems then to disappear inside for some privacy—even the usually privileged (voyeuristic) reader is not permitted to follow them in.

Song of Songs 5, on the other hand, begins with an aborted tryst at the woman's front door. The man beats on the door and a series of double entendres ensue, which most commentators are keen to point out. Garrett indicates the possibility that the man's moist head might refer to seminal fluid on his penis (and, given the rest of the verse, presumably his pubic hair),[97] while Pope understands the mention of feet to be euphemistic for female genitals.[98] The crucial element in any sexual reading of the passage, though, is v. 4: 'My lover thrust his hand into the hole, at which my insides thrilled'. As Pope writes:

> Given the attested use of 'hand' as a surrogate for phallus, there can be no question that, whatever the context, the statement 'my love thrust his "hand" into the hole' would be suggestive of coital intromission, even without the succeeding line descriptive of he emotional reaction of the female.[99]

Exum interprets the 'emotional reaction' described by Pope here as 'orgasm'. Moreover, she extends the sexual overtones of the scene by pointing out the 'erotic suggestiveness' of the woman's 'opening' to her lover in v. 6; the Hebrew term has a sexual second meaning.[100] Pardes cites the woman's myrrh-soaked fingers (the garden produce seems to have remained in the frame) as evidence that the scene is a masturbatory fantasy, or else is suggestive of some extremely heavy petting.[101] At this point in the text, of course, Boer is unable to hold himself back,

---

96. Munro, *Spikenard and Saffron*, p. 134.
97. Garrett, *Song of Songs*, p. 207.
98. Pope, *Song of Songs* p. 515.
99. Pope, *Song of Songs*, p. 519.
100. Exum, *Song of Songs*, pp. 191-92. I also explore the sexual meaning of this term in relation to doorways and spatial meaning in the context of 1 Samuel in Christopher Meredith, 'A Case of Open and Shut: The Five Thresholds in 1 Samuel 1.1-7.2', *BibInt* 18 (2010), pp. 137-57 (21).
101. Ilana Pardes, 'I am a Wall, and My Breasts like Towers': The Song of Songs and the Question of Canonization', in *Countertraditions in the Bible: A Feminist Approach* (Cambridge, MA: Harvard University Press, 1992), pp. 118-43 (132).

Sue's 'innards yearned for him', his hand moving back and forth in an ecstasy reminiscent of the ultimate orgasm of childbirth. She is loose and open now, Frank's hand stimulating her cunt; she grabs his cock and he sprays cum all over her, her hands 'dripped with myrrh, [her] fingers with liquid myrrh, upon the handles of the bolt' (5.5).[102]

Come the crucial moment of the 'opening' in v. 6, however, the man is nowhere to be found. He has fled into the city streets, and the woman goes looking for him.

While searching for him in the city streets, the woman is found by the city guards and beaten (נכה). It is not clear whether this is a single strike or a series of blows but wounding or bruising (פצע) is the result.[103] The watchmen—or, literally, the 'keepers of the walls' (v. 7)—also remove the woman's veil (רדיד). The exact meaning of this term is uncertain. The Septuagint suggests θέριστρόν, a veil or summer cloak. The only other occurrence of this word is in Isa. 3.23, when it appears as part of a list of female clothing. As Carole Fontaine has pointed out:

[T]here it [רדיד] is distinguished from an 'over-tunic' (מעטפה, Isa. 3.22) and a 'cloak' (מטפחת) in the same verse. The loss of this garment is a sign of punishment in Isaiah and fits with the 'stripping' motifs visited upon 'bride' Israel by God and his angry prophets. In addition to 'veil', translators have also used the words 'mantle' or 'wrapper' for these Hebrew terms, *suggesting an outer garment that signals the boundary between the woman inside it and the world outside.*[104]

As Exum stresses, however we render the verse the watchmen's action constitutes a 'contemptuous act of exposure'.[105] After this portion of text the female lover goes on to describe the male to the daughters of Jerusalem and runs gaily off to his garden, where, apparently, he has been waiting for her the whole time (6.2).[106]

In light of these observations, my contention is that the city is constituted in the text by two interwoven processes: a tension between the city's opacity and the characters' attempts to overcome that opacity through surveillance. And, secondly, from the inversions of imagery that that process of attempting-to-render-transparent gives rise to. In chap. 5, the violence, the

102. Boer, *Knocking on Heaven's Door*, p. 66.
103. For a full discussion of this, see Exum, *Song of Songs*, pp. 197-200.
104. Carole R. Fontaine, 'Watching Out for the Watchmen (Song of Songs 5.7)', in C. Cosgrove (ed.), *The Meanings We Choose: Hermeneutical Ethics, Indeterminacy and the Conflict of Interpretations* (London: T. & T. Clark, 2004), pp. 102-21 (116), emphasis mine.
105. Exum, *Song of Song*, p. 197. For further discussion of this veil, see Bergant, *Song of Songs*, p. 66; Bloch and Bloch, *Song of Songs*, p. 182; Longman, *Song of Songs*, p. 169; Murphy, *Song of Songs*, p. 165; Black, *Artifice of Love*, pp. 191-92.
106. Exum, *Song of Songs*, p. 197.

search, and the erotic encounter at the door stem from the fact that the city is an opaque construction.

Opacity and Transparenc(it)y

Even in this relatively compact survey of the material it is fairly clear that the textual city is an opaque structure. Three things mark it out as such. First, even if we think in terms of basic visibility, the city is dark. Unlike virtually every other setting in the Song, the city is shown to us only at night. As a result the streets appear to be quiet, even deserted (aside from the potentially violent guards of course) and this makes the woman's search (appear) more difficult. Second, it is impossible to identify this city, which renders the streets historically and socially opaque. Though a mere lock of the female's hair or the angle of her nose might conjure up a precise grid-reference in other parts of the Song (7.11, for example), the twice-explored city remains oddly anonymous. The city itself resists readerly decipherment, then, since we are not allowed to know which city it is. Like the woman who cannot see where the male has gone or why, we are blind to the overall pattern of the city as a setting in the text.[107] Thirdly, and most importantly, the textual city is opaque because it is presented as an edifice designed to hide the things within it. In fact, that is the city's primary function in the poem. It conceals the male in 3.1 and 5.3, it conceals the female in 5.2, and it conceals the couple entirely (even, as I have said, from the reader) in 3.4. The very *presence* of night watchmen is also suggestive of the possibilities and dangers of concealment that exist within the city; lurking is a distinctly urban practice. This city is a space in which you can be close to something—your quarry, a policeman—and not necessarily know it, or, in the case of the man at the woman's door, without necessarily being allowed access. The processes of searching and finding in the text rely on the city operating as a kind of labyrinthine space, a space that hides things but which encourages us to go looking for them.

Each city scene essentially deals with the characters' varied attempts to unveil what the urban space has successfully hidden. In 3.1 and 5.6 the woman searches for the man in the city's streets and marketplaces. In 3.1 she is successful, in 5.6-7 the city gets the better of her. In 5.2 the male

---

107. Robert and Tournay argue that the Song's city is Jerusalem based on allusions to the temple, but these 'allusions' simply do not stack up with the text. Robert and Tournay, *Le Cantiques des Cantiques* (Paris: Arlèa, 1963), p. 132. See also Pope, *Song of Songs*, p. 417 for discussion on this point. Pope suggests that the city is Jerusalem on the strength of the mention of the 'women of Jerusalem', but these women are addressed without any reference to an urban context at several points in the text (2.7, 8.4); that is, their presence does not automatically imply Jerusalem as the setting in any other part of the poem. Moreover, the Song is not reticent to use geographical references anywhere else, making the lack of an obvious name for the city all the more conspicuous.

searches out the woman who is concealed within her house. In 3.3 and 5.7 the watchmen mark out the entire metropolis as a circle of surveillance, twice making 'rounds' of the city as a peripatetic reminder of the dangers of being in the city after dark. These attempts at bringing transparency are fuelled by the darkness of the city and are what come to constitute the urban space in the text. The 'urban' in the poem is enacted through a series of displacing operations between opacity and transparency.[108] It is this tension that allows for the operation of power between the characters in the text: the power of the woman, safe behind her door, to reject the man; the power of the male to disappear and cause his beloved to fret; the power of the male guards over the dark streets; the power of the male guards to beat the woman; the power of the male guards to get away with it.

DistURBing, duplicAtiNg

The violence of the watchman in 5.7 has been variously interpreted. Murphy believes the violence is as a result of the female not finding her beloved quickly enough.[109] Gordis and Keel feel the woman has probably been mistaken for a prostitute. Keel offers Middle Assyrian laws that prohibited veiled prostitutes in support of this view. This notion is soundly put down by Exum who points out that there is 'no biblical evidence to indicate that a woman on the street would be treated so ruthlessly' and that the Middle Assyrian laws are notoriously severe anyway.[110] Pardes, Polaski and Müller see the violence as a kind of dream-anxiety brought on by the woman's guilty conscience over the erotic scene in 5.2.[111] Garrett believes that

---

108. This term, 'displacement', is a key one since the actions that mediate between the darkness and visibility in the city are on the whole displacements: movements, wanderings, searches. The whole city is written in footprints. 'To walk is to lack a place', says Michel de Certeau in his own treatise on the city: 'It is the indefinite process of being absent and in search of a proper. The moving about that the city multiplies and concentrates makes the city itself an immense social experience of lacking a place—an experience that is, to be sure, broken up into countless tiny deportations (displacements and walks), compensated for by the relationships and intersections of these exoduses that intertwine and create an urban fabric, and placed under the sign of what ought to be, ultimately, the place but is only a name, the City…a shuffling among pretences of the proper, a universe of rented spaces, haunted by a no-where of dreamed-of places' (*The Practice of Everyday Life* [trans. Steven Rendall; Berkeley, CA: University of California Press, 1984], p. 103).

109. Murphy, *Song of Songs*, p. 171.

110. Exum, *Song of Songs*, pp. 197-98; Gordis, *Song of Songs*, p. 91, Keel, *Song of Songs*, p. 195.

111. Pardes, *Countertraditions in the Bible*, pp. 136-39; Polaski 'What Will Ye See in the Shulammite?', pp. 78-79; Müller, *Vergleich und Metapher im Hohennlied* (Göttingen.Vandenhooek & Ruprecht, 1984), p. 78.

the violence is somehow indicative of 'anxiety' over the loss of virginity.[112] Burrus and Moore, by contrast, make violence a legitimate sexual category by walking readers through the lively rigors of BDSM—violence can be a rewarding part of sex, they argue, and the Song begs for such a reading.[113]

The violence also seems to fit as a part of the text's seeking and uncovering motif, however; it seems to stem from the tension between opacity and transparency that I have been tracing here. The guards' violence involves a very particular kind of incursion: a visual one. The guards remove the woman's veil, uncovering her body in some way. This action—albeit brutal—seems to sit within the economy of the urban in the text. It is another example of a tension between opacity (here bodily) and the will-to-transparency. The guards' violence is, then, the very inverse of the search that brings the incident about. The woman resists the city's opacity, searching to make her lover visible to her. Meanwhile, the city resists the woman's bodily opacity, unveiling her to make her body visible. If we take Fontaine's suggestion seriously, that the woman's veil (רדיד) indicates 'an outer garment that signals the boundary between the woman inside it and the world outside' then there is a cruel irony in that the guardians of the city's 'walls' (stipulated as such in 5.7) tear down the outer perimeter of the woman as a bodily subject.

The beating and bruising also draw attention to the contrasting ways in which the woman's bodily boundaries have been treated in the city. The watchmen's beating of the woman is a hallucination of the doorstep tryst. In 5.2 the physical boundary of the urban home doubles as a site of sexual arousal when the threshold of the woman's house becomes interchangeable with the threshold of her body through the use of double entendre: 'My lover thrust his hand into the hole, at which my insides thrilled'. Later, in 5.7, the 'keepers of the walls'—the guardians of the city's boundaries—turn the bodily boundary of the woman into a site of abuse. In the sexual encounter of 5.2-3, then, the male's 'hand', the woman's nakedness ('I have taken off my robe'), and the domestic boundary join as part of a sexual discourse. In 5.7 the male fist, the public boundary ('those keepers of the walls'), and

---

112. Garrett, *Song of Songs*, pp. 409-12.

113. Burrus and Moore, 'Unsafe Sex: Feminism, Pornography and the Song of Songs', *BibInt* 11 (2003), pp. 24-52. Black notes that the outrageousness of the incident in 5.7 is heightened due to the benign interaction the woman has with the watchmen earlier in chap. 3 (*Artifice of Love*, p. 161). Indeed, it is really this innocent interaction with the city's constabulary that makes the text so problematic and not the violence itself. Violence can be explained, abhorred, fetishized, subverted, welcomed, undermined, and submitted to all the other kinds of other political action that biblical discourse routinely makes use of. The inaction-and-then-brutality of the watchmen, and the resulting inconsistency of the poem's police force, makes for a literary problem, a problem which, inevitably, undermines every definitive theory, reading or explanation of the stripping and beating of the woman in 5.7.

a public uncovering converge as (sexual?) violence.[114] The Song's most dis-
turbing scene is an unconscious inversion of its most suggestive one. The
brutal episode transforms the familiarity of the urban dwelling, the security
of the domestic threshold and the intimacy of the body into a violent public
space characterized by losing (the male lover), exposure, and the incursion
of the watchman's fist. Given the spatial economy of the story in chap. 5,
there is something cruelly ironic, then, about the watchmen's actions. Theirs
is not simply violence but a spatial perversion of a very spatial function—
just as the uncovering of the woman is an inversion of her search for her
lover.[115] The public city and the private city collide here and the female protagonist becomes caught, semi-clad, somewhere in the middle.[116]

---

114. Is the episode a rape? Alicia Ostriker (and her students) think so, see 'Holy of
Holies: The Song of Songs as Countertext', in Athalya Brenner and Carol Fontaine
(eds.), *The Song of Songs: A Feminist Compasion*, p. 51. In her early work, Athalya
Brenner thinks not: 'at least she is not sexually molested for her modesty' (Athalya
Brenner, *Song of Songs* [Sheffield: Sheffield Academic Press, 1989], p. 83). Similarly,
Black points out that there 'is no direct evidence for sexual violence in the text'. Black
admits that it would be 'reasonable to consider the possibility of sexual violence if, in
fact, the woman was [entirely] stripped and exposed'. But, ultimately, Black reasons that
'if raped…the [woman's] fear would doubtless not be articulated in the jubilant spirit
in which the poem seems to be written' (Black, *Artifice of Love*, p. 192). I cannot help
thinking, however, that there is little 'direct' evidence for *anything* very much in the
Song of Songs; it is a poem that uses suggestion, double entendre and readerly projection to exert its considerable literary wiles over its readership, who are invited to enter it
and fill its numerous holes. (This is, in point of fact, a thesis of Black's own.) Though not
a violation in explicitly sexual terms, the watchmen's actions in 5.7 are certainly a violation of all the strictures of embodiment, safety and sexual discretion as they sit within
the sexual-spatial economy of the chapter. In a text where the closest we come to orgasm
is a fumble at the threshold, where dexterous fingers play with domestic boundaries and
so point to penetrative ecstasy—'my insides thrilled' (5.3)—what else do we expect a
rape to look like? Can we expect the Song to spell such things out in ways that are totally
uncharacteristic of the rest of the text?

115. The indirect result of the violence is an ambivalence about the nature of the watch
itself. Are the watchmen present to keep outsiders out or insiders in? Are these roving
sentinels for defence or for policing? Certainly, in the name of security, they enable
repression.

116. The potential problem with articulating this point in this way is that it plays too
readily into the hands of scholars like Pardes and Polaski who see the watchman's violence as a manifestation of the woman's psychosexual guilt regarding her doorstep
encounter with her lover. I already touched upon these kinds of readings in my critique of dream rhetoric in Chapter 2. Here I am insisting that we highlight the connections that exist between the events at the door and the events on the city streets in chap.
5, but that we do so without imposing the idea of a conjectural psychic space on the text
at the expense of the self-evident city-space. Any reading of the violence that rests on
our questioning the legitimacy of the woman as a sexual being puts us at odds with the
rest of the Song. Any reading that dismisses this violence, or lets its male instigators off

All this is to say that the proliferation of hidden, obscured, and opaque spaces in the city gives rise to searches and attempts to uncover on the one hand, and, on the other, to disquieting repetitions or inversions of the imagery we have already been presented with: domestic threshold, female covering, the male hand.

Freud and the Labyrinthine City

In Donald's discussion, the 'labyrinth' becomes a useful cipher for this mixture of the familiar and the disquieting, and, indeed, for the mixture of opacity and transparency on which it relies. Donald does not particularly explore the image in its own terms, but it is not difficult to see why the labyrinth comes to operate in his work as a symbol for emotional duality. The labyrinth appears in numerous writings—most notably those of Bachelard,[117] Tschumi,[118]

---

the hook, or which expunges the violence itself from the Song is also obviously deficient. But taking the interactions between identities and spatialities seriously, and looking at the kinds of links that the city draws between rhythms of life, love, desire and terror is instructive in recognizing the complex tensions at work in the poetic presentation of the city.

117. In Gaston Bachelard's essay on the labyrinth as a symbol in materialist psychoanalysis, Bachelard puts it this way: 'le rêveur vit une étrange hésitation: *il hésite au milieu d'un chemin unique*. Il devient matiére hésitante, une matiére qui dure en hésitant. La synthés qu'est le rêve labyrinthique accumule, semble-t-il, l'angoisse d'un passé de souffrance et l'anxiéte d'un avenir de malheurs. L'être y est pris entre un passé bloqué et un avnir bouché. Il est emprisonné dans un chemin. [the dreamer experiences a strange uncertainty: *he hesitates in the middle of a single path*. It becomes a matter of uncertainty, and one's uncertainty lasts. The dream-labyrinth is built, it seems, from synthesis, from anguish over a past of suffering and anxiety about a future of misery. The dreamer is caught between a blocked past and a blocked future. In a way, he is imprisoned.] Gaston Bachelard, *La terre et les reveries du repos* (Paris: Corti, 1946), pp. 211-12. The labyrinth as an embodied experience is what gives power to this sense of duality.

118. The image of the labyrinth became important in architectural discourse because of the writings of Bernard Tschumi. For Tschumi the labyrinth functions as a metaphor for the kind of subjective first-person point-of-view that characterizes all spatial praxis. We all experience the world, Tschumi argued, as embodied nomads, blind to the whole puzzling design of the spaces around us, and able to engage only with the part of the world that manifests itself directly before our eyes: 'Unfolding against the projections of reason, against absolute truth, against the pyramid, here is the sensory space, the labyrinth, the hole. Dislocated and disassociated by language or culture or economy into the specialized ghettos of sex and mind, Soho and Bloomsbury, 42nd Street and West 40th Street, here is where my body tries to rediscover its lost unity, its energies and impulses, its rhythms and its flux', Bernard Tschumi, 'Questions of Space: The Pyramid and the Labyrinth (or the Architectural Paradox)', *Studio International* 190 (1975), pp. 136-42 (137). Tschumi's comments relate to a whole intellectual economy that is interested in the marginal and subjective experiences that come to characterize and create 'city-ness'

Borges[119]—as an emblem of the kinds of inherent contradiction that arise from and through personal experience *in* a space. The labyrinth is a decidedly unsettling space, where every corner, every avenue, is new and untested and yet identical to each of the corners and avenues that have gone before it. In the labyrinth I am caught. Do I move forwards, or do I go back to remake an earlier choice? I am pressed under the cumulative weight of my own shaky decisions (Left? Right? Straight on?), trapped somewhere between the memory of an entrance and the hope of a centre. There is a certain kind of terror that can come alive only in the maze or in the walled city late at night, where one finds oneself cast adrift between the emotions attached to being lost and those of being imprisoned. The space of the labyrinth mixes desire of the prize with a fear of the puzzle, endlessly duplicating the familiar until it becomes alien, until it shocks us by means of its familiarity.

The labyrinth is useful in critical discourse about space because it is a spatialization of Freud's discourse on the uncanny. Strictly speaking, Freud's uncanny, or *Unheimlich* (literally, and poignantly for this discussion, the un-*homely*), describes the emotional effect of a particular range of disquieting experiences that frighten because they involve a collision of the familiar and the alien, or else because they involve a repetition/duplication of the seemingly singular. *Déjà vu* is perhaps the most obvious everyday example, though other oft-quoted examples include the idea of the doppelgänger, the doll made animate, the divided self, the denied death, the undermining of self-determination.[120]

(that is, those writings of Donald, Pile, and de Certeau's that I have already touched upon). To focuses on the seemingly banal, the spectral, those personal mythologies that come to inscribe urbanity with power from the inside is itself a pseudo-labyrinthine approach, then. And the Song's city, as a first-person perspective of the city, is itself already describing, and inscribing, the idea of city from the inside out, that is, from the point of view of the searching woman.

119. Most famously, Jorge Luis Borges, *Labyrinths: Selected Stories and Other Writings*.

120. Sigmund Freud, 'The Uncanny', in *The Uncanny* (trans. Donald McLintock; London: Penguin, 2003 [1919]), pp. 121-62. *Unheimlich* works so much better than its English equivalents; the *Unheimlich* emerges from the *heimlich* (the familiar, or homely), which has become 'hidden' (again, *Heimlich*) in the recesses of the mind. In an intriguing article on the connection between the City monument and the uncanny, Derek Hook stresses: 'It is not just the disjuncture of the body and soul that Freud is interested in here—that is, problems of embodiment—but *disjunctures of history* also, anxieties of "the before" suddenly pre-empting the specific moment of the present, those moments in which that which has been superseded now comes to overrun the sensibilities of the present. It is vital in this respect that we take note of the priority that Freud gives the factor of repetition in his account of the uncanny, underlining the "dominance in the unconscious mind of a compulsion to repeat, a compulsion powerful enough to overrule the pleasure principle, lending to certain aspects of the mind their daemonic character"', Derek Hook, 'Monumental Space and the Uncanny', *Geoforum* 36 (2005), pp. 688-704 (698).

Freud himself relied on urban experiences, in fact, to formulate his ideas about the uncanny in the first place. His 1919 essay on the subject relates an episode in which he flees an insalubrious neighborhood of an Italian town only to find himself back at the junction he started from.

> Strolling one hot summer afternoon through the empty and to me unfamiliar streets of a small Italian town, I found myself in a district about whose character I could not long remain in doubt. Only heavily made-up women were to be seen at the windows of the little houses, and I hastily left the narrow street at the next turning. However after wandering about for some time without asking the way, I suddenly found myself back in the same street, where my presence began to attract attention. Once more I hurried away, only to return there again by a different route. I was now seized by a feeling I can only describe as uncanny, and I was glad to find my way back to the piazza that I had recently left and refrain from any further voyages of discovery.[121]

For the disoriented Freud, the labyrinthine city becomes an arena where places of safety and places of danger slide together, giving rise to a disquieting duplication of experience and the unbidden return of what had been pushed away.

It is this core idea that Donald invokes in order to explain the labyrinthine qualities of the City, tying the image of the labyrinth—characterized as an opaque site that induces search and movement, as in the Song—to the uncomfortable disjunctions of urban life. The uncanny city is thus 'both problem and possibility', a place where 'threat' and 'home' must necessarily coincide.

> How can such a bewildering and alien environment—the city as an unsolvable enigma—provide a home? The disquieting slippage between a place where we should feel at home and the sense that it is, at some level, definitively unhomely links Simmel to Freud, or at least to his premise that the *unheimlich* is rooted in the familiar, the *heimlich*. That suggests why it is necessary to make sense of the individual in the metropolis not only in terms of identity, community, and civic association, but also in terms of a dramaturgy of desire, fascination and terror. This uncanny city defines the architecture of our apparently most secret selves: an already social space, if often a decidedly uncivil form of association.[122]

This idea is crucial in Donald's discussion, which contends that 'the fear of darkened spaces and the opacity of the social marked Enlightenment conceptions of space'. It is therefore important, says Donald, not only to recognize that power works through surveillance (so Foucault), but also to come to understand 'the extent to which the paring of transparency and obscurity is essential for power to operate'. This disquieting mix constitutes the social

---

121. Freud, 'Uncanny', p. 144.
122. Donald, *Imagining the Modern City*, p. 71.

power of the modern city, or as Donald puts it, 'This modern uncanny, imagined as the labyrinth, always returns to haunt the City of Light'.[123]

The lost woman in the Song, searching for her lover in the dark, finds herself in a decidedly labyrinthine city. Not only is her experience of the city—running through streets and squares, looping around the city in circles—reminiscent of one's movement through a maze, this movement gives rise to precisely the same kinds of urban dynamics that Donald and Pile describe at work within labyrinthine cities more generally; there is a coupling in the text of the will to find with the city's ability to hide. There is threat—as the Song's commentators have been keen to point out—in this city, but there is also a prize: the hope of finding one's lover. There is violence in this labyrinth, certainly, but there is also profound sexual intimacy. There are brutal men, but there is a home too, a female, even a maternal home in the midst of the dark *metro*polis (*mother*-city). Between this homely environment, where the intimate sexual scene takes place, and the city streets, where the decidedly unhomely violence unfolds, the woman's experiences of the city also take on the aspects of the labyrinth that could be described as uncanny. The violence of the watchmen duplicates the earlier intimacy; the un-homely moment of the text is, literally un-homely insofar as it is an uncanny inversion of the events that took place in the woman's *home*.[124] In 5.7 the pleasurable teasing of the boundaries, at once bodily and domestic, becomes cruelly recycled as a violent episode where border keepers lift the veil and violate the body. The dashed eroticized hopes of the home life thus resurface as a horrendous public space. In this space, the male element in the text, momentarily lost beneath the opaque surfaces of the labyrinthine city in 5.3, comes bubbling up as a violent almost-repetition of masculinity. It inevitably haunts the sanctity of the original. The home and the unhomely, the urbane and the decidedly uncivil, meet, diverge, and excite each other at the street corner.

It would be tempting, then, to conclude that the city operates in the wider context of the poem as a space of emotional closure, that is, as a symbol of resistance to the unfettered rhythms of love. Marcia Falk insists on exactly this when she writes that 'of all the contexts of the Song, the city is least sympathetic to the lovers'. But to arrive at this kind of conclusion one must,

---

123. Donald, *Imagining the Modern City*, p. 73.

124. Connections between Freud's original essay on the uncanny and the Song are actually numerous. Freud argues that uncanny literary tropes include an uncertainty in the mode of a text's narration, which the dream-rhetoric of 3.1 and 5.2 in the commentaries seems to attest to in the Song. Freud also sees the motif of return as a kind of uncanny womb-fantasy, and since the lovers return to 'the chamber of the one who bore me', in 3.4, this seems to be present in the text too. There simply is not space in this chapter to explore these features of the text further; see Freud, 'Uncanny', pp. 139, 162.

like Falk, arbitrarily strip the urban *house* out of the city context.[125] The themes of urban darkness and urban displacement are potent in the poem precisely because of the contrast they draw with the sexualized encounters in the mother's chamber and at the female's doorstep. The city is powerfully dark precisely because it is potentially intimate.

The City in the Garden in the City

Really, of course, what I have been throwing light on in the city—the processes of concealment, surveillance, efforts to control, and the surprising redeployment of romantic tropes in the enactment of violence—is itself a duplication of what my reading of the garden aimed to effect.

My reading of the garden did not aim to overturn the idea that the garden can, or should, be read as a romantic image of intimacy and seclusion, but sought, rather, to foreground the way the garden works as an image. The garden relies on a set of more sinister—earlier I used the term 'violent'—ideological operations in order to present itself as a symbol of Arcadian bliss. The garden is compiled; in it people attempt to demonstrate their control over the environment; the garden, as a repository of life, comes to be symbolic of women. The garden is bounded; access to it is regulated; gardens naturalize the operations of power by which they are constituted. The garden might work as a romantic image, then, but when we look closely we see that all the elements that make the garden so lovely—its enclosedness, its variety of flora, its association with the sexually aroused body—are reimaginings of less salubrious images: space as claimed, space as penetrated. The city too is built and designed; the city too is enclosed; in it (watch) men attempt to demonstrate their control over the environment once again. The city has some violent moments but look closely and all the elements that make the city so imposing—its enclosedness, its opacity, its association with the sexually molested body—are reimaginings of more tender images: space as claimed, space as penetrated.

I argued in the last chapter that the city emerges out of the image of the garden, that, in the phantasmagorical shifts of scene that characterize the Song, the woman's dwelling emerges as a kind of urban duplicate of the garden. The configuration of the spaces remains the same while the thematic 'overlay' changes. In Song of Songs 6.2, of course, the garden reasserts itself against the city and comes back into the frame. But the

---

125. Falk treats the urban home as an entirely different contextual category in the poem, one unashamedly geared toward passion: in the urban dwelling 'lovemaking will be at its best' she promises us. But she offers no clue as to why the metropolitan love-nest should be treated as any less of an urban situ (Marcia Falk, *Love Lyrics from the Bible*, p. 90).

city seems to lay dormant 'in' the garden, and the garden 'in' the city, in ways than run deeper than the structural make-up of the text. Both spaces rely on remarkably similar operations of concealment, of visibility, of control and influence, and work as settings for the lovers for largely the same reasons; at root, power is parsed out in the two environments in much the same way.

The division between city and garden is largely invented by scholarship. Each space, like the Song as a whole, is a complex web of performances and effacements, which readers can work with in one way or another. The city re-imagines the garden; the garden re-imagines the city, and the whole process of reading the Song thus becomes fraught with incidences of the uncanny, of almost repetitions that use the power of the familiar to instigate moments of arrest. Landy likens the whole text to the garden, as we saw earlier, but perhaps it is just as much an extension of the city: a space of repeats, and circlings, of re-codings and almost-duplications: a labyrinth.

Chapter 4

GENDER, SPACE AND THRESHOLD MAGIC

> Threshold magic. At the entrance to the skating rink, to the pub, to the tennis court, to resort locations: *penates*.[1] The hen that lays the golden praline-eggs, the machine that stamps our names on nameplates, slot machines…[c]hairs beside an entrance, photographs flanking a doorway, are fallen household deities, and the violence they must appease grips our hearts even today at each ringing of the doorbell. Try, though, to withstand the violence. Alone in an apartment, try not to bend to the insistent ringing. You will find it as difficult as an exorcism. Like all magic substance, this too is once again reduced at some point to sex –in pornography.[2]

In this chapter I intend to use the thresholds of the Song of Songs—its door and window images—to critique the poem's attitudes about gender.[3] This discussion will give way to a broader treatment of categorization in the Song. My contention, to put it very briefly, is that the Song cannot maintain its own gender divisions; like all kinds of dyad, the dividing lines are just too crumbly to sustain the definitions. The Song's doors and windows open out onto the problems of gendered identity on the one side and onto the partiality of discourse on the other. This chapter aims, therefore, to illuminate the connections between ideological and spatial positions in the Song and

---

1. Lit: household gods.
2. Benjamin, *The Arcades Project*, p. 214. Here Benjamin describes that same tension Gaston Bachelard famously alluded to, the tension of threshold where two spaces are stitched together and differentiated all at once, Gaston Bachelard, *The Poetics of Space* (trans. M. Jolas; Boston: Beacon Press, 1994 [1958]), pp. 211-12. Benjamin's description goes so far as to figure the paradoxical threshold as a kind of violent magic that mediates between categories, an occult space that contains and subdues radical differences between. Thus to ring the doorbell, to seek to cross the line between inside and outside, is, by Benjamin's reckoning, to awaken powerful social forces of inclusion and exclusion. We may be used to performing the rituals at doorways that appease these forces (tapping key codes, swiping membership cards, presenting passports), but that does not make our 'sorcery' any less potent. Moving between Here and There is always and inevitably a complicated social act.
3. Some of the following discussion has appeared elsewhere in a slightly different form; see Christopher Meredith,'The Lattice and the Looking-glass: Gendered Space in Song of Songs 2.8-14', *JAAR* 80 (2012), pp. 1-22.

to demonstrate that the spatial phantasmagoria we have been looking at thus far (in broad terms in Chapter 2 and in two specific cases in Chapter 3) is in play in the gendering of the lovers too. The process of mapping the gendered spatiality in the Song brings us back to an issue I have been concerned with throughout this discussion: the troublesome line between readers and characters, where the Song's diffuse and flexible politics is again at work.

The Line That is Not One

All thresholds are potent symbols. As Gaston Bachelard once wrote, 'outside and inside form a dialectic of division, the obvious geometry of which blinds us as soon as we bring it into play in metaphorical domains. It has the sharpness of the dialectics of *yes* and *no*, which decides everything.' In other words, thresholds spatialize the fundamental nature of the metaphorical dialectic: yes/no, in/out, present/beyond, even being/non-being, which Bachelard himself calls a 'faint repetition of the dialectics of inside and outside'.[4] The Song itself, of course, is a dialectic between male/female, and, crucially for this particular discussion, the poem frequently seems to merge the dialectic inside/outside with this gendered divide. Existing discussions that pertain to gender issues in the Song are legion, and most tend to treat gendered interactions in isolation from the poem's settings and situs. Despite this, they are often unconsciously spatial.

Numerous feminist scholars have detected a manifesto for gender equality in the poem. Phyllis Trible discerns in the Song 'no male dominance, no female subordination, and no stereotyping of either sex'.[5] Carol Meyers, in her contribution to *A Feminist Companion to the Hebrew Bible*, also points to the prominence of a 'gynocentric' modality in the Song that constitutes a 'reversal of conventional gender portrayal'.[6] Athalya Brenner and Fokkelien Van Dijk-Hemmes adopt a more central line. Their text is 'double voiced'; traces of an underlying phallocentrism compete with the text's strong gynocentric tenors.[7] Alicia Ostriker hails the Song as 'an extraordinarily egalitarian image of mutual love and desire' that enjoys an 'absence of structural and systemic hierarchy, sovereignty, authority, control, superiority, [and] submission' on either lover's part.[8] This is, she says, caused

---

4. Bachelard, *The Poetics of Space*, pp. 211-12.

5. Phyllis Trible, *God and the Rhetoric of Sexuality*, p. 161.

6. Carol Meyers, 'Gender Imagery in the Song of Songs', in Athalya Brenner (ed.), *A Feminist Companion to the Song of Songs* (Sheffield: Sheffield Academic Press, 1993), p. 208.

7. Athalya Brenner and Fokkelien van Dijk-Hemmes, *On Gendering Texts: Female and Male Voices in the Hebrew Bible* (Leiden: E.J. Brill, 1993), pp. 79-81.

8. Alicia Ostriker, 'A Holy of Holies: The Song of Songs as Countertext', in Brenner and Fontaine (eds.), *A Feminist Companion to the Bible*, pp. 37, 49-50.

by the text's continual 'blurring of boundaries'.[9] Though not everybody is convinced. Donald Polanski uses Foucault's panopticon (the ultimate self-policing prison) to argue that the female lover internalizes the male's gaze. The Song's supposed paragon of feminist power is in fact a self-policing subject, he insists, who functions according to a decidedly phallocentric economy.[10] David Clines sees the Song as 'the stuff of pornography', an attempt 'to drive underground the pervasive social [read: patriarchal] reality with pillow talk'.[11] I have already alluded to the work of Fiona Black, which critiques the somewhat arbitrary assumption that the varied, and often patently ridiculous, imagery applied to the female lover is complimentary. This 'hermeneutic of compliment' underwrites scholarly engagement with the Song, says Black, but adherents fail to consider its (often unfortunate) implications for the female body.[12]

The apparently unconscious spatializing that underpins much of this discourse is not too hard to detect. Meyers justifies her gyno*centric* text as such by positing it as 'a product of domestic life'.[13] But placing a paean to love neatly beside the hearth spatializes it in a number of ways, none of which do very much for the text's feminist credentials. Brenner and Dijk-Hemmes's discussion depends upon the language of a 'male-world' versus a 'female-world' (terms they borrow from Rabin) to posit the text's duality.[14]

9. Ostriker, 'Holy of Holies', p. 49.

10. Donald Polanski, 'What will ye see in the Shulammite?', pp. 64-81.

11. David Clines, *Interested Parties: The Ideology of Writers and Readers of the Hebrew Bible* (Sheffield: Sheffield Phoenix Press, 2009), pp. 102, 113.

12. Black, *Artifice of Love*, pp. 29-32. Virginia Burrus and Stephen Moore point out that feminism and heterosexuality are quintessentially modern constructs that have been imposed upon the Song and argue for a broadening of reading strategies to reflect that fact. As I pointed out in the notes to the last chapter, along the way they propose some ferocious readings of their own, which necessitate both 'safe-words' and some specialist equipment. My approach to biblical notions of gender in this chapter reflects something of that fact, see Virginia Burrus and Stephen Moore, 'Unsafe Sex: Feminism, Pornography, and the Song of Songs', pp. 24-52.

13. Elsewhere Meyers cites the Song's prominent 'mother's house' as yet another indication that the poem contains 'little gender stereotyping' but her discussion tends to assume, without much justification, that בית אם transcends the physical 'house' to signify a broader dynasty in the way that בית אב does. The fact that the former seems to denote consistently a bounded domestic space in the Song is simply dismissed out of hand. The use of 'chamber' as its parallel in 3.4 is rejected as evidence to the contrary due to Meyer's rather arbitrary claim that the parallel is female focused rather than space focused. It is not made clear why readers are to disassociate two correlating spatial nouns; Carol Meyers '"To Her Mother's House": Considering a Counterpart to the Israelite *Bet 'ab*', in David Jobling *et al.* (eds.), *The Bible and the Politics of Exegesis* (Cleveland, OH: Pilgrim Press, 1991), pp. 46-47.

14. Chaim Rabin, 'The Song of Songs and Tamil Poetry', *Studies in Religion* 3 (1973–74), pp. 205-19.

For Polanoki, the female comes to embody a Foucauldian *prison*, while Black focuses on the nitty-gritty composition of bodily space. Even Clines's metaphor is subterranean.

But other quarters make far more explicit connections between spatiality and gender than that, with some writers equating femininity with internality, and masculinity with externality, or mobility, or both. In 1970, Leo Krinetzki equated the Song's female protagonist with the Jungian archetype of the vessel.[15] Exum notes that the imagery used by the male character is 'drawn from the domain of economic livelihood'—the public, economic sphere—and that the male 'enjoys a freedom of movement and social autonomy that she does not share'.[16] The male's elusiveness in the poem results, says Exum, from the fact that 'we see him from her point of view, going where he pleases, while she is more often associated with the domestic setting'.[17] It is Munro, however, who is most vocal on this score:

> While spatial relationships are in a state of permanent flux, it is however possible to discern a pattern in the kinds of places with which each lover is associated. As already noted, the woman is most often associated with images of enclosure or hiddenness. She it is whose lively eyes and ruddy cheeks are sheltered from the direct gaze of her lover by a veil (4.1, 3; 6.7), she too it is who is likened to a shy dove hiding in the mountain-side (2.14) and who is borne on a litter that hides her from view (3.6-11). On three occasions she waits indoors for her lover (2.10-14, 3.11 5.2-6) and on two occasions she wanders the streets of the city, itself a kind of prison (3.2-3, 5.7). There are also the images of the spring (4.12), the garden (4.12–5.1) and the vineyard (1.6; 8.11-12), each of which is symbolic of her. Even her lover's embrace shelters (2.3) and enfolds her (2.6, 8.3).[18]

Munro's brief survey is fairly compelling evidence that the text seems profoundly aware of the ways in which the spaces it describes work as concretizations of gendered identity and ideology; the open public sphere is male; the closed domestic setting is more appropriate for a woman. Feminist discourse may unconsciously spatialize the poem and its lovers, but perhaps only because spatiality already plays such a key role in the fixing of gendered identity in the text.

My initial question, then, is, how far does the text push these exclusionary gender politics; how far is the Song willing to go in its contrasting of male/outside with female/inside, and, come to that, do these dialectical

---

15. Leo Krinetzki, 'Die Erotischen Psychologie des Hohenliedes', *TQ* 150 (1970), pp. 404-16; this designation is discussed (and eloquently critiqued in psychoanalytic terms) by Landy, *Paradoxes of Paradise: Identity and Difference in the Song of Songs* (Bible and Literature Series, 7; Sheffield: Almond Press, 1st edn, 1983), pp. 63-65.

16. Exum, *Song of Songs*, pp. 25-26.

17. Exum, *Song of Songs*, p. 27.

18. Munro, *Spikenard and Saffron*, p. 123.

divisions always necessarily stand firm? Does the Song's phantasmagorical 'flux' really stop at the lovers' doorstep as Munro so charmingly implies? As we shall see, if recent developments in philosophy, gender and literary theory have taught us anything, it is that the archetypal dialectical 'divisions'—in/out, being/non-being, present/absent—are not always as divided as one might first think. It seems prudent to ask if the lines between inside and outside always hold in the phantasmagorical Song, then. If they do not, we might legitimately wonder what their collapse might tell us about the text's approach to gendered categorization, and to the notion of the dialectic itself.

I want to begin by looking at how collusions between gender and space have already been mapped out by the wider academy. How do gendered identities take on spatial forms? This should add some critical flesh to Song scholars' observations on the lovers' gendered world. First I want to look at Irigaray, whose seminal work on the female as sepulcher would appear to account adequately for the Song's patterning of male/outside, female/inside, and, indeed, articulates the phallocentric underpinnings of such an equivalency. Is this entirely satisfactory, though? A reading of post-Irigarian discussions on feminism and space, and of responses to Irigaray's patently exclusionary politics—male *versus* female—particularly, indicates that it might not be so simple an issue. Gillian Rose argues that exposing divisions between men and women does not, indeed cannot, challenge exclusionary strategies; on the contrary, it only reinforces them.[19] Rose refigures

19. Gillian Rose, *Feminism and Geography: The Limits of Geographical Knowledge* (Cambridge MN: University if Minnesota Press, 1993). Rose's work is a methodologically significant choice here because of Soja's use (and abuse) of it. Feminist approaches to spatiality are not dealt with at all in Soja's earlier writings and the androcentric ordering and conceptualizing of urban spaces was thus left entirely un-critiqued, as Massey pointed out for us earlier (pp. 13-14, n. 33). In a later book, *Thirdspace*, Soja seeks to address some of the criticisms, adopting Rose into his thirdspatial paradigm. At first glance, Rose's Paradoxical Geography seems comparable to Soja's emancipatory Thirdspace. Rose also looks to break a traditional dichotomy and embrace a third-way of reading space (an approach which we shall be looking at in some detail in the present discussion). This seeming similarity is precisely the grounds on which Soja appropriates her work: '[Rose's geography] travels…very close to the Thirdspace I have evoked from her [Rose's] writings' (*Thirdspace*, p. 125). The connections between Thirdspace and Rose's discussion are not necessarily as compelling as Soja would have us believe, though. The Sojan project splits up 'space' into its constituent parts, while Rose seeks to do precisely the opposite, collapsing the binary into a single interpenetrating continuum, an 'elsewhere', as she terms it. While both studies deal with social structuration and social experiences of space, they treat these issues in fundamentally different ways. Soja parses *out* as a means of *analysis* while Rose facilitates an interpenetration as a means of resistance.

The converse ways in which these two theorists treat space speaks to the fundamental divergence in the aims of their respective projects. The Sojan categories of First, Second

the dichotomy of inside/outside in an attempt combat separatist modes of thinking, and, in so doing, offers us another way to approach the collusions between gender and space in the Song of Songs, collapsing divisions, rather than extolling or ignoring them. What is particularly interesting about the biblical poem, as we shall see, is that it rather neatly fits *both* these theoretical frameworks. The text's merging of gender and space is always very clear but readings of this gendered spatiality are multiple, even contrary, which itself says something about the openness of spatiality (and potentially gender) in the poem.

Gendered Space and Irigaray

The analysis of gendered space is the analysis of the manifestations of gender ideology in the spatial patterning of society. It critiques both spatialized gender positions and the ways in which space is used to inscribe gender upon individuals, whether by its use, disuse or misuse. I borrow three examples from feminist architect Jane Rendell:

> Toilets (rest rooms in the US) are 'sexed' male or female because they are occupied by men or women, while the domestic kitchen is gendered feminine because the activity of cooking is something that is socially connected with women. However, how do we consider the kitchen of the public restaurant where the cooking is done by the chef, who is usually male?[20]

A public toilet is a gendered space not only because it is designed with one gender specifically in mind but because its use is exclusively gendered. To enter the restroom is to associate oneself with a gendered position.

and Thirdspace articulate the *structure of our spatial experience.* Rose on the other hand articulates *our experiences of spatial structure*—the particular, the gendered, the embodied structures that characterize life and social engagement at the everyday level. Rose and Soja engage with the same analytical vehicles (hence the ease with which Soja makes the link between his work and hers) but they take them in different, indeed opposite, directions. Perhaps this accounts for the curious absence of any two-way interface between trialectics and feminism in Soja's own writings. Soja spends time subsuming feminists into his own Thirdspatial project but an outline of what Thirdspace may have to offer feminist debate remains curiously absent in his work. Soja fashions a functioning intersection between his project and Rose's, but all the intellectual traffic is moving one way. Arguably, as with his earlier work, Soja's politics of emancipation only functions by means of a kind of cultural and gendered hegemony, which his rhetoric then attempts to efface. His feminist engagement, that is, ends up subsuming feminist geography into an avowedly male, white, and Western thesis. My treatment of Rose here is designed to circumvent Soja's use of Rose by putting her discussion back to work on its own terms.

20. Jane Rendall, 'Introduction: Gender, Space', in Jane Rendall, Barbara Penner, and Iain Borden (eds.), *Gender Space Architecture: An Interdisciplinary Introduction* (London: Routledge, 2000), p. 101.

To enter the wrong door is either an embarrassing *faux pas* or an active statement of defiance, and either way the ideological division is maintained. Domestic kitchens are gendered because of the social connotations of home cooking as a female preserve, an extension of the nurturing, maternal typecast in which women support male life and the fruits of reproduction (best achieved, apparently, by baking, roasting and making jam). The gendered space of the kitchen, then, more likely represents a space made 'female' by men as an envelope of a very particular kind of female identity. Gendering the kitchen differentiates the domestic woman from the public (male) sphere and mediates social power in the male's favour. The restaurant kitchen on the other hand is a competitive, often aggressive, and, importantly, an *economic* arena and is gendered very differently from the hearth, despite their analogous uses. The restaurant kitchen is public, representing the sphere of production—as opposed to that of *re*production in the home—and so escapes the buxom shadow of Mrs Beaton to become dominated by men.

Discussions about space have therefore come to form a necessary part of feminist reflection. For how, feminists have asked, could systems of oppressive interrelations be renegotiated without acknowledging the field in and through which these oppressions occur? Luce Irigaray makes precisely this point in *Je, Tu, Nous: Toward a Culture of Difference*: '[T]he transition to a new age requires a change in our perception and conception of space-time, the inhabiting of places and of containers, or envelopes of identity'.[21] Irigaray sees these discrete envelopes of gendered identity working in very specific ways in the West. Phallocentric modes of thought, she argues elsewhere, have sought to scoop out the male sense of self in order to project it outwards upon society.[22] This projection leads to an external, public cultural environment that reflects and rewards male identity at the cost of the contribution of women and the maternal body—a body that society owes for its very existence.[23] Such a phallocentric march to occupy heaven and earth leaves cavities in its wake, spurned internal spaces that the penis passes by. Women come to dwell in these cavities, refashioned as supports for the hollowed-out male cultural cosmos that is projected onto society's surfaces. Women thus come to embody the internalities left behind by the scooping/projecting endeavor of a transcendent masculinism: home, kitchen, and emotionality featuring particularly prominently. The womb in turn becomes a passive symbol of female interiority, a corporal confirmation of female insideness. These numerous 'sepulchers', as Irigaray famously termed them,

21. Luce Irigaray, *Je, Tu, Nous: Toward a Culture of Difference* (New York, Routledge, 1993), p. 7. My own discussion of Irigarian space is indebted to the work of feminist architect Elizabeth Grosz. See her essay, 'Woman, *Chora*, Dwelling', in *Space, Time and Perversion, The Politics of the Body* (London: Routledge, 1996), pp. 111-24.

22. Luce Irigaray, *Elemental Passions* (New York: Routledge, 1992), pp. 14-17.

23. Irigaray, *Elemental Passions*, pp. 53-54.

are designed to contain, limit and thus delete the female and her body.[24] Kitchens, nurseries, and chauvinistic re-presentations of the female form all come to excise the female contribution, working as cultural parentheses to neutralize through delineation:

> Everywhere you shut me in. Always you assign a place to me. Even out-side the frame that I form with you... You set limits even to events that could happen with others... You mark out boundaries, draw lines, surround, enclose. Excising, cutting out. What is your fear? That you might lose your property.[25]

'Shutting in' comes to be reflected in social dividing lines which have tra-ditionally linked women with domesticity, stasis and the inner world of the heart and spirituality on the one hand, and men with action, mobility and sober public life on the other. Such dividing lines are a product of and are highly productive of closely regulated genderspaces. They sire physical thresholds in the social world and actualize ideological patterns to reinforce these cultural stereotypes over time.

Rose and Paradoxical Geography

This 'separatist' analysis, exposing the thresholds of separation and dom-ination that run between men and women, remains a significant mode of feminist critique. As Marylin Frye points out, separatism is an effort by women to control how definitions of 'woman' are negotiated.[26] But impor-tant counter-critiques have been offered too. The main problem with the separatist position is that it fails to address the violent male-female divide at the heart of phallocentrism. Separatism lays bare both male power and the often hidden means by which that power is exercised (and maintained and recharged), but it does so primarily to eject the male from his high-place, so retaining the claims of an exhaustive male/female binary. Separatism might seek to reorganize the power coursing through gendered relationships but it does not, indeed it cannot, trouble the constructedness of its own polarized gender categories. A successful separatist feminism may replace the rank-ing personnel in a male/female hierarchy, but the inherently abusive nature of the hierarchy would remain.[27]

---

24. Luce Irigaray, *Speculum of the Other Woman* (trans. Gillian C. Gill; Ithaca, NY: Cornell University Press, 1985), pp. 143-44.

25. Irigaray, *Elemental Passions*, pp. 24-25.

26. Marylin Frye, *Politics of Reality: Essays in Feminist Theory* (Trumansburg, NY: Crossing Press, 1983), p. 105.

27. For a fuller discussion of this reasoning, see the volume by I. Diamond and L. Quinby (eds.), *Feminism and Foucault: Reflections on Resistance* (Boston, MA: Northeastern University Press, 1988).

An important attempt to broach this problem comes from Gillian Rose in her 1993 work, *Feminism and Geography: The Limits of Geographical Knowledge.* Wishing to be 'neither victim nor perpetrator in the experiences of displacement, exile imprisonment and erasure', Rose recognizes that feminist discourse should comprize a full gamut of female experiences, experiences that go beyond merely those of the white, the middle-class, the heterosexual, the able-bodied.[28] If it is to include this kind of diverse complexity, feminism must, she says, embrace 'a fragmented and rich geographical imaginary': 'this geography can no longer simply be a mapping of social power relations onto territorial spaces: masculine and feminine onto public and private, for example'.[29] To do so is not only to leave the In/Out, Same/Other binaries untroubled, it is to imbibe a simplicity that an emancipatory project cannot afford to entertain. We need a 'geometrics of difference and contradiction'.[30]

Rose's answer (though of course it is really a question too) is the 'paradoxical geography'. Beginning with a recognition that Same/Other form parts of one field of perception, Rose goes on to describe the ways in which some feminists (Sintow, Hill Collins, Frye) have sought to resist phallocentrism and its army of binaries by enacting an oscillation, a continual switching of their analytical viewpoint between the two positions of centre and margin. However, as Rose goes on to point out:

> All these discursive spaces depend on a sense of an 'elsewhere' for their resistance. The subject of feminism has to feel that there is something beyond patriarchy in order to adopt these strategies of subversion. Thus the paradoxes described in the previous subsection [Sintow, Hill Collins, Frye etc.] themselves depend on a paradoxical space which straddles the spaces of representation and unrepresentability. This space of unrepresentability can acknowledge the possibility of radical difference, as de Lauretis argues.[31]

Paradoxical geography finds its ultimate expression as a kind of manipulation of the (single) field of Same/Other to produce an interpenetrative Elsewhere. In this Elsewhere the female subject is recognized as being neither 'in' the dominant clique nor 'out' of it, she is grounded neither at the centre nor at the margin of discursive spaces and comes to be acknowledged instead as an occupant of both realms simultaneously. To explore a paradoxical geography is to explore the ways in which women are prisoners and exiles of the phallocentric system at the same time. This

28. Rose, *Feminism and Geography*, pp. 149-50.
29. Rose, *Feminism and Geography*, pp. 150-51.
30. Donna Haraway, *Simians, Cyborgs, and Women: The Reinvention of Nature* (London: Free Association Press, 1991), p. 170. For discussion of Haraway's comments see Rose, *Feminism and Geography*, p. 151.
31. Rose, *Feminism and Geography*, pp. 153-54.

approach pushes this 'oscillation' between categories to its next level, that is, to the point of broaching a dynamic tension between poles. Rose's feminism strives to be a 'multidimensional geography structured by contradictory diversity'.[32]

The simplest examples Rose uses to illustrate her paradoxical geography are the experiences described by black women working in white homes (as discussed by Hill Collins) and the trope of the homosexual 'closet' (as discussed by Fuss and Frye).[33] Black women working as domestic servants in white homes have often articulated their position as an 'outsider-within stance'; they are on close terms with the children of the family and occupy space at the centre of a hegemonic universe, yet they are made to feel absent from that universe too. Black feminist politics ends up claiming the identity imposed upon it by white racism—as a basis for resistance—and refusing to be interpreted as the white man's Other. The sustained contradiction creates a paradoxical space in which identity is adopted and rejected in the same discursive movement. In a similar vein, for gay men and lesbian women to come 'out' is really for them to come 'in'—in the sense of becoming visible, knowable, and 'culturally intelligible'. But of course to come out is not necessarily to be embraced by social 'in'clusion. As Frye points out, by acting straight, gay men and lesbian women can end up 'inside', watching as outsiders, a paradoxical position that is at once oddly privileged and 'painfully disempower[ing]'.[34] Rose maintains that embracing these kinds of paradox as a means of subverting the field of Same/Other is the very substance of true feminist/liberationist discourse. In 'threatening polarities' she hopes to 'allow for the possibility of a different kind of space in which difference is tolerated rather than erased'.[35] But how do these gender/spatial paradigms affect the way one reads the Song's poetic world?

The Woman and the Window

> I live only here, between your eyes and you,
> But I live in your world. What do I do?
> —Collect no interest—otherwise what I can;
> Above all, I am not that staring man.[36]

32. Rose, *Feminism and Geography*, p. 155.

33. Patricia Hill Collins, *Black Feminist Thought: Knowledge, Consciousness, and the Politics of Empowerment* (London: Harper Collins, 1990), pp. 11-12; Diana Fuss, 'Inside/Out', in Diana Fuss (ed.), '*Inside/Out: Lesbian Theories, Gay Theories* (New York: Routledge, 1991), pp. 1-10; Rose, *Feminism and Geography*, pp. 151-55.

34. Rose, *Feminism and Geography*, pp. 149-51.

35. Rose, *Feminism and Geography*, p. 155.

36. Elizabeth Bishop, 'To Be Written on the Mirror in Whitewash', in *Complete Poems* (London: Chattow & Windus, 2004), p. 205.

As we have already seen, while phantasmagoric slippage is part of the text's wily charms certain genderspatial patterns have been noticed in the Song.[37] The female is usually internal and bounded, placed within the poem's numerous cavities: boudoir (1.4), locked garden (4.15), private vineyard (1.6), city (3.2, 5.7), latticed lookout (2.9). She is, moreover, frequently construed *as* a cavity for male inhabitation. Her chest is a vineyard of En-Gedi in 1.14. The female body has walls, doors and bulwarks in 8.9-10. The female protagonist is *in* the garden of 4.13 and yet she *is* the garden too (v. 12, 'a locked garden is my sister, my bride'). The patent innuendos of 5.2-5 superimpose her body onto her house. In 3.1-5 the lovers head through a city to a conspicuously maternal dwelling to a tryst in a maternal chamber centered upon the conceiving womb (v. 4). Even when the female makes the (allegedly) unorthodox move of frequenting the streets, the city is twice stressed as an *enclosure* policed by a circle of roving males (3.3; 5.7). If the female is to move, it is to be under male supervision (4.8; 6.12; 8.5).

The male suffers no such inconvenience. He is a wild, free and unbounded being with powers of unfettered movement. In Song of Songs 3 and 5, for instance, the woman is contained by the city and spends the first half of each chapter shut in her room wishing her footloose lover were tucked up beside her (3.1-2; 5.2-6). He, meanwhile, leaps across hills and spiced mountains (2.17; 8.14), frequently appearing or disappearing over the horizon: 'flee my beloved...over the mountains of spices' (2.17; 8.14). Similarly, the broad landscapes conjured by the so-called *wasf* passages in chaps. 4, 6 and 7 are voiced by an apparently well-travelled male, while the analogous passage of the woman's in 5.10-16 describes only a civic statue, as though she has never been beyond the city to see Carmel, the tower of David or the pools of Heshbon. In short, the male's perpetual motion means that he is never at rest, at 'home', in quite the same way that his beloved is.

What is the significance of the theoretical frameworks I have just sketched for the Song? Let us look at two sections of the Song of Songs, 2.8-14 and 5.2-6, which would seem to exemplify the overall patterning of the poem as I have just mapped it. The significance of these passages is that they are centered upon thresholds—a window in chap. 2 and a door in chap. 5—and therefore allow us to look at inside spaces, outside spaces *and* their interaction. How do these spatial interactions inscribe gender on the poem's lovers and do they contribute to the mediation of gendered power? I start with Song of Songs 2.

---

37. These have been noted by a handful of scholars, though comments are very much in the vein of *imagery* rather than their spatiality. The most extended discussion is probably Munro, *Spikenard and Saffron*, pp. 121, 127-37.

The sound of my lover!
Look! He comes![38]
Leaping over the mountains,
    springing[39] across the hills.
My lover is like a gazelle,[40]
    or a young stag.
Look! He's standing outside our wall,
    he's peering[41] through the windows,
    gazing through the lattices.

My lover answered and said to me:

'Arise my beloved, my fair one,[42]
    and come away.
For look! Winter has passed,
    the rain is over and gone.
The blossoms[43] appear on the earth,
    the time of pruning[44] has arrived,
    and the voice of the turtle dove is heard in our land.
The fig tree flavours[45] its first fruit
    and the budding vines give off fragrance.

38. As Exum point out here, the demonstrative works with the הנה to emphasize present action (*Song of Songs*, p. 121).

39. This verb קפץ appears in the *piel* here. In the *qal* the root means 'to draw together' On the strength of this, Exum translates the term 'bounding' (Exum, *Song of Songs*, p. 121). Given this sense of the movement as a series of contractions and extensions, 'springing' seems the most faithful to the original terminology.

40. Murphy notes a pun at work here in the term צבי, gazelle, which has a homonym meaning 'beauty'; see Murphy, *Song of Songs*, p. 139.

41. Perhaps poignantly, Murphy writes of this verse that the term for 'peering' is a *hiphil* form of a word that usually means 'blossom'. It is the parallelism and context that demand the sense of 'look', which the ancient versions reflect in their translations (Murphy, *Song of Songs*, p. 139).

42. The Septuagint adds 'my dove', both here and after 2.13. Fox muses the 'my dove' was probably 'a scribal elaboration in different Hebrew texts'; see Fox, *Song of Songs*, p. 113.

43. This term is a hapax. A cognate form is used in Gen. 40.10, Job 15.33 and Isa. 18.5. A similar form appears in Song 6.11 and 7.12 for pomegranates; in Eccl. 12.5 this amended form reappears for almond blossom; see Exum, *Song of Songs*, p. 121.

44. The Hebrew term here, זמר, has a homonym meaning 'singing'. Exum translates 'singing' accordingly (*Song of Songs*, pp. 120-21), as does Fox (*Song of Songs*, p. 113). I, along with Pope, as well as the ancient versions and authorities (Septuagint, Aquila, Symmachus, Vulgate, Targum) opt to retain the horticultural flavour of the verse and translate the term as 'pruning'. For the relevant discussion see Pope, *Song of Songs*, p. 395.

45. The verb here indicates ripening, and in other contexts (cf. Gen. 50.2) is used of embalming, of, in Exum's words, 'an 'infusion of aromatic mixtures' (*Song of Songs*, p. 122). The sense here is of ripening as a process of sweetening, of adding sensuous flavour to the fruit.

Arise my beloved, my fair one,
  and come away.
My dove in the clefts of the rock,
  in the hiding-place of the cliff,
  let me see your form.[46]
Let me hear your voice.
For your voice is sweet and your form is lovely' (2.8-14).

The scene consists of a springtime landscape and an inside room. This room has a latticed window through which the impressive vista is visible, its suggestive mountains and foothills marking the horizon. The male is outside, enjoying his mobility: 'leaping upon the mountains, bounding over the hills' (v. 8). The female is static and inside, watching the outside world but obscured from view by the lattice, which acts here as a mediating threshold between her world and his. The male—importantly, in the form of a gazelle—arrives, peers through the window, invites the female outside ('Arise my love…come away', v. 10) and then, speaking as to his 'dove', asks both to see and hear her: 'O my dove, in the crags of the rock…let me see your form, let me hear your voice' (v. 14).

These verses from chap. 2 are easy to map along familiar genderspatial lines. The female is enclosed, surrounded and contained in the passage. This configuration is underlined by the fact that even when she is disguised as a dove she remains passive and ensconced, this time within the rocky 'crag'. The male on the other hand is a free creature of the natural world. All the verbs (actually participles) in the passage are his and the request for the face and voice of the dove are grammatically reflexive: 'let *me* see…let *me* here'. The action is all his. This dynamic male is placed outside as an almost elemental force and by virtue of his considerable descriptive powers, in fact, he becomes the cervine harbinger of the springtime itself (vv. 10-13).[47]

The difference between male and female in the text is sustained through a system of binaries: visible/invisible, active/passive, public/private, mobile/static. In the case of each of these binaries the dividing line between terms coincides with the threshold between outside and inside affected by the latticed window. The female's space is a classic Irigarian sepulcher: a constructed edifice, it is physically restrictive and an imposition upon the landscape that serves to delete the woman from view. She is free to look out

46. This is often translated 'let me see your face' (Murphy, for example; *Song of Songs*, p. 138), but in Hebrew the sense is of form more generally. I have translated here along with Fox, that is, literally (Fox, *Song of Songs*, p. 113).

47. The Hebrew participle used to denote his 'peering' in v. 9 (מֵצִיץ) has a homonym that means, literally, 'blossoming' (e.g., Num. 17.8; Isa. 27.6; Ps. 72.16). It is perhaps too much to see the male's 'peeking' as itself an extension of the rampant springtime here, that is, as another kind of feral 'bloom' at the woman's windowsill. But, given the context, it is an interesting pun that sits behind the poetry.

but not to be seen or incorporated into the world (without male help). Conversely, the transcendental man is free to disappear over the mountains at a moment's notice (as indeed he does in v. 17). He appears in the text here as the would-be mediator of her release, a release incidentally that is offered on the grounds that he have a first-hand experience her body ('let me see your form, let me hear your voice'), another potential envelope of imposed space to be sure. 'Everywhere you shut me in. Always you assign a place to me. Even outside the frame that I form with you.'

Actually, the male's imposition of a bodily space upon the female is a key issue at other points in the passage. In recoding his beloved as a dove the male exhibits a measure of 'embodied perspective'; what he says carries the imprint of the space from which he says it and as readers we begin to see what *he* sees from his embodied and 'spaced' point of view. Throughout the whole scene, the raw shape of the textual space remains unaltered: the female stays obscured within an inaccessible enclosure. But in v. 14 the male takes the female's own description of this configuration from v. 9, 'there he stands behind our wall, gazing at the windows, peering through the lattice', and recodes it according to his own vernal spatiality.

> My dove in the clefts of the rock,
>   in the hiding-place of the cliff,
>   let me see your form.
> Let me hear your voice.
> For your voice is sweet and your form is lovely.

When the male speaks in v. 14 the woman is still as bounded, enclosed, and visually concealed as she was several verses earlier. But through the gazelle's eyes she is not bounded by a wall—as *she* has said—but by a cliff face. He is not looking through a window any longer but a cleft in the rock. The woman's face remains obscured (as the request itself implies), but now it is a craggy outcrop rather than a lattice that conceals it. In Hebrew even the conspicuous plurals remain, the lattices of the windows mirrored in the clefts of the cliff. The two characters are viewing the same image, the same underlying spatial configuration, but are doing so from different genderspatial perspectives. She sees through a pair of domestic spectacles, he sees through a pair of gazelle's eyes. On one level this suggests the degree to which the poem's constructions of space are concomitant with its notions of gendered identity. Space, identity and outlook are mutually re-enforcing elements in these verses. On another level, this move—subtle as it is— quietly slips the reader into the man's shoes.

But making the male perspective commensurate with public, open, natural and active space has other implications for the scene. The crucial issue is that the male's projection of his own spatiality onto the woman and her room is reminiscent of the scoop-project-conquer process that Irigaray describes as being at the heart of the phallocentric drive. In the text the world is remade from the gazelle's point of view, who uses his own sense of space as a template. This organic, elemental, male identity is projected outwards to recreate the woman and her situ, fashioning both the woman and the world in a way that reflects the male's own identity in the text. The female's body and the female's space are little more than hollow scaffolds for this projection, which takes over (masculinizes) the reader's gaze. Moreover, once naturalized into the springtime cordillera, the constructed-ness of the female's enclosure becomes invisible to both the reader and the male lover. The male protagonist recognizes the enclosure, certainly, but not its nature as an imposition upon the world; his view cannot acknowledge the woman's sepulcher as a constructed framework, as a structure *designed* to limit. Her obscurity is regrettable, lamentable even, but no longer intentional.

The Man in the Mirror

The scene in 2.8-14 appears to be a comparatively sturdy part of the Song's imaginarium; its gendered positions, its spatial scenario and the trellised division that marks out basic categories may be destined to dissolve silently into an urban vignette (3.1), but for the moment these images appear clear and intelligible and stable. Or do they? As Cheryl Exum has pointed out in her commentary, something extraordinary happens in 2.10: the woman becomes a storyteller, 'My lover answered and said to me', she says. Foregrounding this narrative activity produces a very different spatial reading. Exum writes:

> For the first time, the Song acknowledges the presence of a narrator. This narrator is also a character, as distinguished from the poet as narrator, whose narrative presence throughout the Song is deftly effaced. The poet puts words into the woman's mouth, creating her speech (2.8–3.5) in which she puts words into her lover's mouth, creating his speech (2.10-14)... The beginning of the woman's speech (v. 8) is vividly situated in the present (the lover is approaching). The narrated story that follows (what the man *said*) is transformed, through the illusion of immediacy, into the present, as we overhear him *saying*, 'Rise up, my love, and come away...'. The blurring of boundaries between past and present is also a blurring of the distinction between the woman as narrator and the woman as a character in her own narrative. We cannot tell the storyteller from the story.[48]

Exum's point is twofold. Firstly, she highlights the fact that the male and his words (2.10-14) originate from the mouth of the female, who is telling the story. In short, the male in this passage is a literary creation of the female character herself (and, as Exum stresses, the female in the Song is in turn the creation of an original real-life poet, whose decision to speak

48. Exum, *Song of Songs*, pp. 123-25.

only through the mouths of the lovers slyly obscures his or her own pres-ence in the text).[49] The second issue is regarding temporal progression. The poet blurs the connection between past and present in the woman's story, causing an ongoing disruption of temporal continuity, contributing to what Exum calls the 'illusion of immediacy', which draws readers into the emo-tive content of the poetry.[50] The poetic fluidity of the passage blurs other ref-erents too, referents that are best understood spatially.

In the text there is a smudged distinction between the woman as a literary creator *beyond* the space of her narrative and her status as an *inhabitant* of the narrative itself: 'we cannot tell the storyteller from the story', as Exum puts it. In narrating, the female protagonist necessarily evokes a world. But is she in this world or beyond it? On the one hand, in v. 10, her story world is a distant space ('My lover answered and said'), though, on the other, the whole episode was originally set up in v. 8 as a current experience: 'Look! He's standing outside our wall'. In one sense the male's words themselves imply that the woman is *in* a narrative space *with* him ('Come with me'), but, in another, the whole speech has already been set out as something akin to a relayed account, as a story ('he said to me'). These vocal and temporal paradoxes mean that it is impossible to choose between possibili-ties; whichever position one tries to ground, one simply ends up suppress-ing other elements in the passage. The paradox that these blurred lines and literary smudges generate is a familiar one. The woman is both inside her text and outside it, both transcendent over her story and wrapped up into it, both its lattice-rattling prisoner and a mountain-bound exile. The Song's ready adoption of this dual position, its amenability to a kind of own-brand paradoxical geography, opens up the text to a secondary, perhaps a more resistant reading of gender/space collusions. In this reading we can see the paradox I have highlighted here—which arises from the *fact* of the woman's narration—replicated in, and working with, the nitty-gritty details of *what* she actually narrates. She is above and within a story *in which* she is both the female-imprisoned and the male-exiled (the male is, after all, sent away at the end of the story in v. 17).

Shifting tack and foregrounding the woman's storyteller role in a reading brings these paradoxes into focus.

---

49. It is important to remember that the double voice in this chapter—the female who speaks as the male—is herself the product of a poet. In actual fact, then, the polyphony in Song of Songs 2 is triple layered: the poet's voice is given to a female character who then gives her voice to a male character. Since my discussion is focused on the mechan-ics of the text itself, and on the processes of readerly engagement with the text, I have chosen to circumvent questions of authorial voice in this discussion. Such questions, after all, could merit a book-length discussion in their own right.

50. For a full discussion of this see Exum, *Song of Songs*, pp. 3-6.

> My lover is like a gazelle,
>   or a young stag.
> Look! He's standing outside our wall,
>   he's peering through the windows,
>   gazing through the lattices (2.9).

In v. 9 the woman is looking through a window at her cervine lover, but what the narrator-female looks through the lattice *at* can be nothing more than a landscape of her own imaginative creation. Read the poem-within-the-poem and the space beyond the lattice ceases to be an exterior world at all. Rather, it is a blank canvas awaiting the female's imaginative projections. The gazelle is her creation. His words are devised by her. The spring, too, is the woman's territory. In which case this lattice is more mirror than window since it contains only extensions of the female, reflections, that is, of her own consciousness. The masculine elements of the text—the male, his words, the panorama they create—can therefore be read as images that actually better reflect the female's own sense of self, as indeed can the male's demands to see the woman's beautiful body, which we must now recognize as narcissistically self-created. They are all part of a story, which, ultimately, she tells about herself. In turn, the invitation to tumble out into the flowery wilds becomes both a longed-for escape and an exercise in subtle introspection. Moving 'out' through the window simply moves the female-narrator deeper into the reflective, further through the looking glass into the psychologically self-imposed. Going 'out there' is really delving deeper 'in here'. The spring is her mind *realized.*

As a result, trying to locate a definitive Inside and Outside in the text-world quickly becomes a nonsense. If the outside is an extension of the female's *inner* psyche, the male's public space is now her private mental landscape, his mobility is now her stasis, and her passivity is now an imaginative action. The clear-cut divides between inside and outside and between male and female all become messy and confused. The dichotomies on which the chapter *seems* to be built rely on the clarity of the lattice-threshold, manipulate it and these hard and fast divisions become strangely interpenetrative. The spatial collapse peaks with a collapse of gender divisions. He *is* her because here *is* there. Here *is* there because he *is* her. And because of these blurs and smudges the lines between male and female, of latticed prisoner and hill-bound exile, need not be so definite after all. The lovers are more inter-readings than binary opposites, more of a mutually constituting reflection than a polarized pair. The 'positions' of male and female in the text are, in fact, more akin to spatial performances, performances that play with the ideas of Self and Other through a manipulation of the field inside/outside (inside/outside the lattice on one level, and inside/outside her storytelling on another).

An important consequence of this interdependence is that the power play of the male's embodied perspective—his recasting of his lover as a dove—is turned on its head. On reflection it is the *woman* as the storyteller who is ultimately responsible for the imposition of new imagery upon the female form and for the male's enculturation of her space more generally. These are changes wrought by the woman. And yet the gazelle's perspective still speaks in terms of his male-ness; v. 14 still recodes the constructed dwelling in terms of the gazelle's *own* textual identity rather than the woman's. So do we ultimately read these words as male voiced or female voiced? Indeed, we might read v. 14 as a female internalization of the male gaze. We might read it, in other words, as a kind of genderspatial double bluff in which the woman re-imagines herself through male eyes. That is what her story *does*.

This male gaze that the female adopts, however, does not perform the functions one might initially expect. Instead of performing the Foucauldian panoptical function (policing and limiting her from the inside) that Polanski affirms, she seems to be putting this synthetic male perspective to good use, using male enculturation as a means of getting what she is after: an escape from her neatly latticed prison. Seeing oneself from another's perspective has a power of its own, after all, and here the woman uses *his* view to achieve a liberating transformation. The 'male' gaze in v. 14 shifts the tenor of the poetic imagery toward the wide, the outward, and the open. Essentially, viewing herself through male eyes causes the out-of-reach countryside forcibly to invade, transforming her boudoir into an untamed crevasse and her into a creature of the air. With the dove as her avatar, the woman is both liberated from the inner room to occupy this springtime world poetically with her lover, and, moreover, she has the wings to make latticed boxes a thing of the past. The lovers come to share the spring poetically, transcending the inside room by playing with the magic of gazing between spaces.

While the woman is both prisoner and exile in her stories, she is also represented as being both within and without the story itself: she is both its narrator and a character within it. This is possible because the divides are not merely thresholds between springtime and bedroom, or between bedroom and street. They also act as a connecting point between the world that precedes the woman's stories and the world created by the woman's stories. She clambers out, so to speak, of her story to have a narratorial overview of it, and, a little later, tumbles back inside the story. The thresholds thus multiply meaning and voice and destabilize genderedness in the text through a continual renegotiation of the textual space. The positions of inside and outside the room become confused with inside and outside the story. Furthermore, the positions of male and female become confused with the positions of narrator and character: the female's role as a creator of the story merging with her role as the character within it.

This is all possible because at the eye of this perfect storm of spatial and sexual processes the window-threshold remains as a kind of paradoxical fixed point. The window is the spatial coordinate that allows for the crystallization of Man versus Woman (window space) and it is the point at which the power to differentiate between male and female is overthrown (looking-glass space). The threshold's dialectics fuse the gendering and spatializing processes in the poem, but they do not make these processes identical. The relationship between gendered and en-spaced categories may be formed (consummated?) at the window, but these gender and spatial categories do not fully merge or form a single unity. The threshold, according to its own basic paradoxical structure, both asserts categories and pulls them into fluid relationships.

In part these observations indicate the degree to which one can read space and gender as collusions in the Song, as interpenetrative parts of a continuum that both invites and resists delineations. But the duality of my spatial readings—the text is Irigarian and Rosian all at once—also suggests that these gendered and spatial constructions are not finished. Their paradoxes mean that readers must inevitably decide to construct the Song's literary spaces in certain ways rather than others. The textual world, even in its most economical state, is not a fixed quantity. It is undecidable. The thresholds are the scars left by the possibility of these Other spaces and the point at which new reading trajectories can be plotted in the text. The social construction of space is not restricted to the making of 'real' worlds on one side of the text and the making of spaces by character interactions on the other. Spatial production continues between person and page, the surface of which acts like the window in the poem, or the scrim in the phantasmagoria, inviting projections and (con)fusing the image and the imaginer.

Crucially, then, the social, sexual, and political geometries we use to construct our imaginary landscapes can, like the biblical lovers' own imaginarium, have a dramatic effect on a reading. That is to say, what my Rosian and Irigarian readings show up is that readers inevitably find themselves making spatial decisions as part of reading the text. Just as the spatial and ideological suppositions of the lovers in the Song shape their worlds, imposing or manipulating spatial frameworks onto each other, our own geometries dictate the type of textual worlds we find ourselves participating in as readers. If the lovers can project gendered ideologies onto each other's bodies through poetic interplay, readers too can project spatial values onto the corpus of the Song by virtue of the way we participate with the text, reading one world, then reading another.

The Song is transgressive, not because it is an erotic text or a protofeminist one, but because it holds together two contraries, on the one hand the expected gender dichotomy and, on the other, dissolution. Indeed, that is perhaps a more honest appraisal of our own gendered identities anyway; space and gender are textual systems that point us in several directions at once. In other words, space and gender are open, interpretative networks of potential relationships between. Space and gender must be translated in a critical reading, and, as a result, can be retranslated, mistranslated, over translated, and so on. Gendered meaning and spatial meaning are mutual reinforcing systems in the text, but, like textual signification itself, are ultimately unstable.

Doorstep Sex

So far, I have been using the division between spaces to look at gendered identities and at their simultaneous delineation and collapse in the text. What is perhaps more interesting, or at least more fundamental to the make-up of the Song as a text, is the other categorical divisions that seem marked out by these thresholds: the lines between authors and characters (which I have touched upon with regard to the narrating female in Song of Songs 2), and, most importantly, between readers and the text itself. As I want to argue in this section, the lovers must deal with each other at the threshold in precisely the same way that we must deal with the poem as readers, by means of engaging with an obscuring partition that invites and resists decipherment—a kind of internalized poetic 'scrim'.

Indeed, the thresholds (con)fuse the most fundamental categories of the poem—that of the text and the not-text. It is this that gives rise to all the dualities we have looked at so far, with the paradoxical geography of gender being simply the most visible. I turn now to the second threshold of the Song, the doorway of Song of Songs 5, in order, first, to demonstrate the repetition of the gendered and spatial paradoxes I have been looking at in Songs 2.8-14, and, second, to think about how the thresholds within the text both delineate and confuse the thresholds between the spatialities of reading and loving.

In Song of Songs 5.2-6, the narrative again begins with the woman as both character and narrator. Her story also begins with her being called a 'dove' by her beloved.[51] Here, however, the male protagonist seems to be seeking entry to the female's room rather than looking to encourage her outside.[52]

> I slept and my heart was roused.
> Listen! My lover is knocking!
>
> 'Open to me, my sister, my friend,
>   my dove, my perfect one;
> for my head is wet with dew,
>   my locks with night sprinkles.'

51. The difference here being that we never get to see anything else through his eyes, so the passage remains female/urban in theme.
52. For notes on the translation see Chapter 3 above.

I had taken off my robe,
    am I to put it on again?
I have washed my feet,
    am I to soil them?

My lover thrust his hand into the hole,
    at which my insides thrilled.
I rose to open to my lover,
    and my hands dripped with myrrh,
my fingers with liquid myrrh,
    on the handles of the bolt.
I opened to my beloved,
    But my lover had turned and gone.
My soul failed me because of him.

In the first part of the text, vv. 2-4, the poem sets out a series of familiar oppositional differences between the lovers, with the domestic threshold functioning as a line of differentiation between categories. Most obvious, of course, is division between inside and outside, visible and invisible, and between public and private space.

The relative positions of inside and outside give rise to a number of the lovers' characteristics in this passage. These, in turn, seem to come to relate to a male/female binary. So, inside connects to cleanliness (the ability to bathe and stay clean/dry), and to enclosure, and to invisibility or inaccessibility, and to stasis/passivity (being inside, you stay in the same place). Outside gives rise to dynamism (the ability to move around, or away), an elemental quality (covered with dew), wetness ('night sprinkles'), a desire to enter inside, etc. What develops in the text is a contrast between the inside/urban/clean-footed female and an outside/elemental/wet-headed male. The threshold marks the couple as opposites. As we saw in Song of Songs 2, the in/out apparent/concealed oppositions come to be mapped onto male/female.

Space seems to contribute to the gendering of the couple in particularly poignant ways here, though, because of the highly suggestive nature of these oppositional images, which appear to play with common ideas of the sexually aroused male and female bodies. The dynamic transcendental male character (he will run off and disappear without trace in the next verse) is made synonymous with the male sex organ. As Garrett has noted, it is possible to read the male's dew-soaked head and his 'night sprinkles' as innuendos for male sexual fluids, particularly if, following Pardes, Bergant and Boer, we take the accompanying myrrh (5.5) as suggestive of the same.[53] The male is a wet sylvan head banging up against an opening. The female

---

53. Garrett, *Song of Songs*, p. 207; Pardes, *Countertraditions in the Bible*, p. 132; Bergant, *Song of Songs*, p. 65; Boer, *Knocking on Heaven's Door*, p. 66.

character by turns is the owner of that opening, and the passive subject of the male's noisy attempts to gain entry.[54] If the male's 'head' has been understood to represent the penis, the female's 'feet' have been understood (principally by Pope) as its opposite number, the female's genitals.[55] Two sets of images seem to be at work here: one contextual, the other carnal. This overlap between the contextual and the carnal results in a series of familiar gendered and spatial stereotypes: the dynamic, mobile, public external male, and the internal, passive, domestic female, whose home represents the space into which the penis wishes to pass. The scene is a kind of spatialization of gendered politics and a passage in which the act of penetrative sex is concretized as a doorstep scene.

While in vv. 2-4 the division between inside and outside is the key spatial reference in the text, the idea of the threshold itself becomes the focus in the succeeding verses. The categories of inside/outside become secondary to the dividing line that creates them as the threshold takes centre stage.

> My lover thrust his hand into the hole,
>   at which my insides thrilled.
> I rose to open to my lover,
>   and my hands dripped with myrrh,
> my fingers with flowing myrrh,
>   on the handles of the bolt.
> I opened to my beloved.

Here the lovers 'hand'—a well attested ancient euphemism for penis— enters the woman's 'hole' or 'opening'. Her body thrills. The sexual tension has apparently moved from the wider head/feet, inside/outside oppositions and become focused on the surfaces of the doorway itself. His hand crosses the threshold, exciting the woman's 'insides', and her hand reaches out to touch the 'bolt', which is now wet with 'flowing myrrh'. While the male incursion into the woman's hole here seems to be a fairly unambiguous suggestion of coitus, the female's playing with the bolt is, like the door, two sided in its significance. Is the woman's toying with the bolt a suggestion of masturbation (playing with her clitoris, perhaps), with the flowing myrrh representing the female's sexual fluids? Or is the phallic 'bolt' a metaphorical stand-in for the inserted penis, the wetness of which is carried over from the proceeding line? I am not sure we necessarily have to choose between these possibilities. After all, since this account is a story told/imagined by the female character, all its sexual activity is, in a sense, masturbatory. All the sex in her story is auto-arousal, however mutually it is figured in the narrative.

---

54. She will surprise us, and countless commentators, in a moment by engaging in a search, but that is, very pointedly, after the sexual part of the scene has concluded.

55. Pope, *Song of Songs*, p. 515.

In either case, then, the threshold—the point at which outside and inside rub up against each other and 'where' space is negated—becomes synonymous with a sexual mingling in which male and female rub up against each other, and, indeed, become lost and merged in each other. As my comments on the 'bolt' of v. 4 indicate, it becomes difficult, even, to distinguish male and female sexual organs amid all the fluidity. The space between inside and outside becomes a space between male and female in which there is differentiation and comingling all at once. If sexual categories are made distinct through spatial differentiation in the first part of the passage, the indistinctness of spatiality found 'within' the threshold—as a space between spaces—comes to stand in for the indistinctness of gendered expression in the sexual act.

In a recent article, Yael Almog argues that the use of 'fluids' in the Song—flowing myrrh, nectar, wine, milk, etc.—undermines the idea of bodily boundaries in the text.[56] The lovers' physical fluidity facilitates a kind of social fluidity between gender roles, she argues, figuring the lovers as radical transgressors of 'normal' gender mores. But Almog's conclusion focuses on the mingling and fluidity of the lovers at the expense of those moments where gendered and bodily distinctions are clearly drawn by the text, as in the first part of this passage from Song of Songs 5. That is, I would respond to Almog's claims that bodily fluidity gives rise to a fluidity of gendered roles in the poem by pointing out that the very notion of fluidity and dissolution relies upon, indeed assumes as its precondition, a series of distinctions that are undone, or eroded, by the fluids. Fluidity is relative. Fluidity in a world without distinctions is not transgressive. The lovers' fluidity—physical, social and gendered—is potent because the text enjoys moments of fixity (of 'hardness'?) that the dissolution works against, a little like the phasing of the phantasmagoria we looked at in Chapter 2, where continuity and dissolution must co-exist in a complex alliance. This is also what I have been arguing is in play in Song of Songs 2.8-14; the text's fluidity emerges from its undermining of its own binaries, not because such binaries are entirely absent from the text. Almog seems reluctant to acknowledge those moments of gendered distinction in the text, or, in fact, that fluidity and 'hardness' are, like male and female, a mutually constituting pair. Song of Songs 5.2-6 seems to figure the lovers as inhabitants of distinct realms and then uses the complex spatiality of the threshold to undermine their differences. As with all penetrative acts, fluidity and hardness must work together here. The text's erotic tenor emerges from that interplay, on the one hand a fluidity and hardness of the lovers' bodies, and, on the other, a fluidity and hardness in gendered and spatial categories; now standing fast, now giving way.

---

56. Yael Almog, 'Flowing Myrrh upon the Handles of the Bolt: Bodily Border, Social Norms and their Transgression in the Song of Songs', *BibInt* 18 (2010), pp. 251-63.

Of course, as with Song of Songs 2.8-14, the spatial structure of the text-world in chap. 5 is considerably more complex than I have outlined above. This complexity arises once again because of the woman's role as both a narrator of a story and a character within that story: 'I was sleeping... Listen! I hear my lover knocking'. Again, the spaces in this part of the poem are created by the female character. Again, the notions of inside and outside become double-jointed and self-referential since they are both played out in the woman's mind. Moreover, since everything originates from, and ultimately points to, this female storyteller, ideas about Otherness, an elsewhere, and gender become readerly contrivances designed to allow certain readings of the poem to function; we separate out the woman from her story as we choose, and thus come to separate out male from female, and inside from outside, on largely our own terms.

There are profound similarities between the Song's two threshold stories. On a first reading, both the window and the door delineate gendered spaces with the mobile male associated with exterior, public, elemental spaces and the static female associated with interior, enclosed private, architectural spaces. In chap. 5 the pair are characterized by yet more oppositions: head/feet, bathed/dew-soaked. In each story Irigarian stereotypes would seem to hold firm. Of course, as we have seen in Song 2.8-14, these divisions are not necessarily that simple. The woman's role as storyteller makes the notions of spatial divisions and of gendered difference hard to ground definitively in the text. The thresholds between inside and outside, and between narrator and character, come to be superimposed on each other. The woman's vacillation between modes of narrator and character make these divisions break down somewhat. Similarly, in Song of Songs 5, the woman is a storyteller again, again the male is her creation, again the text is a fantasy turned in on itself and again the 'lines' between male and female and inside and outside turn out to be blurry.

Since I have given a thorough account of the ways in which narrative spaces collapse on these terms in Song of Songs 2.8-14, duplicating that account in any more detail for Song of Songs 5 would be unnecessary (not to mention tiresome for the reader). Instead I intend to look here at the way in which the threshold of Song of Songs 5 works as a space of projection. I touched on this with regard to Song of Songs 2 as well—specifically with regard to both the male's projection of his own values onto the woman's space, and the male's world as a space of the female's imaginative projection. Here we can tie these threshold encounters to the phantasmagoric structure of the Song and to my ongoing discussion on the spatiality of reading process.

Doors as Scrims

Somewhat oddly, the sexual episode at the door of Song 5.2-6—arguably the most sexually explicit encounter of the whole poem—unfolds only because the woman locks the man outside. It is closure and exclusion that creates the sexual possibilities of the text rather than intimacy, presumably because maintaining the threshold as a forbidden space gives the poet more scope to explore the tropes of mingling, sexual incursion, and the teasing open of rheumy boundaries. Unfettered access is not very sexy, apparently. On the other hand, and as Bachelard points out, there is 'an entire cosmos of half open' that can be poetically explored.[57]

The upshot of this is that the door of Song 5.2-6 functions as surface onto which the lovers are able to project their (frustrated) sexual desire. The projection of the male's desire onto the surfaces of the door is perhaps the most obvious, thrusting his hand into the hole in such a way as to, literally, 'stir' the woman's 'insides' (v. 4). The woman responds to the male's suggestive fumbling by toying with the phallic 'bolt', as I have already discussed. Each side of the door comes to stand in for the body of one or other of the lovers. In communing with the threshold they commune with each other. The door thereby ends up standing in for the body of the other lover, hence its almost-hermaphroditic status, having both a sexualized 'opening' and a sexualized (and well lubricated) 'bolt'.

Strictly speaking, of course, neither lover sees the other in this section of the text because of this door. The paramours project their desire onto the door while the door itself hides each of them from the other's view. From the characters' perspectives, their lover is a disembodied voice that speaks from behind a partition. Of course, the most interesting aspect of this is that the obscuring of the lovers seems to intensify their sexual anticipation. Their mutual invisibility, their nature as disembodied voices, and the blankness of the door that allows for an imaginative projection, intensifies the sexuality of the episode.

Earlier, in Chapter 2, I discussed the way the Song works by means of a spatiality of projection. I want to explore the possibility here that the threshold space in Song 5.2-6 functions in exactly the same way. The door functions as a scrim that hides one lover and encourages emotional projections on the part of the other by means of a politics of concealment. In other words, the door in Song of Songs 5 works as an internalized scrim, causing the lovers to interact with each other in the same way that the readers must engage with the text. When we read Song 5.2-6, we are not simply reading about lovers, we are reading our own processes of reading. Our phantasmagoric interactions with the page mirror the characters' interactions with the door.

Each lover's beloved is invisible, a disembodied voice that emanates from the concealed space behind the opaque partition. As with the Song itself, the blankness of the scrim/door invites a double projection. A lover's words act on the scrim-cum-door from one side and the other lover's

---

57. Bachelard, *Poetics of Space*, p. 222.

desire is projected on to the other. The whole erotic episode becomes a kind of self-constituting milieu based on these mutual projections. The threshold of Song of Songs 5 is the Song's spatial phantasmagoria in microcosm. Indeed, this microcosm can be seen at work in Song of Songs 2 as well, where, again, the male listens for the voice of his beloved even though she is obscured from him. Both episodes create gendered distinctions using spatial distinctions, and neither episode can maintain these divisions; the lines between categories, spaces and bodies simply cannot be trusted. What are the implications of this paradox for the relationship that exists between the lovers and their readers?

Derrida's Hymen

An important tool in gauging the significance of the text's categorical 'undecidability' is Derrida's essay, 'The Double Session' from *Dissemination*.[58] 'The Double Session' is a treatise on mimicry and on the idea that literature is an activity of the 'in-between'. For Derrida it is always the gap between, the *différance* between categories that produces the effect of meaning, and literature as an entire *oeuvre* fits into that formulation of meaning and liminality. Fittingly, Derrida's essay itself takes place 'between' two texts: the texts of Mallarmé and Plato. Derrida's is an attempt to disrupt the commonly assumed opposition between literary and philosophical discourse, and his essay comes around to explore the nature of the copy and the quotation, and thus of all writing, as an act which endlessly multiplies and undermines connections betwixt. Writing, Derrida argues, consists of both a conjoining and a holding apart: it takes place between texts and titles, between readers and writers, between copies and quotations; writing functions only as a result of the gaps between the words on the page.[59]

In *Dissemination*, the term 'hymen' comes to operate as shorthand in for the point 'between' categories, where there is a simultaneous conjoining

58. Jacques Derrida, 'The Double Session', in *Dissemination* (trans. Barbara Johnson; London: Athlone Press, 1981), pp. 187-237.

59. In order to understand the context for this idea, we need to go back to that infamous saying of Derrida's that we encountered in Chapter 1: *il n'y a pas de hors-texte*, 'there is no outside-text', or, perhaps better, 'text knows no bounds'. As I said earlier, this axiom is not an affirmation that only text matters. Instead, Derrida's adage is intended to articulate the fact that writing has no outside. Any demarcation 'between' literature and non-literature would itself constitute a kind of textuality. The threshold between text and non-text would itself be a kind of literary mark, like the upstroke of a glyph, or the line on the page. As Derrida himself puts it: '[T]here is no experience of *pure* presence, but only chains of differential marks'. Every threshold is an opening as well as an ending, marking as Other, assimilating as Same; Jacques Derrida, 'Signature Event Context', in *Limited Inc* (Evanston IL: Northwestern University Press, 1977), pp. 1-25 (10).

and delineation that gives rise to meaning. 'Hymen' is a handy term for this kind of complex paradox because the word is itself dual. On one hand, it means 'wedding' (the Greek god of marriage was named Hymen)[60] and, on the other hand, it refers to the vaginal membrane that is breached during heterosexual intercourse.[61] The hymen is thus a name for that which joins together and that which holds apart. Derrida takes the term from Mallarmé's work, where the term 'hymen' functions in just this way—as a symbol for the simultaneously separated-and-conjoined: 'In a hymen…tainted with vice yet sacred, between desire and fulfillment, perpetration and remembrance: here anticipating, there recalling, in the future in the past, under the false appearance of a present. Thus operates the Mime, whose acting is limited to perpetual allusiveness without breaking the glass: it installs, thus, a medium, purely, of fiction.'[62]

In Derrida's expansion of this idea we find a crucial launching point for his treatise on the Hymen:

> 'Hymen' (a word, indeed the only word, that reminds us that what is in question is a 'supreme spasm') is first of all a sign of fusion, the consummation of a marriage, the identification of two beings, the confusion between the two. *Between* the two…there is no longer difference but identity. Within this fusion there is no longer any distance between desire (the awaiting of a full presence designed to fulfill it, to carry it out) and the fulfillment of presence, between distance and non-distance; there is no longer any distance between desire and satisfaction. It is not only the difference (between desire and fulfillment) that is abolished, but also the difference between difference and nondifference. Nonpresence, the gaping void of desire, and presence, of fullness of enjoyment, amount to the same. By the same token, there is no longer any difference between the image and the thing, the empty signifier and the full signified, the imitator and the imitated, etc. But it does not follow, by virtue of this hymen of confusion, that there is now only one term, a single one of the differends. It does not follow that what remains is thus the fullness of the signified, the imitated or the thing itself, simply present in person. It is the difference between the two terms that is no longer functional…this hymen eliminates the spatial heterogeneity of the two poles in the 'supreme spasm', the moment of dying laughter. By the same token, it eliminates the exteriority or the anteriority, the independence of the imitated, the signified, or the thing. Fulfillment is summed up within desire; desire is (ahead of) fulfillment, which, still mimed, remains desire *'without breaking the mirror'*.[63]

60. Hymen usually appears in depictions with a torch and a veil—the first a symbol of penetration, the second of resistance.

61. Leslie Hill, *Cambridge Introduction to Jacques Derrida* (Cambridge: Cambridge University Press, 2007), p. 47.

62. Derrida, 'The Double Session', p. 219; see also Mallarmé and Jacques Scherer (ed.), *Le 'Livre' de Mallarmé* (Paris: Gallimard, 1957).

63. Jacques Derrida, *Dissemination* (trans. Barbara Johnson; London: Athlone Press, 1981), pp. 209-10, emphasis original.

For Derrida, the term 'hymen' thus refers to a strange suspension of meaning. The term articulates a conjoining 'between two', but not so that there is only a brand new One left in their place. There is fusion between two, but they remain two. The two have not stopped functioning as two; only the idea of a *différance* between them has been negated. The separations between anticipation and fulfillment have, in other words, become null—a little like Mallarmé's mention of the mime, where the action of engagement with an absentee object negates the absence of that object without inaugurating its presence. (The mime artist pressing against the fictional glass does not create a window but rather causes the difference between the window's absence and its presence to disappear. The window becomes an unbreakable hymen, conjoining and delineating absence and presence all at once.) This paradox, argues Derrida, is the achievement of every textual system. 'The virginity of the "yet unwritten page" opens up space for that paradox.'[64]

> [This hymen] is nothing other than the space of writing: in this 'event'—
> hymen, crime, suicide, spasm (of laughter or pleasure)—in which nothing
> happens, in which the simulacrum is a transgression and the transgression a
> simulacrum, everything describes the very structure of the text and effectu-
> ates its possibility.[65]

Specifically, in a text this duality of meaning/non-meaning manifests itself as various systems of potential sense rubbing up against one another without ever being finalized. Leslie Hill helpfully sums up Derrida's position on the hymen:

> But the word [hymen] not only alluded to itself, it also referred to a strange
> suspension (neither real nor unreal, true or untrue)…various separate but
> cohabiting layers of sense jostle equally for attention [in a text]. Meaning
> is not finalized, but suspended. It hovers, so to speak, between terms. What
> counts here, though, for Derrida, is not in itself the serendipitous con-
> vergence of two contrary meanings within the same word [hymen], but
> the syntax that, in this specific text [Mallarmé's 'Mimique'], affirms and
> exploits the strange marriage between the two senses of the word *hymen*,
> which comes to signify itself and its opposite, twice over.[66]

The mechanics by which meaning is continually suspended within a text in this way is termed the 'undecidable': the nature of texts to have so many interpretative options that readers cannot, in the end, *interpret*, but must rather *choose*. Hill goes on:

> If *hymen* can mean both conjunction and separation, in the same way that
> the word *between* serves to join together two nouns, adjectives, prepositions,
> adverbs, or verbs, while also keeping them apart, how might it be possible to

64. Derrida, 'The Double Session', p. 222.
65. Derrida, 'The Double Session', p. 218.
66. Hill, *Introduction to Jacques Derrida*, p. 47.

select one of the positions rather than the other? Is one not forced to refuse
the alternative, and opt for a third possibility: not the one nor the other, but
both—and neither.[67]

Taking all of this together and turning, finally, to Hill's summary of Derrida's reading of *Mimique*, we see that the undecidable quality of text is inscribed into Mallarmé's principle character, Pierrot, in such a way as to suggest some resonances between Derrida's sense of the hymen and the sense of the threshold that I have been sketching out here. Pierrot is 'comic but also sad, silent but also eloquent, the perpetrator but also the victim, male but also female, himself but also another, alive but also dead: a spectre, dressed in white, like the unwritten page'.[68]

Threshold/Scrim

The door of Song of Songs 5 and the window of Song of Songs 2 have two functions in the text, splitting the lovers up and regulating the social-sexual differences between them and allowing for a mutual connection, even a sexual fusion.

Earlier I looked at the double structure of the text in Song 2.8-14 at some length, where male and female become troublesome terms because there are equivalent problems with grounding inside and outside as discrete spaces. As I have pointed out, a similar phenomenon can be observed in Song of Songs 5.2-6. Fixing an inside and an outside 'in' the world of the text, and fixing male and female personae along with it, relies on readers making decisions about how to figure the lines 'between' by which categories are formed and regulated in these passages. Readers can figure these lines-between in very different ways, giving rise to very different interpretative frameworks: narcissistic woman or damsel in distress? Autonomous male or fantasy puppet? Sexual congress or masturbatory fantasy? Our readings necessarily depend on how we shift our gaze on the lines that crisscross through the 'undecidable' text. The threshold does not simply have two functions, then, but two opposing functions that it performs simultaneously. The threshold structures difference in one reading and negates it in another. Each reading, however, is preserved in its opposite's shadow. Strictly speaking, readers must either 'choose' one spatial configuration—and thus one interpretative framework—over the other, or else we must embrace the text as a space of the both-and-neither, in which case the project of gendered reading, and of feminist reading in particular, becomes more troublesome than has been previously recognized.

67. Hill, *Introduction to Jacques Derrida*, p. 48.
68. Hill, *Introduction to Jacques Derrida*, p. 48.

This is because, firstly, readings that wish to foreground the Song's lack of gendered inequality and gendered stereotyping are confronted with a text-world that offers plenty of both. She is bounded. He is liberated, and worse, liberating. However, deeper readings do not necessarily improve things. The paradoxical geography may illuminate the text world as a mutually interpenetrative environment, but it takes the 'female' and the 'male' of feminist discourse with it into the collapse. What kind of 'fem' is it that we are left with in a Paradoxical feminist reading? It is certainly not clear from the text of Song 2 and 5, where genderedness has become a little tricky to pin down. If it is difficult to affirm gynocentrism in a poem with an aversion to 'centre', it is even more difficult when the Presence of the 'gynological' is ever unstable too. It is trickier still to posit sexual equality in a text where stable sexual identities and stable boundaries (the prerequisite of the balancing act of equality, surely) are more a product of the reader than they are of the poem.

In other words, the dyads of male/female, inside/outside visible/invisible are differentiated, maintained, and regulated by the thresholds in Song of Songs, and yet these positions are, by virtue of the Song having its character as its own narrator, also mutual performances. These roles are interpenetrative and fluid acts where inside and outside (and, by extension, male and female, narrator and narrated) become hard to ground definitively as polarized ideological positions. To reiterate Derrida's point:

> [T]his hymen eliminates the spatial heterogeneity of the two poles in the 'supreme spasm', the moment of dying laughter. By the same token, it eliminates the exteriority or the anteriority, the independence of the imitated, the signified, or the thing. Fulfillment is summed up within desire; desire is (ahead of) fulfillment, which, still mimed, remains desire '*without breaking the mirror*'.[69]

If each threshold negates the difference between the lovers without necessarily negating them *as two*, the narratives themselves also negate a more profound difference, that between desire and fulfillment.[70] The woman is, in both the texts I have been occupied with here, living in the very story she is telling. Each of these passages is a recounting of itself, an infinite loop of self-copying in which the woman tells the story about how she comes

---

69. Jacques Derrida, 'The Double Session', pp. 209-10.
70. This feature of the text has, of course, already been indicated in the work of Exum that I discussed earlier. Exum talks of the Song's blurring of distinctions between desire, anticipation and fulfillment as one of its controlling poetic strategies: 'The blurring of the boundaries between past and present is also a blurring of the distinction between the woman as narrator and the woman as a character in her own narrative' (*Song of Songs*, pp. 124-25; 9-11). I am, in a sense, seeking to show how the Song's world works as a kind of topographizing of those literary dynamics.

to be telling a story. Her sexual desire, its fulfillment, and the formulation of the narratives, though apparently different and suffused with a sense of difference, are all coterminous. The woman desires by means of stories, is satisfied by means of the stories—which she enters into and forms a part of—and climaxes by means of linguistic slippage (double entendres and the like; cf. Song 5.2-5). She has sex by means of language, and she communicates by means of her sexuality. The difference between desire and fulfillment thereby becomes negated in the text. A story told because of longing and the experience that satisfies that longing are completely merged.

If we take the following passage of Derrida's as a kind of critical commentary on these threshold texts, we can see just how similar the 'scrims' of the Song and the Derridean hymen are. The following works as a critical Targum with either threshold text of the Song, though given its specific imagery, keeping the doorway of Song 5.2-6 in mind sharpens the equivalency:

> The hymen, the consummation of differends, the continuity and confusion of the coitus, merges with what it seems to be derived from: the hymen as protective screen, the jewel box of virginity, the vaginal partition, the fine invisible veil which, in front of the hysteria, stands *between* the inside and the outside of a woman, and consequently between desire and fulfillment. It is neither desire nor pleasure but between the two. Neither future nor present, but between the two.[71]

What makes both these threshold texts so complicated, then, is the fact that the line between inside and outside, and between male and female, is not the only politics of 'between' at work in these two texts. The texts work at a temporal intersection too, and, indeed, at an intersection between modes of textuality. If the troublesome nature of spatial division in these passages points us toward the instability of gendered positions in the Song, the issue of gender itself points us toward more profound concerns of how the lines between text/reader and narrator/character are managed by the poem in these two threshold narratives.

The duality of the threshold as a line that *both* conjoins and separates allows the poem to differentiate the gendered lovers and overthrow this distinction in the same spatial operation. The threshold is a kind of hymen, one that points back to the nature of these texts as projects of the in-between— not simply in their subject matter but in their very structure—'like the unwritten page'.

The Song as a whole, of course, is a 'space of writing', to borrow Derrida's phrase. In fact, the Song could be described in precisely the same way that Derrida describes '*Mimique*': a text, an event, 'in which nothing happens, in which the simulacrum is a transgression and the transgression

---

71. Derrida, 'The Double Session', p. 223.

a simulacrum, everything describes the very structure of the text and effec-tuates its possibility.[72] All that happens in the Song is a recounting or con-juring of love. The Song is all words and no action, a kind of inverse mime, a space in which simulacrum is eroticism, and where all eroticism is a simulacrum—where romance and poetic composition have become identical.

We can see the poem's numerous self-duplications right across its chap-ters of course—from the reuse of particular words and phrases ('I adjure you, daughters of Jerusalem...', 2.7; 3.5; 8.4; 'who is this coming up from the wilderness?', 3.6; 8.5) to the almost-repetition of whole sections, like the two city scenes, the two episodes in the garden and so on. Obviously, the two threshold texts I have been reading here are essentially retellings of each other. But they are also copies of the structure of the Song. As I indicated above with regard to Song 5 (though the same holds for Song 2 as well, if less obviously), the surfaces of the thresholds in the text medi-ate between the lovers in the same way that the surfaces of the page medi-ate between the reader and the characters. The door/lattice obscures the Other lover like a phantasmagorical scrim hides the mechanical phantoms. The lovers must engage with each other through imaginative projections, through a mixture of performance and concealment that duplicates, almost exactly, the way in which readers must engage with the text. These lovers become to each other creatures of pure voice, obscured behind a surface that imaginatively recreates them. The male/female, reader/character never meet, and yet the threshold-cum-hymen-cum-page allows for a consumma-tion that is neither just desire nor just fulfillment but a both—and a neither. The thresholds are to the lovers what the page is to the reader, a hymen to be projected upon, a lattice '*between* the inside and the outside of oneself, and consequently between desire and fulfillment'.[73]

The Elusive Line

The notion of the threshold, and of the categories of identity which it would seem to delineate in the text, is far more complicated than yes/no, male/female, being/non-being. Thresholds are a both-and-neither place, liminal zones that function in the text to delineate and to circumscribe identities—readerly and gendered. And yet these thresholds also seem to function as coordinates where division is broken down. Therefore, the gender politics that are played out at the Song's threshold spaces trouble the notion that the text has entirely fixed gender categories; the Song, try as it might, cannot maintain its gendered binary. More significant, though, is the fact that this

72. Derrida, 'The Double Session', p. 218.
73. Derrida, 'The Double Session', p. 223.

topography of the in-between works as a cipher for the wider spatiality of the Song itself. The dialogic Song, the betwixt-text, the text that relies on the indeterminacy of spatial relationships for its very functioning, is unable to maintain 'reader' and 'read' as discrete categories either; what we read between the lovers is a reading of our reading. The lovers, negotiating processes of projection by which they become 'like the unwritten page', are doing precisely what the Song's readers are doing: becoming part of a process of projection, a process by which we must navigate the as yet unwritten, unconfigured, surface of the page.

The spatiality of the Song's phantasmagoric textuality and its internal topography are analogous, and it is difficult, even, to see where one stratum of meaning ends and another begins. Though, as we shall see in the next chapter, the problems of stratification in the Song go much further than that, implicating the bodies of the lovers and the textual corpus itself as similarly indecipherable spaces, as figurative hymens of a very different order.

Chapter 5

The Corpus without Organs
(Can be used as a Surrealist Kingdom)

> A man sets out to draw the world. As the years go by, he populates a space
> with images of provinces, kingdoms, mountains, bays, ships, islands, fishes,
> rooms, instruments, stars, horses, and individuals. A short time before he
> dies, he discovers that the patient labyrinth of lines traces the lineaments of
> his own face.
>
> —Jorge Luis Borges[1]

Gilles Deleuze and Felix Guattari once painstakingly reconstructed the pro-
ceedings of a lecture given by that great twentieth-century mind, Professor
Challenger (the same Challenger in fact who was so closely associated with
Sir Arthur Conan Doyle).[2] In this chapter I am going to use that lecture to

1. Jorge Luis Borges, *Dreamtigers* (Austin, TX: University of Texas Press, 1985
[1960]), p. 93.
2. For anyone who is not aware of the great Professor Challenger, and thus of
the kind of rhetorical move being made by Deleuze and Guattari here, it is worth my
noting that Challenger is a fictional character of Conan Doyle's. Challenger is, like
Conan Doyle's other great creation, a kind of sleuth, although as far as personality is
concerned Challenger could not really be more different from Sherlock Holmes. Challenger first appears in Conan Doyle's *The Lost World* (London: A.L. Burt Company,
1912), where the narrator (one Edward Malone) describes the professor in the following way: '[h]is appearance made me gasp. I was prepared for something strange, but
not for so overpowering a personality as this. It was his size, which took one's breath
away—his size and his imposing presence. His head was enormous, the largest I have
ever seen upon a human being. I am sure that his top hat, had I ventured to don it,
would have slipped over me entirely and rested on my shoulders. He had the face and
beard, which I associate with an Assyrian bull; the former florid, the latter so black
as almost to have a suspicion of blue, spade-shaped and rippling down over his chest.
The hair was peculiar, plastered down in front in a long, curving wisp over his massive forehead. The eyes were blue-grey under great black tufts, very clear, very critical, and very masterful. A huge spread of shoulders and a chest like a barrel were the
other parts of him which appeared above the table, save for two enormous hands covered with long black hair. This and a bellowing, roaring, rumbling voice made up my
first impression of the notorious Professor Challenger' (p. 16.) Deleuze and Guattari's
have their own reasons for using the fictitious Challenger in their mock-up of a lecture. Challenger is worth mentioning here, of course, because he seems (at least in

think about the correlations between bodily space and landscaped space in the Song of Songs, linking my observations here to the previous chapters to build up a picture of both the spatial and ideological functioning of the Song's bodies, and the spatial nature of the Song as a corpus. Challenger's lecture lends itself to this kind of project because, as Deleuze and Guattari report, Challenger's address was the direct result of his mixing of biology and geology textbooks. In other words, Challenger's subject matter seems to map on to the Song's tellurian bodies rather nicely, since they too are a curious mixing of biology and landscape.

Challenger's disquisition began, we are told, with a little look at the planet earth:

> The Earth—the Deterritorialized, the Glacial, the giant Molecule—is a body without organs. This body without organs is permeated by unformed unstable matters, by flows in all directions, by free intensities or nomadic singularities, by mad or transitory particles. That however was not the question at hand. For there simultaneously occurs upon the earth a very important, inevitable phenomenon that is beneficial in many respects and unfortunate in many others: stratification. Strata are Layers, Belts. They consist of giving form to matters, of imprisoning intensities or locking singularities into systems of resonance or redundancy, of producing upon the body of the earth molecules large and small and organizing them into molar aggregates. Strata are acts of capture, they are like 'black holes' or occlusions striving to seize whatever comes within their reach. They operate by coding and territorialization upon the earth…the strata are judgments of God: stratification in general is the entire system of the judgment of God (but the earth, or the body without organs, constantly eludes that judgment, flees and becomes destratified, decoded, deterritorialized).[3]

Thinking through the openness of the body in this way does something to both our sense of what a body is and what the bodies of the Song might signify. Ultimately, my argument in this chapter is that what we might call bodily space in the Song of Songs could be more accurately described as an 'act of capture', just as Deleuze and Guattari's earth is. There are no bodies in the Song, there are only readerly judgments that strive to seize molecules large and small and organize them into Organisms. But the Song, remarkable— if frustrating—piece of literature that it is, also constantly eludes that judgment. It flees and becomes destratified, decoded, deterritorialized. The Song

---

Malone's estimation) to embody the gargantuan faunal, composite bodies I am looking to explore in the Song of Songs. And since his lecture will lead us on to questions of discourse and the fictive nature of these bodies, Challenger, as the fictional originator of some of the theory I will be employing, seemed too wonderful an incidence of the methodological uncanny to leave in the margin.

    3. Gilles Deleuze and Felix Guattari, *A Thousand Plateaus: Capitalism and Schizophrenia* (London: Continuum, 2011 [1987]), p. 45.

of Songs might have no bodies then, but what it does have is something akin
to a Body without Organs (a BwO), an open body, a constellation of images
which can be folded into a corpus or unfurled into a cosmos. In the Song it is
not described bodies that we find (beautiful, grotesque or otherwise), but the
act of description posing as a body. In analysis this distinction is crucial, and
ties the Song in to a broader scholarly landscape of work on the body, which,
for the moment at least, may be neatly summarized by Spivak:

> If one really thinks of the body as such, there is no possible outline of the
> body as such. There are thinkings of the systemicity of the body, there are
> value codings of the body. The body, as such, cannot be thought, and I cer-
> tainly cannot apprehend it.[4]

It is my contention that this kind of observation on the body ties the
approaches to spatial and textual indeterminacy that I have been looking
at in the book so far with the Song's bodily lovers. The Song's bodies, like
the Song itself, and like the spatial and textual structures emphasized in earlier chapters, are giant molecules, ideological conglomerations that are not
discrete units but open and malleable systems. Thus we might suggest that
what Derrida's *il n'y a pas de hors-texte* puts literarily and spatially Deleuze
and Guattari put geologically and physiologically. This chapter is engaged
with mapping the possibilities of such an equivalency. If bodies, like texts,
are open systems then perhaps all bodies, both literary and fleshly specimens, are nothing more than modes of description, spaces that articulate
articulation itself. We begin by looking at the relevant texts.

Well-sung Bodies

In this discussion I am opting to look at three iconic texts from the Song that
deal with the lovers' bodies in reasonably explicit terms, 4.1–5; 6.4–7; and
7.2–8. Further treatment of embodiment in the Song is simply not possible
in the present study (and since Fiona Black has already undertaken a book-
length work on the Song's bodies—and on the history of interpretation that
comes along with them—there seems little point in attempting to be similarly exhaustive in my treatment here).[5] More to the point, and as Spivak's
comments above seem to suggest, I need to impose some parameters on my
chosen corpus if I am going to make a start at all! It is hoped, though, that
since other allusions to the body in the Song are fairly similar to my selec-
tions here (i.e. often metaphorical, reasonably geographically preoccupied

---

4. Galati Chakravorty *Spivak*, 'In a Word', Interview with Ellen Roony, quoted in
Judith Butler, *Bodies that Matter: On the Discursive Limits of Sex* (New York: Routledge, 2007 [1993]), p. xi.
   5. Black, *Artifice of Love.*

and thoroughly obscure), my observations in this chapter will be readily applicable to the Song as a whole.[6]

The three texts I am looking at are generally recognized as formal poetic exercises—though their boundaries are, of course, disputed—that 'describe' the bodies of the lovers in metaphorical terms. For the sake of ease, and to avoid the problematic designation *wasf*, 'description', I will term these particular sections of the Song 'body-texts' for the time being, since that is what they seem to be preoccupied in depicting. The most obvious connection between these body-texts is their use of metaphorical language. Each

---

6. These three texts focus on the female body. It is worth noting that I will be more concerned with the female body in this chapter than with the male's. There are a number of reasons for this. There is a view that the bodies of the male and the female are substantively different in the poem. Black notes, for example, that one could not link the male with the processes and cycles of life in the way that one can with the woman (*Artifice of Love*, p. 162). The male's body is hard and rigid, she says, rather than pastoral and verdant like the woman's. His arms are golden rods, his legs are pillars of marble on a foundation (feet?) of gold, his loins are like a tusk of decorated ivory (5.14-15). As such, much of his body appears as a closed edifice; he is made to look like a statue. To Black, the male appears to be a hard, fixed point around which other things must be organized, forming more of an erectile imposition on the landscape than a bodily world.

There are key differences between the male and the female bodies in the text but these have perhaps been overstated by Black. The male's face is formed from very explicitly floral and faunal images: hair like the raven, eyes whose waters flow from the streams, lips that drip like lilies, and cheeks like beds of rich perfume. There is, then, a degree to which the male's face coalesces from a constellation of parts taken from the landscape, just as the woman's body does. Later, in v. 15, the male is likened to Lebanon, which enhances the sense that his body, like hers, takes its cues from the landscape. Like his lover, this male emerges from the natural world and might be returned to it. In fact, the male's jeweled body could also be said to suggest a world of natural produce—gold and precious metals are as naturally occurring as doves and wheat, after all, and presuppose as vibrant and valuable a world as fawns or clean sheep. The woman's towers (4.4; 7.4) are 'hard' images after all, but they do not make her, in Black's reckoning, a kind of erectile edifice. What I want to signal at the outset of my discussion, then, is that I take the view that the male and female bodies are reasonably structurally similar in the text, and that many of the broader observations I will make in this chapter regarding the politics of constructing poetic bodies therefore will apply as much to the male as to the female. That said, for the sake of consistency, space, and focus, I have opted in this discussion to focus on the female's body only. The three female-oriented body-texts of the Song already provide too much material for as full an analysis as I would like in the space available. Furthermore, my concern here is to discuss the politics of bodily composition, rather than the connections between bodily composition and gendered ideologies. With that in mind, stripping gender out of the equation seemed a prudent move to focus an already broad discussion. This chapter does certainly raise questions about the gendering of bodies in the text, but that issue is of only limited relevance to this volume at this point. I aim to look instead at the way in which the images function rather than how we can use them to stake a claim on certain ideological positions pertaining to gender.

takes body parts in turn and compares them to non-body images, or, more specifically, to non-*human* body images (ovine bodies stand in for a human organ every now and then). The results of these metaphorical mash ups are, quite obviously, phantasmic. In 4.1-2, for example, the male says to his beloved: 'Your hair is like a flock of goats, streaming down from Mount Gilead'. He follows up with an equally lovely sentiment: 'Your teeth are like a flock of shorn ewes that have come up from the wash, all bear twins, none has lost a lamb'. The descriptions continue in this vein throughout each of the three texts, progressing in vague physiological order, either from the head downward (4.1-5, 6.4-7) or the feet upwards (7.2-8). Here is a fuller example from Song of Songs 6.4-7:

> You are beautiful as Tirzah, my love,
>   comely as Jerusalem,
>   awesome as these commanding sights.
> Turn away your eyes from me,
>   for they overwhelm me.
> Your hair is like a flock of goats,
>   moving down the slopes of Gilead.
> Your teeth are like a flock of ewes,
>   that have come up from the washing;
>   all of them bear twins,
>   and not one among them is bereaved.
> Your cheeks are like halves of a pomegranate
>   behind your veil.

Fiona Black's aforementioned work on the Song is significant for this chapter, not simply because of its astute and erudite treatment of both the body-texts and the reading traditions that have grown up around them, but because Black gets right to the heart of virtually all existing discussions on the Song's bodies, exposing the unspoken rules that have tended to condition their treatment. In short, what Black identifies in the Song's interpretative tradition is a kind of modernist imperative, a striving for 'proper' readings of the text's bodies that proceeds oblivious to the fact that one's sense of 'proper' is always predetermined. Black thus highlights the highly subjective nature of the interpretative methods deployed to decode the lovers' bodies over the last thirty years or so, and argues that at root these methods are idiosyncratic to each scholar's own literary (and romantic?) predilections.

By way of an example, here are some of Black's comments on Roland Murphy's treatment of the Song of Songs and its metaphorical language (specifically his take 4.3, 'your cheeks are like halves of a pomegranate behind your veil'). Black by no means singles Murphy out but her comments on his approach to metaphor fairly succinctly sum up the problems of mainstream approaches to these texts:

Murphy's bias in interpretation is made quite clear. It is affected by two things: realism (or logic) and his expectations that the descriptions are meant to compliment and flatter, to show evidence of the adoration of the one who is creating the description.

It is evident, however, that Murphy's system is problematic. The images that he uses as examples for each of the three groups [read: types of imagery: literal, non-literal and natural] may actually be used in any one of them and his evaluation is really quite idiosyncratic. For instance, the comparison of the cheeks to a pomegranate requires the hermeneutic key of colour (imposed by Murphy) to make it make sense or to be 'straightforward' for the cheeks. But suppose the basis of comparison were the seeds of the pomegranate, or its smell, or its roundness, or some other feature of the fruit. Different bases of comparison would, thus, naturally affect Murphy's interpretation. Equally, the spirit behind the interpretation is important to the result. These are all pleasant connotations (colour, smell, shape), but one could entertain alternative bases of comparison, such as the spoilt nature of pomegranates...[7]

Black traces various formulations of this trend in a range of scholarly texts on the Song: the cultural/contextual readings of Keel, Pope, and Fox, the romantic and idealized readings of Munro and Goulder, the evocative readings of Falk and Soulen, and the so-called readings of excess: Landy's psychoanalytical study and Boer's (in)famous work on pornography.[8] The result of these interpretative idiosyncrasies is a body of work on the Song that has unconsciously enshrined certain readerly decisions, namely that 'behind the images [is] a realistic and attractive woman'.[9] As Black says in conclusion of her review of the literature:

7. Black, *Artifice of Love*, pp. 31-32.

8. Keel, *Song of Songs*; Pope, *Song of Songs*; Fox, *Song of Songs*; Munro, *Spikenard and Saffron*; Falk, *Love Lyrics from the Bible*; Michael Goulder, *The Song of Fourteen Songs*; Richard Soulen, 'The *wasfs* of the Song of Songs and Hermeneutics', in Athalya Brenner (ed.), *A Feminist Companion to the Song of Songs*, pp. 214-24; Landy, *Paradoxes of Paradise*; Boer, *Knocking on Heaven's Door*, pp. 53-70.

9. Black, *Artifice of Love*, p. 32. This 'realistic and attractive woman' lurks around in Song scholarship in various guises. Brenner's 1993 reading, for instance, relies on the 'presumption that behind the image is a real woman who has an identity and a social location' (Athalya Brenner, '"Come Back, Come Back the Shulammite' (Song of Songs 7.1-10): A Parody of the *wasf* Genre', in Brenner [ed.] *Feminist Companion to the Song of Songs*, pp. 234-57). And those whose reading of the metaphorical body centers upon the speaker's emotional affectation—Soulen and Falk, for example—build their case on a similar premise: 'The writer is not concerned that his hearers be able to retell in descriptive language the particular qualities or appearance of the woman described; he is much more interested that they share his joy, awe, and delight' ('The *wasfs* of the Song of Songs and Hermeneutics', p. 223). Can we be so sure that the Song has such a direct real-life precedent? Black's treatment of Murphy (quoted at length above) points to the same problem of course, and her comments mirror Exum's observation that the Song scholar's have an 'unfortunate tendency of historicizing the Song', of mistaking its events for a loosely conceived 'account' of real-life; Exum, *Song of Songs*, p. 45.

First, the obvious: many interpreters are visualizing a 'real' person behind the images—though not necessarily one with a particular historical identity—and they seem unable to suspend their expectations for how real bodies should be represented. This seems an expected response for texts that deal with the matter of embodiment.[10]

Black terms this overall 'organizing principle' in Song scholarship a 'hermeneutic of compliment', by which she means: 'the drive evident in readings to interpret the imagery in such a way that it gives a picture of the one that it describes that is realistic, but…only if that realism is flattering and beautiful'.[11]

Black counters this hermeneutic of compliment by developing the grotesque as a heuristic reading strategy. She employs the work of Bakhtin, Harpham, Barthes and de Certeau to figure 'the grotesque body' as a kind of critical reading tool. Black thus seeks to 'privilege the unexpected, variability and difference' in her reading of the text.[12] In reading for/with the grotesque Black does not seek to affix yet another kind of 'meaning' on the Song's poetic bodies, launching instead an enquiry into the nature of bodily dissonance that focuses on the duality and hybridity of the lovers. Black goes on to explain (as I have already touched upon in earlier chapters) that the Song, as a text, works as another kind of grotesque body, a corpus that is always in-process and which both invites and resists the interpretative advances of its lovers-cum-readers.

As rigorous (and witty) as Black's analysis is, it prompts a set of key questions that the grotesque is not quite able to address, and to which I want to direct some attention here. What if the most significant assumption of scholarly work on the Song was not the kind of body 'behind' the Song's descriptions, but the very idea of textual description itself? Is the notion of description more ideologically troublesome than the kind of description undertaken? Importantly, if we take recent developments in bodily theory seriously, we should use the term 'body' only with certain caveats in place anyway.[13] I want to begin addressing these issues by grounding a series of propositions. First, that there are no bodies in the Song, only collections of organs. These organs only form 'bodies' because of the way in which readers impose the expectation of a body over and against the text's partiality. Second, that bodies—the Song's and everyone else's—are products of discourse that pose as their own precondition. And third, that the formulations

10. Black, *Artifice of Love*, p. 62.
11. Black, *Artifice of Love*, p. 32.
12. Black, *Artifice of Love*, p. 124.
13. In a sense, in what follows I am being reasonably pedantic about the kind of rhetoric we use, even in passing, to discuss the Song's bodies. My aim is not to score cheap points based on academic style. Rather, the point is to indicate that if bodies are linguistic and conceptual products, how we talk about them has implications for how we imagine their ideological workings—in texts and elsewhere.

of landscaped space and bodily space are more mutual in the Song than is sometimes suggested.

Some Assembly Required

It is problematic, or at least arbitrary, to assume that a 'body', a whole being, exists in or emerges from the Song. The Song's body-texts give us only packets of human parts, and with a good deal of the expected material missing (who wants a lover with no tongue?). There are no bodies in the text except in kit form. The text gives us the organs and we, like the good Doctor Frankenstein, must do the rest. Athalya Brenner notes something very similar to this when she writes that 'no "description" is actually obtained [by the body-texts]: by the end of the poem we still have no idea what the loved person looks like, in the sense that no *complete* image is communicated'.[14] If there were a complete image, of course, the Song would be infinitely longer. Articulating the whole body is always an impossibility; patience for description would inevitably break down long before the lower intestine, or the individual bacteria within it, could be adequately sketched. Bodily lovers may result from a reading of the Song but they are nowhere on the page. One cannot really interpret the bodies of the Song, for the idea 'body' is already a kind of interpretation.

We might add to Brenner's sentiment by pointing out that the bodies of the Song are not only incomplete, their parts are disconnected. There is no systemicity to the text's 'bodies'. The numerous parts are not related or wired up, so to speak, with one another. Landy indicates something akin to this when he stresses the linguistic qualities of the body-texts: 'if the [body] passage is isolated, distinctly bounded from its neighbours, without logical connectives, each sentence within it duplicates this isolation. There is no syntactic frame…merely the association of tropes by contiguity.'[15]

Sewing Landy and Brenner's observations together, we might go so far as to say that there is thus no predetermined 'whole' in the Song's body-texts of which hair, or eyes, or nose could be said to form a part. The temptation in the face of this partiality, and one which I have already indulged in the last two paragraphs, would be to label the bodies collections of 'parts'. But if we are going to be very particular about it, this will not do either. The term 'body parts' simply indicates partial aspects of an absent whole. But there is no bodily whole in the text; there is only the isolated organ. The only systematic whole with 'parts' is the one imposed by the reader upon the text, one that disregards the partiality of the text in order to posit a One, a Body that we can attribute to one or other of the Song's characters but that

14. Brenner, 'Come Back, Come Back the Shulammite', p. 235.
15. Landy, *Paradoxes of Paradise*, p. 67.

the text itself never mentions. That is, in referring to body parts we imply a whole body as our conceptual starting point, even when the Song contains no such thing. In practice, readers must imagine bodies where there is only a series of organs floating in isolation. 'The body', the collation of various nooks and crannies into a 'whole', is a result of readers synthesizing the disparate images, stitching the disconnected parts together and using them to project a One; this One is then imaged to have preceded the 'parts', to be their original site, from which they are taken and to which they might be returned. In actual fact, of course, the parts are not contingent on the whole. It is the other way around, the whole body that scholars have read into the text is entirely contingent on (a) a smattering of parts, and (b), the denying of the partiality of those parts. If we take 4.1-7 as an example:

> Look at you! You are beautiful, my friend!
> Look at you! You are beautiful!
> Your eyes are doves
>   behind your veil.[16]
> Your hair is like a flock of goats,
>   streaming down[17] from Mount Gilead.
> Your teeth are like a flock of shorn ewes[18]
>   that have come up from the wash,
>   all bear twins,
>   not one among them is bereaved.[19]
> As a crimson thread are your lips
>   and your mouth[20] is lovely.
> As a slice of pomegranate is your cheek[21]
>   behind your veil.

16. The term for veil (צמה) proved troublesome for the translators of the ancient versions, and a variety of possibilities were raised (Septuagint translated it as silence, the Vulgate: 'without that which lies within'. Rashi understood the terms to refer to locks of hair). See the discussion in Pope, *Song of Songs*, pp. 457-58.

17. The term for 'streaming down' (גלש) appears only here at in Song 6.5. Exum suggests 'winding down' on the basis of a Ugaritic parallel meaning 'to flow in waves'. I have opted to follow Pope, Fox and Murphy here who translate on the basis of the aquatic associations of the word in extra-biblical usage (Pope, *Song of Songs*, pp. 458-60).

18. Literally 'shorn ones (feminine)'.

19. Of this verse Exum writes that the Hebrew words for 'teeth' and 'shorn ones' are both feminine, and the pronominal suffixes on 'all of *them*', and 'among *them*' are masculine, and that 'this type of disagreement in gender is not uncommon in the Song' (Exum, *Song of Songs*, p. 153). Whatever the original linguistic or lexical reasons for these gender disagreements, they take us back to the kinds of arguments on the indeterminacy of gendered positions in the Song that I looked at earlier in Chapter 4.

20. The word for mouth here (מדבר) is a hapax with something of a contested meaning, though it derives from the verb to speak (דבר). See the following discussion (under 'Flashes of Tellurian Flesh') for more details on the issue of lips, borders and deserts.

21. The meaning of 'cheek' here is contested; the term may refer to the cheek, the temple or to the brow; see Exum, *Song of Songs*, p. 153.

As the tower of David is your neck,
  built in courses,[22]
  a thousand shields are hung on it,
  all the warriors' bucklers.
Your two breasts are like two fawns,
  twins of gazelle,
  grazing among the lilies.
Until the day breathes
  and the shadows flee
I will make my way[23] to the mountain of myrrh
  and the hill of frankincense.
Everything about you[24] is beautiful, my friend,
  and flawless.

Here the 'woman'—clearly a woman only because of the breasts and the Hebrew possessive suffixes—consists just of eyes, hair, teeth, lips (no tongue for kissing, or speaking), a single cheek, a neck, and two breasts. Naturally, the 'lack'—if that is not too loaded a term—of one body-part or another does not make a body any less human, or any less attractive (as the work of disability critics in Biblical Studies would surely remind us).[25] That said, it is worth pointing out that one could earn a pastoral living, defend oneself, wash and get lost on this lover's body, but, and as Brenner has similarly observed, one could have only oral (and possibly cleavage-) sex with it, and certainly no conversation afterwards.[26] The real problem with terming this collection a body, though, is not the absence of legs, ears, hands, arms, or a heart, but the absence of any connection between the organs she does have. There is no functionality or systemicity at work between the 'organs', which, aside from the sense-making operations of the reader, are entirely independent from one another. From a purely bodily perspective, this text better resembles dog-food than date since the lover is not a person at all; she is a jumble of offal.

22. On this translation see A.M. Honeyman, 'Two Contributions to Canaanite Toponymy', *JTS* 50 (1958), pp. 59-61.

23. Following Fox and Exum in translating this sense of the ethical dative (Exum, *Song of Songs*, p. 154; Fox, *Song of Songs*, p. 128).

24. Exum translates this 'you are wholly beautiful' (Exum, *Song of Songs*, p. 152), while Pope translates it 'You are all fair' (Pope, *Song of Songs*, p. 452). My translation here attempts to foreground the fact that a unified whole is not necessarily implied by the Hebrew phrasing; the term used (כל) can designate an assemblage or collection of things as well as a single unified 'whole'. That is, the Hebrew designation does not necessarily confer unity on the woman's body.

25. See, for instance, Jeremy Schipper, *Disability Studies and the Hebrew Bible: Figuring Mephibosheth in the David Story* (Library of Hebrew Bible/Old Testament, 441; London: Continuum, 2009).

26. Brenner, 'Come Back, Come Back the Shulammite', p. 241.

The bodily organs of the Song's body-texts are often said to be narrated head to toe (or toe to head) as in the Arabic *waṣf* genre; Black notes this aspect of the text, as does Pope, and, at greater length, Bergant, Brenner, and Falk (among others).[27] It would be tempting, therefore, to use the anatomical structuring displayed in these body-texts to counter what I have been suggesting so far. One might try to ground the idea of a coherent body—a whole into which the parts fit as parts—by recourse to the text's use of anatomical structure. Black refers in passing to these body-texts as representing the lovers in 'systematic fashion' by virtue of this ordering, and one could find this phrase suggestive of just such a reading, with the systemicity of the body-texts standing in for the systemicity of the lover's body.[28] One might thus render the unified body present in the textual world, by giving it a systemic presence outside of the presence of the individual organs themselves.

The problem with this formulation of the text is that anatomical order is not at work in these body-texts in the first place. Readers must in fact overlook certain aspects of the text in order to find systematic description in the body texts at all (a process, as I have been suggesting, with which we are all over familiar in our readings of the Song anyway). By means of an illustration one could take Song of Songs 4 and 6. In the body-text of that chapter the order of the organs runs: eyes, hair, teeth, lips, cheeks, neck, and breasts. The order in 6.5-7 is identical except for the omission of the lips. In what body though is hair the obvious structural neighbor of eyes on the one side and teeth on the other? The text must be assumed to move away from the 'face' and back again. Similarly, how can one assert that a progression from eyes to teeth and only *then* to lips is governed by bodily structure? Necks and breasts tend to be below one's face, admittedly, but this is where the text's adherence to anatomical order stops.[29]

27. On the use of the term in biblical scholarship, see Black, *Artifice of Love*, pp. 21-22, and Pope, *Song of Songs*, pp. 66-68. For early use of the *waṣf* in readings of the Song see Friedrich Horst, 'Die Formen des althebräischen Liebesliedes', in Rudi Paret (ed.), *Orientalische Studien Enno Littmann zu seinem 60 Geburtstag* (Leiden: E.J. Brill, 1935), pp. 43-54. As Black notes, a full history of the genre can be found in Wolfram Hermann, 'Gedanken zur Geschichte des altorientalischen Beschreibungsliedes', *ZAW* 75 (1963), pp. 176-96. See also Bergant, *Song of Songs*, pp. 42-49; Brenner, 'Come Back, Come Back the Shulammite', pp. 241-43; Falk, *Love Lyrics from the Bible*, pp. 80-81.

28. Black, *Artifice of Love*, p. 20.

29. We could go further. The order in chap. 7 continues: breasts, neck, eyes, nose, head, and hair. This construction more obviously abandons anatomical order, moving from the neck up to the eyes, then down again to the nose, then out to the head and hair. Even if one argues that the interpolation of hair between eyes and teeth in chap. 4 was anatomically warranted (perhaps her hair was over her face, or she was being built with a moustache?), the sudden change in what constitutes a sensible anatomical 'order'

Few scholars' arguments hinge on the absolute systemicity of the lovers' bodies, of course. Brenner, for example, rightly notes that the body-text of Song 4 proceeds only 'more or less' in an orderly fashion.[30] But being very strict with ourselves about how we talk about the Song's bodies means considering those aspects of the Song within which the assumption of a whole, unified body has tended to hide. And this issue of an assumed anatomical order can have a subtle effect on the ways in which we read key parts of the text.

Song 7.1-6 is a good example. Here the bodily order runs: feet, thighs, navel, belly, breasts. The navel has been encountered before the belly, disrupting the alleged anatomical order (of Bergant, Pope, and Falk). In response to this, Pope, while fully acknowledging that the Hebrew root for 'navel' here (שרר) is most often linked to the umbilical cord, and, by extension, to the navel, nevertheless recommends that we read the term more obliquely. He suggests we read שרר as a euphemism for vulva based on an more obscure Arabic cognate [*sirr*], meaning 'secret'.[31] To say that this is a stretch is probably understating things somewhat. Tellingly, Pope grounds this reading decision on the very same bodily ordering that he is imposing on the text: 'Since the movement of the description of the lady's charms is from the feet upward, the loci of the evermoist receptacle between the thighs and the belly would seem to favour the lower aperture'. Saucy. But rather circular in logic. The idea of the unified singular body brings itself into being here. Pope's interpretative amendment is not earth-shattering for readings of the Song, naturally, but his discussion of the navel serves as an object lesson on the way in which the body can tend to function in discourse. Bodies can operate as circular arguments that pose as their own preconditions (which is precisely how critical theorists would describe the body, as we shall see in a moment).

Some scholars have gone further and used anatomical order to build new bits of the body that are not in the text at all; the body therefore manages to dictate itself into the text. When Dianne Bergant writes of 4.1, for instance, that 'the primary feature of the image seems to be the movement of the flock...this movement suggests...the cascading movement of her hair down her head, neck and shoulders', she has used the context of the image, the landscape itself, to form the woman's head, neck and shoulders—which the

---

between Song 4 and Song 7 would seem to suggest that physiological structure—that potential grounding point of the Song's bodies—is subject to readerly whim.

30. Brenner, 'Come Back Come Back the Shulammite', p. 241. Though, that said, others indicate the progression of the body texts to be more 'systematic', Black, *Artifice of Love*, p. 20; 'strict', Falk, *Love Lyrics and the Bible* p. 80; or 'orderly', Bergant, *Song of Songs*, p. xv and Pope, *Song of Songs*, p. 67, according to the physiology of the human body.

31. Pope, *Song of Songs*, pp. 617-18.

text of the Song never mentions.[32] Rashi's suggestion that the female of 4.1 should be imagined as bald (given that the goats have quit the mountain) would seem to indicate that he has read Gilead in precisely the same way, as the woman's head, though nothing in the text speaks beyond the woman's hair.[33] Similarly, while the image of the breasts in 4.4 is primarily faunal, Landy argues that the image serves to underline connections between woman's torso and the earth: 'the fawns, grazing among the lilies, are feeding off the earth, which in the Song, as in the Bible in general, has a maternal function, and is associated with the Beloved'. Landy thus sees the female's torso as a 'meadow dotted with lilies, as in a pointillist painting'.[34] There is no torso in the text. Though the text can be seen to encourage us in this interpretative direction, opening the woman's body out to the world from which its organs are composed, the words on the page do not always specifically constitute the body as it is discussed by the Song's readers.

This premise holds for the whole assemblage as well as individual organs. Exum writes that 'he [the male lover] distances himself from the whole person [of the female] through the breakdown of parts—eyes, hair, teeth, lips, mouth, cheeks, neck and breasts—each inchoately anticipating a successful assemblage'.[35] The suggestion here seems to be that the body parts represent a breaking down of a whole person, and that they anticipate another whole, an assemblage that results from the description. Exum's work is always acutely aware of both the textuality of the Song and the role of the reader in configuring meaning in the poem, but we might legitimately enquire after the location of these whole persons. Is the female character a whole body *before* the description, and broken down by it? Or does her body result only from the description—that is, in Exum's terms, is her body conjured by means of the male's words? In which case, how is he overawed by a body he alone creates? It is not just that the body parts 'anticipate' here; the male's response anticipates too—it anticipates a body it has not yet built. His response to the female body is what creates that body in the text, and yet the response is just that: a response, predicated on her body. The lines between cause and effect break down insofar as the male anticipates his awe at his lover's body, and her body emerges only from the expression of that awe. Her body, then, poses as a vindication of his feelings, when in fact his feelings conditioned the body in the first place. In other words, the woman's body 'poses as its own precondition'; it is a self fulfilling loop of

32. Bergant, *Song of Songs*, p. 44.
33. Judah Rosenthal, 'Rashi's Commentary on the Song of Songs (From Mss, Edited and Annotated)' in S. Bernstein and G.A. Churgin (eds.), *Samuel K. Mirsky Jubilee Volume* (New York: Jubilee Committee, 1958), pp. 130-88.
34. Landy, *Paradoxes of Paradise*, p. 68.
35. Exum, *Song of Songs*, p. 160.

affective inscription, just as I described space itself in the earliest chapters of this thesis: socially conditioned and the prerequisite of sociality.

We will come back to these links in due course. For the moment, this phrase 'posing as its own precondition', one I have borrowed from Judith Butler's work on the body, requires some more detailed attention with these kinds of issues in mind.[36]

Positing a Prior Body

When discussing those passages of the Song that are said to image the lovers' bodies for us, scholars understandably talk of the texts 'describing' the couple (see Bergant, Munro, Keel, Pope, and most others).[37] Or else scholars talk of the writing 'imposing' on the paramours' forms (Black),[38] or of geographical references 'disintegrating' one or other of the lovers' features (Landy),[39] or of the curious metaphorical language working 'to hide the body as much as to display it' (Exum).[40]

This kind of language is almost unavoidable, and on the whole these commentators do not use such terms as ideologically weighted provisos to advance an argument that posits a 'real' body behind the text. Exum and Landy of course are quite clear—clearer than most, indeed—on the fact that the bodily lovers are poetry and nothing more. But the use of such terms as impose, describe, hide, display, etc., regardless of the overall argument they serve, inadvertently suggest a particular kind of relationship between the text and its bodies, namely that the text is a kind of agent that works upon the lovers' forms, hiding, displaying, describing them, and so on. As I say, these authors do not intend this terminology to suggest that the Song has bodies aside from the ones in the text. And this is particularly curious, that scholars who intend to foreground the textuality and partiality of the poetic body must nevertheless become tacitly reliant on the body as a discrete, unified conceptual entity that the poetry then engages with (displaying, imposing upon, etc.) Even in writing of the textuality of the body we must inevitably fall back on a rhetoric that unconsciously privileges the body over the text, treating bodies as a prior object that the Song's 'descriptive' passages can work upon: distancing the body, dissecting the body, describing the body.

---

36. Judith Butler, *Bodies that Matter: On the Discursive Limits of Sex* (New York: Routledge, 2007 [1993]), p. 4.

37. Bergant, *Song of Songs*, p. 84-85; Munro, *Spikenard and Saffron*, p. 125, Keel calls several parts of the text 'Description Songs', *Song of Songs*, pp. 138, 196, 230; Pope, *Song of Songs*, pp. 69-77.

38. Black, *Artifice of Love*, p. 130.

39. Landy, *Paradoxes of Paradise*, p. 67.

40. Exum, *Song of Songs*, p. 20.

In fact, the Song does not describe a body. Rather, we might say description is a mode of embodiment in the poem.[41] This issue of embodiment as a discursive mode of becoming is precisely what Judith Butler takes up in her seminal *Bodies that Matter*, which develops her earlier thesis of 'performative gender' into a case for the body, and for matter generally, as a social and discursive fabrication. In short, the idea of the body as operating prior to social discourse is problematic for Butler because such an idea turns the body into a kind of transcendental signified, a pure *a priori* category. But the 'body' is in fact a cultural idea, says Butler, and our notion of it is both socially determined and linguistically mediated. It is insufficient to say that social experience emanates only *from* the body since culture and language inevitably feed back into perceptions of and ideas about the body too. Our notions of embodiment, the way we figure our individual experiences, are to some degree socially conditioned and we go back to substitute these ideas as original and innate, as the body and discourse's own starting points. As Butler puts it,

> What I would propose in place of these conceptions of construction is a return to the notion of matter, not as a site or surface, but as a *process of materialization that stabilizes over time to produce the effect of boundary, fixity, and surface we call matter.*[42]

This all comes back to the fact that the body is not a fixed monolithic One, even on an individual level. We are a viscous cocktail of humors and hormones, a stream of saliva and piss and plasma, a marvelous constellation of organs and electrical signals. Each of us is several and metastable (we have seen this partiality at work in the Song already under my heading 'Some Assembly Required'; the significance of Butler's work is that the partiality of the Song's bodies thus makes them more, lot less, 'realistic'). What the partiality and multiplicity of embodiment causes us to do in so-called real life is to posit a One to whom our experiences and bodily processes are said to be happening. We could rearrange that sentiment quite easily though: experience and bodily processes continually bring the 'I' into being. In readings of the Song, things are not much different. We posit a body to whom the itemized 'descriptions' of the body-texts 'happen', when we might just as easily read the descriptions as inaugurating a body. In other words, what if instead of imagining the body as an object, we understood

---

41. I should stress that this observation does not indicate failings within existing approaches to the Song, literary or otherwise. Nor does it seek to downplay the literary sensitivities of existing work on the Song. But the issue of the way in which the body works as a conceptual category tends not to be spoken about in the literature in explicit terms: continually brought into being by action (physical or textual) but continually posited as an object to which that action happens.

42. Butler, *Bodies that Matter*, p. xviii. Emphasis original.

the body to be 'a happening'? The sensation of bodily unity would cease to be a starting point in our readings and unity would instead become recognized as being merely an aberrant side effect of the process of body-ing.

If the body is indeed a social idea, the very fabric of which constitutes a claim to originality,[43] then 'body' is simply the name that social discourse gives to that which it needs to presuppose in order to function, and to obscure the circularity of the operations by which it goes on functioning. Butler's point is that one cannot elevate materiality over experience or process. Bodies are nexuses of becomings; there is not an *a priori* body to be assumed and then culturally operated upon. Discursive operations are the means by which 'the body', as both an idea and as an experience, continually comes into being. It is thus 'body-ing' that produces the effect of fixity rather than fixity that defines the body. Put simply, critical theory foregrounds the facts that the body cannot operate as a pre-given in social theory and that it is not a unity in social practice. The body is instead understood to be an idea that emerges from culture, an idea that serves to summarize and collate a series of bodily processes into the ongoing illusion of a singular, solid state. We constantly become. The effect of that becoming is the misnomer of fixity. We go back and presume this fixity to be the site of our numerous becomings, when it is actually their effect.

We face inevitable difficulties in talking critically of bodies, then, because all bodies, and especially the Song's, always pose as their own precondition. We saw this process in miniature with regard to Pope's re-categorizing of the navel a little earlier but it is visible in plenty of other ways too. The Song's bodies pretend to be subjected to the very same poetic operations that bring them into being, and in talking about the Song's bodies—even when we do so only to posit them as text—we can end up assuming their conceptual coherence aside from that textuality.[44] As an example, here are a number of comments of Black's that relate to the Song's body-texts:

43. Butler, *Bodies that Matter*, pp. 4-7.

44. Thus I have already fallen foul in Chapter 4 to processes and rhetorical devices that I want to challenge and critique in this chapter. This is, to a degree, entirely necessary if Chapter 4 was to be intelligible and if the present discussion was to be properly critical of the body. After all, the body should not be ignored as a tricky category, nor should every discussion that mentions a body descend into a discussion of Judith Butler and the performativity of matter. What I have opted for in this thesis, then, is to treat bodies in simple terms up until this point in the knowledge that this chapter provides ample opportunities to think about the word body in more nuanced ways. This does not make my observations in Chapter 4 obsolete, however. Rather, this chapter's sense of the body as a continually unfurling process of signification could be reinserted into my foregoing discussions with relative ease. As we shall see, in fact, this discussion on the body takes us on to precisely that kind of project; I shall be replaying the issues raised by the body for other parts of this thesis in due course, and in the process drawing together Chapters 2-4.

Imposed on her body are fruit and animals, along with the physical lines of
the land and its marks of human habitation and destruction.[45]

The image is startling and somewhat grim in its dehumanizing of the body
through architecture and the gore of war.[46]

The pools and Carmel also seem to take us in another direction, one that plots
the woman's body across the topography of Israel, in effect merging her not
only with certain features of geography, but mapping her body, as one might
tread from place to place as if on a journey.[47]

Nature, as we saw with the preceding sections, incorporates her into the
topography, stretching her as if she might be a path to be trodden or a hill to
be climbed.[48]

These features (the building and the building*s*) trouble the body: they threaten
to do much to estrange it; they border dehumanization.[49]

Black's comments here—chosen because they are summaries of her various discussions on the different (female) bodies in the Song—relate various
ways in which the male's gaze performs political operations on the woman's form. In all of these texts the Song is imagined to be a tool that works
upon the surfaces of the lover's body. The woman's body is described. It is
imposed upon by the life cycle of the earth, coded by the machinations of
power and the military machine, and submitted to a kind of cartographic
fetishizing.The problem is that we need two bodies to make these readings
work, one created by the text and one to whom the text 'happens'. We can
describe a body as lovely or unlovely, but a 'description', like an 'imposition' or a 'dehumanization', must have a body as its necessary precondition. Which is to say that existing discussions on the Song's bodies—even
Black's, which eschews a historicizing rhetoric—can slip into the rhetoric of a body that exists somewhere beyond the creative operations of the
poem's discourse. Where is the pre-existent body of the Song located, and
of what is it composed?[50]

The Song's bodies, in fact, more obviously resemble Butler's intellectual
formulation of embodiment as a discursive product. The lovers themselves,
after all, explicitly speak their bodies into being. Moreover, the Song's textual 'bodies' are in as many pieces as ours; they are messy, wet, incomplete

---

45. Black, *Artifice of Love*, p. 130.
46. Black, *Artifice of Love*, p. 131.
47. Black, *Artifice of Love*, p. 155.
48. Black, *Artifice of Love*, p. 158.
49. Black, *Artifice of Love*, p. 154.
50. Few would openly suggest that the female lover exists outside of the Song, of
course. What I am getting at is the logic that lies behind these discussions, the question
of how the text that composes the body can also impose, dissect, hide or display that
body.

portions of a perpetually undisclosed whole. The danger is that we can underplay these dynamics in the text by relying too heavily on our innate sense of bodily unity, reading the body-texts as a description of a body rather than as the discursive constitution of one. We read whole persons into the text, imposing unified wholes that collate the disparate pieces into a One that serves, primarily, to efface our experiences of the text as a kind of continuum of fragmentary organs. The body posited as prior to the poem becomes, by virtue of being posited, its own effect in the scholarly literature.

We could reframe our thinking of the Song's bodies relatively simply, however. It might be legitimate to say of the Song that 'imposition upon' and 'constitution of' seem to be simultaneous processes in the poem's presentation of the body. That is, while scholars like Landy and Exum and Black have already eloquently stressed that the Song's bodies are only text, I wish to draw attention to one particular facet of that fact: the Song's bodies are not simply texts about the body, they are texts about the articulation of bodies: they are texts about body-ing. And that makes a difference, as we shall see.

The Lover in the Song is Mae West

> Who shall conceive the horrors of my secret toil as I dabbled among the unhallowed damps of the grave or tortured the living animal to animate the lifeless clay?[51]

If we try to move away from the idea of a body posited before the text, and acknowledge that the bodies are always the result of taking a particular view of textual process, we are left with an approach that treats the images that comprize the lovers' organs not as an imposition upon already-bodies, but as a mode of becoming-bodies. And this is where we come back to space. There is no question that the body is a spatial category in its own right, but the particularly curious thing about the body parts of the Song is that their spatiality tends to be borrowed from that of the landscape, one spatial index constituted by another. This will already be perfectly plain from the texts from Song of Songs 4 and 6 that we have looked at briefly already. But we can see the same thing at work in chap. 7:

> Your two breasts are like two fawns,
>   twins of a gazelle.
> Your neck is an ivory tower.
> Your eyes are pools in Heshbon,
>   by the gate of Bath-Rabbim.[52]

---

51. Mary Shelly, *Frankenstein: Or, The Modern Prometheus* (London: Penguin, 2007 [1818]), p. 43.

52. Literally: 'by the gate of the daughter of many'.

Like a tower of Lebanon is your nose,
   overlooking Damascus.
Your head crowns you like Carmel
   and your flowing locks[53] are like purple;
   a king is held captive in the tresses.[54]

These womanly parts also 'cohere', if that is not now too troublesome a word, as a geography, a surreal and partial kingdom admittedly, but a kingdom nonetheless.

Obviously, it would be a mistake simply to posit a prior Kingdom at the expense of a Prior Body. My suggestion instead is that these two spatial indexes—body and landscaped context—are a self-constituting and self-sustaining milieu in the Song. The body is the landscape's mode of becoming, just as the landscape is the body's. In this reading, I move closer to Landy's sense of the relationship that exists between bodies and landscapes in the Song: 'a collage, a web of intricate associations and superimposed landscapes that serves to blur the distinction between the lovers, and between them and the external world'.[55] Where Landy focuses on correspondences between images in the text, however, I want to focus on the partiality of the bodily and contextual spaces, and how the partiality of the Song's world mirrors the partiality of textual signification in the Song as a whole.

To illustrate what I mean, let us turn to a particular to a particular work of Salvador Dali's. Dali's *Face of Mae West (can be used as a surrealist apartment)* (gouache on newspaper, 1935) depicts what seems on first impression to be a surrealist image of Mae West's face. As one looks harder though one sees that the image can also be taken as the view through a door into an apartment. Curved stairs form Mae West's neck, her hair is a pair of curtains, her lips are a sofa (or a sofa forms her lips?), her nose is the mantelpiece (you can tell because it has a carriage clock perched on top of it). The framed images hanging on the back wall of the 'room' are painted to resemble heavily made-up eyes. (Look closely, however, and one sees that they are not images of mascara-painted eyes at all but cityscapes that give the 'optical' illusion of being eyes; using pictures of eyes to play with visual apprehension sums the whole work up.) What seems at first glance to be a bold facial portrait turns out to be a work of quite considerable spatial complexity; Mae 'can be used as a surrealist apartment'.

---

53. The term for hair here (דלל) indicates thread on a loom elsewhere (Isa. 38.12), and signifies ' that which dangles or hangs and is descriptive of female hair, presumably unbound' (Hess, *Song of Songs*, p. 197).

54. I follow Exum here with the translation 'tresses'. Elsewhere, as she notes, the Hebrew term refers to canals through which water flows.

55. Landy, *Paradoxes of Paradise*, p. 65.

What is at issue in Dali's *Face of Mae West* is the politics of perception and inhabitation. There is no body and no apartment in the piece; there are rather two collections of incomplete patterns (one body-ish, one apartment-ish) held in a network of simultaneous connections that borrow from each other. Look at the painting in one way and the patterns coalesce into the image of a body. Change your perceptual priorities and you find yourself at the threshold of an apartment. Each 'pattern'—body and apartment—is incomplete and each requires and resists the other. The work is not simply about the potential inhabitability of the female/celebrity body, then, but about the inhabitability of the textual system; change one's perspective, one's position within the conceptual network presupposed by the work, and the image itself changes: the body dissolves as the apartment rises out of the female face, or the apartment drops away and we are looking into Mae's metropolitan eyes. Altering our relationship with the textual network between the patterns of 'place' and 'body' changes what we view.

The apartment and the face are not the only symbiotic pair implied by the work, however. The onlooker and the canvas form another self-constituting spatial milieu. Really, there is neither body nor apartment in Dali's image, since the turning of disconnected parts into a whole, or wholes, is a readerly contrivance. West's face cannot be sustained by the 'text' itself. The text only sustains a network of connections, a network open enough to invite readerly inhabitation and thus interpretative reconstitution. The body and the apartment are the products of these readerly reconstitutions. Dali throws us a world that responds to the decisions we make about inhabiting it.

My contention is that the Song's body-texts work in a similar way. What we think of as bodies in the poem are actually constellations of organs organized into bodies by the sense making operations of the reader. Like Dali's *Mae West*, the component parts cohere into a recognizable 'pattern' only because of the relative position adopted by the onlooker. To alter one's reading position is to alter the image. Organs are being heaped up and spread out to form a landscape in one reading of the Song, and the landscape is being fashioned into a collection of bodily parts in the other. In neither, though, is a 'body' being 'described'. Instead of bodies—systemic unities operating as One—the text has two mutually reinforcing but incomplete patterns: one pattern of organs and one pattern of images (the most prominent and persistent of which are the spatial images taken from the Israelite landscape). These two patterns are mutually reinforcing. They operate in parallel through a network of literary connections and equivalencies.

Becoming Body

While Dali's portrait/landscape of Mae West represents this mutually reinforcing nexus of relationships for us nicely, it is necessary too to talk of the politics implied by this kind of bodily formation. For this we come back to Deleuze, Guattari and their BwO. The BwO, Challenger's open and dynamic constellation of foldable images, helps us map the forces of attraction and repulsion by which these two schemas are held together in the text. The BwO gives us a vocabulary and syntax for the written body that does not lapse back into a sense of the body as a discrete categorical *a priori* concept. This is another way of saying that Deleuze and Guattari offer us a discussion on the body which attempts to explore embodiment outside of the binding categorization of The Organism, of which the Song scholar's 'prior bodies' are, I would argue, an archetype. Particularly significant in contextualizing the BwO, however, is Deleuze and Guattari's approach to the idea of 'becomings'.

Deleuze and Guattari prioritize becomings in much the way Butler does, arguing for a reversal of the traditional kinds of relationships and models of agency that we usually assume to be at work in the world. Like Butler, Deleuze argues that individuals are formed through their performances of actions; from a nexus of becomings we organize Beings.[56] Thus for Deleuze and Guattari literature has more of a constitutive role than an imitative one. The power of literature, they argue, is not the power of signification or the power to describe human experience but the power to wrench individual human perception out from its usual moorings; it is the gift of an alternative perspective. When we read we must surrender to another pair of eyes, when we read, they say, we must re-become. Literature thereby *produces* us. By extension there is a danger or limitation when we read as though literature *signifies* because we overlook this re-becoming and its potential to transform us. This is the same limitation we succumb to when we permit the positing of a body prior to the Song: embodiment becomes something that is reported rather than something the reader undergoes. Claire Colbrook explains Deleuze and Guattari's position on these issues in a fairly direct fashion:

> *Moby Dick* can (and has) been read as a novel about the search for human meaning, such that Ahab imagines that if only he conquers Moby Dick he will achieve integrity, sense and order… Deleuze and Guattari typically read literature against such manifestly interpretative (or hermeneutic) methods. Indeed, they select just those authors, such as Kafka and Melville, who have been read as producing the image or sign of meaning that lies forever

56. This is contrary to Freud, who understands desire as the operation of sexual relationships between people. Deleuze sees individuals as being formed by means of the organization of desire; the Oedipus myth is not a representation of familial dynamics for Deleuze, familial dynamics come into being as a result of Oedipus, and stories like it. See Claire Colbrook's insightful summary (and Deleuze and Guattari need all the summarizing that can be mustered) in Colbrook, *Gilles Deleuze* (New York: Routledge, 2001), p. 141.

out of reach. Instead of reading literature as a quest for meaning and interpretation, Deleuze and Guattari argue that literature shows that literature is
about affects and intensities. It is only the reactive literary critic who wants to
interpret Melville's whale and Kafka's insect as 'signifiers' of some ultimate
meaning. It is always possible to read literature as an art of recognition, as
about 'ourselves' and 'the' human search or meaning. This art of interpretation for hermeneutics requires that we 'overcode' literature, seeing each text
as an expression or representation of some underlying meaning...[57]

Essentially, this same premise underlies those existing works on the Song
that Black discusses, namely those attempts to 'decode' the body, or to
figure the correct interpretative approach to the body images. Only the reactive critic wants to read the Song's bodies for what they might mean.[58] Colbrook goes on:

> Alternatively, literature can be read for what it produces, for its transfor-
> mations. Instead of reading the 'animals' of literature as symbols—what do
> they mean?—we can see the animal as a possible opening for new styles of
> perception. In this case, becoming-animal would indicate a tendency in lit-
> erature, and art, of rendering perception open to what is not itself. Literature
> would not be about the expression of meaning but the *production* of sense,
> allowing new perceptions and new worlds.[59]

It is perhaps not unreasonable to suggest that we read the bodies of the
Song not for what they signify but for what they produce, not to interpret
them but to map the new perceptive worlds they allow, and to trace the
blazing lifelines that lead out of what is intelligible and into what is farther
off. This is what I have been edging towards so far. What realities are produced by the text? What is the text's approach to bodily space? How do the

57. Colbrook, *Deleuze*, p. 137.
58. Soulen and Falk are potential exceptions here, since they argue that the writing is
designed to evoke the same joy that the male lover/poet experiences. That is, they seem
to argue that the text exists to evoke a particular perspective. The problem with their particular deployment of this idea is that they tend to un-read, or disengage, with the Song's
imagery, thus turning this 'becoming-animal' (becoming-Other) of the text into a transcendental meaning all of its own; for Soulen and Falk it is the *author's* original feelings
that we are supposed to be 'discovering'; Soulen 'The *wasfs* of the Song of Songs and
Hermeneutics', pp. 222-24; Falk, *Love Lyrics from the Bible*, pp. 80-87.
59. Colbrook, *Deleuze*, p. 137. The men themselves put this idea a little more exuberantly: 'For it is through writing that you become animal [/anomalous], it is through colour
that you become imperceptible, it is through music that you become hard and memory-
less, simultaneously animal and imperceptible: in love. But art is never an end in itself; it
is only a tool for blazing life lines, in other words, all of those real becomings that are not
produced only *in* art, and all of those active escapes that do not consist of fleeing *into* art,
taking refuge in art, and all of those positive deterritorializations that never reterritorialize
on art, but instead sweep it away with them towards the realms of the asignifying, asubjec-
tive, and faceless' (Deleuze and Guattari, *A Thousand Plateaus*, p. 208).

processes of embodiment in the text go about constituting the bodiliness of reading? These questions necessitate our inevitable return to Deleuze and Guattari's BwO, which explains and experiments with the textual bodies in ways that fit the Song surprisingly well.

Sediment as Syntax: The Body without Organs

Deleuze and Guattari, in *A Thousand Plateaus* in particular, treat the body as a compact interweaving of processes, a continuum of becoming that loosely resembles the formulations proposed by Spivak and Butler that we looked at a little earlier.[60] Mariam Fraser and Monica Greco sum up Deleuze and Guattari's dizzyingly complex approach to the body:

> The body for Deleuze is not a unified entity, nor is it organized around a central governor. It is not defined by intentionality, biology or by psyche. It is not a property of the subject, nor is it an expression of subjectivity. It is not a locus of meaning. Indeed, a body is not to be deciphered or interpreted at all. Instead, the convergences between bodies (whether they be human or non-human, organic or not, natural or artificial) are there to be made and surveyed: mapped. For Deleuze is a cartographer, who situates all bodies on the same flat ontological plane (the plane of immanence), and defines them by what he calls longitude and latitude... Deleuze argues that a body must be understood not in terms of a form or function, but with reference instead to its relations of speed or slowness (longitude), and to what it can do, by its capacity to affect and to be affected (latitude).[61]

If the body cannot be interpreted, it can be mapped instead. The body does not have to be situated against a world of meaning since it can be traced as a nexus of relationships-between. This mappable body, opened up and explored as a complex interweaving of processes, is the Body without Organs, the BwO. Let us return to Professor Challenger for a reiteration of the sketch of the ultimate BwO that we began with:

> The Earth—the Deterritorialized, the Glacial, the giant Molecule—is a body without organs. This body without organs is permeated by unformed unstable matters, by flows in all directions, by free intensities or nomadic singularities, by mad or transitory particles. That however was not the question at hand. For there simultaneously occurs upon the earth a very important,

---

60. As Deleuze puts it, 'the important thing is the principle of the simultaneous unity and variety of the stratum: isomorphism of forms but no correspondence; identity of elements or components but no identity of compound substances'; the body is, for Deleuze and Guattari, a 'connection of desires, [a] conjunction of flows, [a] continuum of intensities' on which a variety of activities are played out (Deleuze and Guattari, *A Thousand Plateaus*, p. 46).

61. Mariam Fraser and Monica Greco, 'What is a Body', in Mariam Fraser and Monica Greco (eds.), *The Body: A Reader* (New York: Routledge, 2001), p. 45.

inevitable phenomenon that is beneficial in many respects and unfortunate in many others: stratification. Strata are Layers, Belts. They consist of giving form to matters, of imprisoning intensities or locking singularities into systems of resonance or redundancy, of producing upon the body of the earth molecules large and small and organizing them into molar aggregates. Strata are acts of capture, they are like 'black holes' or occlusions striving to seize whatever comes within their reach. They operate by coding and territorialization upon the earth…the strata are judgments of God: stratification in general is the entire system of the judgment of God (but the earth, or the body without organs, constantly eludes that judgment, flees and becomes destratified, decoded, deterritorialized).[62]

The BwO is a continuum of all entities as though they were laid out flat in a single spectrum. What we might call 'bodies'—animal, vegetable, mineral—are the strata in that spectrum. They are not discrete wholes but the concentration and capture of phenomena into organized 'Belts', or zones of intensity. What we call bodies, entities, categories and the like are in fact the effects of these acts of capture, just as we have seen with regard to the Prior Body in Song scholarship. We draw lines around certain interrelationships and call them discrete wholes, or 'Organisms'. But one can break apart these organisms by suspending, bit by bit, one's expectation of the system that circumscribes them:

> Dismantling the organism has never meant killing yourself, but rather opening the body to connections that presuppose an entire assemblage, circuits, conjunctions, levels and thresholds, passages and distributions of intensity, and territories and deterritorializations measured with the craft of a surveyor.[63]

One can zoom into the Organism and see the contrivance of the 'strata' that make it up; the formations of organs and that have been folded into the boundaries of the 'Organism'. One can also zoom out to look at Earth and see the human body itself as yet another kind of 'organ' in a wider stratum—of which each body is only a tiny, singular part. One can try to perform both of these imaginative camera moves simultaneously, pushing the body out of its place within a codified strata and pulling it into other possible linkages and connections. We can thus come to think of the body on the edge of its other numerous possibilities and dependencies, the connections it might form, or might form part of. Or, as Deleuze and Guattari put it, the body swings 'between the surfaces that stratify it and the plane that sets it free'. The BwO is always about to be folded into an Organism, and always about to be unfurled as a cosmos.

62. Deleuze and Guattari, *A Thousand Plateaus*, p. 45.
63. Deleuze and Guattari, *A Thousand Plateaus*, p. 177.

It is the BwO that is stratified. It swings between two poles, the surfaces of stratification into which it is recoiled, on which it submits to judgment, and the plane of consistency in which it unfurls and opens up to experimentation. If the BwO is a limit, if one is forever attaining it, it is because behind each stratum, encased in it, there is always another stratum.[64]

The BwO is not antagonistic to *organs* but to the organization of organs into an Organism. The Organism is, on the face of it, just another line of 'sediment' on the BwO of the Earth, an arbitrary act of capture.

However, in practice the Organism is not just another stratum. Deleuze and Guattari stress that because the Organism sets itself up as *the* legitimate form of relations, the unit to which the world-wide-map of the BwO should be scaled, one should be naturally suspicious of it. For Deleuze and Guattari the Organism is actually the result of power relations that legitimize certain kinds of relationship. Deleuze and Guattari term these power relations 'Theology'. The Organism is Theology's product and its staunchest champion.

The system of the judgement of God, the theological system, is precisely the operation of He who makes an organism, an organization of organs called the organism because He cannot bear the BwO, because He pursues it and rips it apart so He can be first, and have the organism be first... The BwO howls: 'they've made me an organism! They've wrongfully folded me! They've stolen my body!'[65]
[He replies.] you will be organized, you will be an organism, you will articulate your body—otherwise you're just depraved. You will be signifier and signified, interpreter and interpreted—otherwise you're just deviant. You will be subject, nailed, down as one, a subject of the enunciation recoiled into a subject of the statement—otherwise you're just a tramp.[66]

In this passage the BwO howls in response to the abuse of being 'folded' into a form—an Organism—in order to be interpreted. Its body has been 'stolen' by the theological system through the Organism's circumscription of it. The consequence of the BwO not conforming to this recoiling, its clinging to permeability and openness, is the charge of illegitimacy. The open network is epistemologically slutty: deviant, delinquent, 'a tramp'. In short, the BwO becomes an open thoroughfare of connections at the expense of the notions of the closed, original, virginal One. Its hymen has been broken.

Crucially, in this passage the theological violence the Organism directs at the strata is manifest in its drive to be posited as prior to the very discourse that gives rise to it. This links Deleuze to Butler, or at least to her suspicion of the transcendental status that is so often afforded biological systems. By extension, the Prior Body of Song scholarship comes to resemble the

64. Deleuze and Guattari, *A Thousand Plateaus*, p. 176.
65. Deleuze and Guattari, *A Thousand Plateaus*, p. 176.
66. Deleuze and Guattari, *A Thousand Plateaus*, p. 176.

Organism and its Theology. The Prior Body is a Theological product that poses as a precondition in order to maintain its primacy as a conceptual category. The Prior Body is just another kind of theological allegory.[67]

The BwO is an attempt to apprehend the body, all bodies, outside of the controlling demands of the Organism. The BwO is a body where systemicity and the expectations of scale have been suspended so the body can be viewed afresh: as a set of processes, and as an open network of wider possible linkages and potential chains of meaning. Bodies do not have limits, they are not discrete categories. Bodies are loci where the connections-between—the relationships that exist between all objects—are particularly intense. The body is one zone in a potential cosmos-wide constellation of material. The BwO is that body poised, frozen on the threshold of every action (becoming) that it might be able to undergo. Brian Massumi sketches if for us:

> Call it a 'body': an endless weaving together of singular states, each of which is an integration of one or more impulses. Call each of the body's different vibratory regions [bits of the body that 'do' stuff] a 'zone of intensity'. Look at the zone of intensity from the point of view of the action it produces. From that perspective, call it an 'organ'. Look at it again from the point of view of the organ's favourite actions [tasting, seeing, defecating, arousal etc.], and call it an 'erogenous zone'. Imagine the body in suspended animation: intensity = 0. Call that the 'body without Organs'. Think of the body

---

67. As Black's work on the interpretative traditions surrounding the text indicates, the Song's bodies are, like Deleuze and Guattari's BwO, constantly in danger from the claims of this Theological allegory. By which I do not simply mean that the proponents of the religious allegory appropriate the lovers along with the rest of the poem (though they do), but that the Song's lovers are most often subjected to interpretative strictures that seek to organize the lovers into an Organism. This is done it seems in order to render the openable lover as a closed, literary construct: a body. Black's history of interpretation outlines various modes of circumscription that we might call Theological on these grounds, the cultural/contextual readings of Keel, Pope, and Fox, the romantic and idealized readings of Munro and Goulder, the evocative readings of Falk and Soulen. Each tries to organize the strata of the bodies, and one could quite readily lend these ideologically secular interpretative traditions the voice of Deleuze and Guattari's imagined deity: 'you will be organized, you will be an organism, you will articulate your body—otherwise you're just depraved. You will be signifier and signified, interpreter and interpreted—otherwise you're just deviant. You will be subject, nailed down as one, a subject of the enunciation recoiled into a subject of the statement—otherwise you're just a tramp' (*A Thousand Plateaus*, p. 176). The Prior Body of Song scholarship, as a theological product, thereby comes into being like all theological products: by being pincered between two strata until the pressure makes it a Thing. It is by this logic that Deleuze and Guattari reason that 'God is a Lobster'. (In fact, since this theological pressure seems to be networked into all perception, able to boom into whatever context it wishes, one might go so far as to say that God is a kind of mixture of the lobster with the telephone: Dali again.)

without organs as the body outside any determinate state, poised for any action in its repertory; this is the body from its point the view of its potential, or virtuality.[68]

The organs outside categorization are nexuses of relationships-in-potential. The BwO prizes the possibilities of the organ, and understands the organs as a series of intensities of virtual connectedness that come into being by relating. The organs of the BwO are concentrated might-bes, they might allow a range of possible becomings. To make a BwO is to explore all those lines of flight.

> We treat the BwO as the full egg before the extension of the organism and the organization of the organs, before the formation of the strata...because the organs appear and function here only as pure intensities... No organ is constant as regards either function or position...sex organs sprout anywhere... rectums open, defecate and close...the entire organism changes colour and consistency in split second adjustments. The tantric egg.[69]

While the overlap here between geophysical and physiological terminology makes the use of the BwO in reading the body/land-texts in the Song attractive from a rhetorical viewpoint, Deleuze and Guattari's attempts to make us reassess our relationship with the world and their descriptions of the BwO's own resistances and rejections of signification, seem to produce the same kind of perceptive worlds that are produced in the Song of Songs. In other words, the reality of the body that the Song enacts and the modes of becoming-body that we undergo through our engagement with the text, is so similar to the kind of bodies described by Deleuze and Guattari as to beg an interreading. This is not to say that the Song's approach to the body is the same as Deleuze and Guattari's, nor that one allows for an *interpretation* of the other, but rather that an *exploring* of the Song with the BwO in mind would seem to open up and articulate the mutuality of landed spatiality and bodily space in the biblical text in interesting ways. To begin the process of mapping the BwO alongside the LwO, the Lover without Organs, let us experiment with some of Deleuze and Guattari's texts alongside key aspects of the Song's body-texts, beginning with this notion of the geographical giant.

Flashes of Tellurian Flesh

> It is the BwO that is stratified. It swings between two poles, the surfaces of stratification into which it is recoiled, on which it submits to judgment, and the plane of consistency in which it unfurls and opens up to experimentation.

---

68. Brian Massumi, *A User's Guide to Capitalism and Schizophrenia: Deviations from Deleuze and Guattari* (Cambridge, MA: MIT Press, 1992), p. 70.
   69. Deleuze and Guattari, *A Thousand Plateaus*, p. 170.

> If the BwO is a limit, if one is forever attaining it, it is because behind each
> stratum, encased in it, there is always another stratum.[70]

Connections between bodily space and geographical space are already well established by scholarship on the Song. As Albert Cook puts it, 'the many geographical metaphors (Kedar, Heshbon, Tirzah, En-gedi, etc.), by their repetition, persistently suggest identifying the contour of the country with the body of the beloved'.[71]

The importance of the land in the body-texts is pushed to its most breathtaking extremes by the geographical allegorizing of Robert and Tournay, who read the Song's bodies according to a strict topographical schema. For Robert and Tournay, each and every part of the textual woman is made to correspond to a real-world geographical landmark of some kind or other. In Song of Songs 7, for instance, the woman's feet (v. 2) are said to allude to a return from exile (cf. Isa. 11.15) and thus represent the Nile; her hips (thighs, v. 2), a little further north, are synonymous with the coastline. The navel (or vulva) of v. 3 represents, through geographical approximation, Jerusalem (the 'navel' of the world).[72] Pope, who understandably thinks little of this geographical allegorizing, points out that Robert and Tournay's reading really does not work with the actual topography of the region. For one thing the proposed 'schema' places the eyes oddly out of line with the neck and head (Pope, *Song of Songs*, p. 626). Though 'with sufficient devotion', Pope notes, 'it would be possible to find an allegorical explanation, geographical or otherwise, for eccentric eyes' (p. 626). Pope has a point. Robert and Tournay's reading really tells us more about their own topographical preoccupations than it tells us about either the text or the 'bodies' contained therein. But while this unusual reading of the woman's body as a complete geography may present us with serious problems—not to mention a great deal of eisegesis—it is worth remembering that the idea of a complete body has its own problems. The eyes, noses and mouths of the Song are already eccentric, whether Pope likes it or not.

Black is no more convinced than Pope of its accuracy or veracity, but she helpfully equates the overall effect of Robert and Tournay's reading with a kind of cubist disintegration that serves to underscore the grotesqueries

---

70. Deleuze and Guattari, *A Thousand Plateaus*, p. 176.

71. Cook, *The Root of The Thing*, p. 127.

72. The two gazelle-breasts must, Robert and Tournay reason, also corresponds to an actual location. They become, somewhat implausibly, the mountains Ebal and Gerizim: Le contexte nous invite, ici encore, à découvrir sous l'image en question quelque caractéristique physique de la Palestine. Comme tout à l'heure il était question de Jérusalem assimilée au nombril, et de la montagne de Juda figurant le ventre, comme par ailleurs l'auteur remonte du Sud au Nord, on serait tenté de voir dans les seins l'Ébal et le Gerizim' (Robert and Tournay, *Le cantique des cantiques*, pp. 192-94).

of the reading process itself: 'Robert's attempts to link the woman to the land in effect further tie her to it, and sometimes more grotesquely than the lover originally did. With Robert's reading, the body is cut up and spread across the land, a little like the victimized woman of Judges 19, and reassembled, Picasso-like, as the pieces are gathered into a geographical portrait'. [73] Black's problem with Robert and Tournay's reading, then, is, like Pope's, the overzealous enthusiasm for body/land connections. In tying her so closely to the land, Robert and Tournay make both the female lover's body and the lovers' landscape too disparate to cohere realistically.

But is our allegiance to 'realism' not precisely what Black wants to circumvent in her study? If expectations of what a body *should* look like are objectionable by Black's reckoning, why is the expectation of what a landscape should look like not similarly problematic? While there is indeed a problem with arguing for total historical/anatomical coherence between body and land in the Song, Robert and Tournay seem to be edging towards a counter-reading of the idea that the woman constitutes a landscape in the text: that we might instead read the landscape as constitutive of the woman. We need not necessarily assume that an accurate geographical picture will emerge in order to undertake such a reading, nor that the body parts need be effaced in order that the landscape be prized. Rather we need only assume that the male can find his love everywhere in his world, encased within any plateau he cares to give attention to. 'Within each stratum, encased in it, is always another stratum.'[74] Or, in other words, within each organizational schema there is always another one waiting to break free.[75]

73. Black, *Artifice of Love*, p. 156.
74. Deleuze and Guattari, *A Thousand Plateaus*, p. 176.
75. The disparate and obscure references to the land can, after all, provide a counter-schema to that of physiological ordering which I looked at earlier. An often overlooked aspect of the body-texts is the movement from 'high' images to lowland ones. Deckers mentions this in terms of the lovers' movements in the poem more generally: 'Close reading shows that this description moves from spatial high to low and from low to high. In the Chant of Beauty (1.15–4.1a) as well as in the Chant of the Bride (4.1b–6.7), the description of the subject moving through the landscape is always from spatial high, asking her to walk with him through the fields (2.8-13); and the bride comes down from Lebanon and arrives in a garden (4.8–5.1). Furthermore, in both chants the description of the beloved's body, the so-called *wasf*, proceeds from high to low (4.1-5; 5.10-16; 6.4-7)' (M. Deckers, 'The Structure of the Song of Songs', in Brenner, [ed.], *A Feminist Companion to the Song of Songs*, pp. 185-89 [186]). Whatever one might think of applying this notion to the text as a whole—and it seems to me to depend on assuming a good many things about both the lovers' placements and their orientations in the textual landscape—the idea that the imagery pertaining to the land moves from high to low in the body-texts seems to bear out. (At least, it is no more misleading than the idea of strict physiological ordering in these texts.) In chap. 4, the lover moves from mountainous images to lowland lily fields via (mid-height?) architecture; in chap. 6 the lover starts at the hilltop settlements of Jerusalem and

Often in these body-texts, the woman's features emerge out of the landscape in an uncomplicated way. In 4.6, for instance, we come to 'see' this woman because of a pair of aromatic mountains:

> Until the day breathes
> and the shadows flee,
> I will make my way to the mountain of myrrh
> and the hill of frankincense.

Similarly, in 7.6 the male lover tops off his lover with Carmel ('Your head crowns you like Carmel'), where her head is poetically fashioned out of the mountainside. A verse earlier in 7.5, the male uses architecture and features of the landscape to evoke a nose, a neck, and eyes.[76] This last equivalency is all the more direct since עין means both eye and water source in Hebrew.[77] The waters of the eye flow directly from the water table. Even the architectural features that the male mentions—the ivory tower in 7.4, the tower of Lebanon in 7.6, and the 'tower of David' in 4.4—are as suggestive of *landscape* as they are of masonry. These towers tend not to appear as shelters with stairases and buttresses, but as landmarks apprehended from without and as part of the vista (sometimes they even boast a fine view).[78] These architectural features do not simply evoke their structure but a conspicuity and function within a wider realm.[79]

Tirzah and moves down Gilead's slopes (again), and in chap. 7, where the discourse starts at the feet, the images move in reverse from the harvests of the land, up to towering architecture and hilltop lookouts and then on to the great Mount Carmel (which Robert and Tournay would stress is not only the highest image but the most northerly as well, a kind of headland). The landscape is just as ordered as the 'body'. This idealized landscape does not adhere to geography, perhaps, but it does not adhere to the laws of physics or the rules of supply and demand either, as the ivory tower of 7.4 indicates. Why insist on realistic maps while positing unfeasible economics?

76. Heshbon is indeed well supplied with water and archeological excavations have uncovered evidence of reservoirs, while there is disagreement as to whether the nose in 7.6 is represented by a 'mountain-tower or a towering mountain'; see Pope, *Song of Songs*, pp. 236-37.

77. Following the Vulgate [*piscinae*], the KJV has them as being for fish, see Murphy, *Song of Songs*, p. 186.

78. This is partly due to a very loose sense of perspective implied by some of the images themselves. As Landy writes: 'Your nose is like the tower of Lebanon, overlooking Damascus' is one of the most notorious images in the Song. Marvin Pope (1976: 627) makes the point well: 'If our lady is superhuman in nature and size, then the dismay about her towering or mountainous nose disappears as the perspective and proportions fall into focus'. It is not a huge nose, but well-proportioned and slender as a tower, seen from a distance, against the background of Lebanon and the prospect of Damascus. Scale is provided by the context (from this point of view of the nose is rather tiny); it is also that of the *wasf* as a whole' (*Paradoxes of Paradise*, p. 79).

79. This tends to give rise to readings of the woman's body as a reflection of a broad

Language sometimes ties the woman's body to the earth in ways that our English translations of the images do not. Take, for instance, the crimson mouth of 4.3. As Black writes, 'the noun used for her lips (שׂפה) might also be translated as "edge", as in the bank of river, or the shore of the sea…in short they are the markers of territories that are being challenged or in need of defense, and in whose interest blood is sometimes spilt'.[80] She goes on to point out that in 4.3 מדבר is also used to denote the woman's mouth. 'There is a pun here', she says, 'for the noun also means desert or wilderness'.[81] The ideas of topographical liminality and of the wilderness lurk behind this image, it seems. Black takes her cue from Fox, who writes of the spatial peculiarities of 4.3 in some detail:

> *Midbareyk na'weh* [in 4.3] alone is an adjectival predication, and a rather pale one at that, in a series of vivid sensual metaphors. Furthermore, the poet, who elsewhere uses common words for parts of the body, here chooses a strange word for mouth, *midbar*, a hapax legomenon apparently meaning 'speaking place' or the like. Both these peculiarities are explained when we recognize a double pun here. *Midbar* can be taken as a 'wilderness', and *na'weh* can be heard as *naweh*, 'habitation', an area contrasted with *midbar.*

and inclusive landscape on which the individual items are smaller, almost toy-like objects. This is most potently realized in Ginsburg's translation of the difficult 4.4: 'Thy neck is like the tower of David, reared for the builder's model' (Christian D. Ginsburg, *The Song of Songs: Commentary, Historical and Critical* [London: Longman, Brown, et al., 1857], p. 156). For more on this issue, see Ian Morley and Colin Renfew (eds.), *The Archaeology of Measurement* (Cambridge: Cambridge University Press, 2010). Jack Sasson understands the woman to be lying down, like a three-dimensional human model of the landscape, by virtue of these map-like qualities of the text: 'What if these eyes watch her lie on a couch and then take up a position at her feet? What if they begin gazing toward her head, from a position level with her sandaled feet? Staring at these sandals, the eyes will first discover that the woman has not cast away the tools of her trade. They will then admire her thigh, not for its power and firmness, but its jeweled roundness, perfect in its confection. They will catch the circular edge of the navel, the raised heap of the belly and the velvety browns of the nipples. Of the neck, they will perceive only its ivory hue, but because the head appears so distant, they will imagine that a tower stretches to separate it from the torso. The proportion for each feature is, so far, just perfect. Inspecting the head, our sight will notice that the woman's own eyes are yet to be seen for, like sunken pools, they are decidedly not the most prominent feature of that imposing head. From the angle and direction of our gaze, however, the nose now looms tower-like, far above the surrounding features. Its nostrils seem cavernous, like huge orifices that stare into far away distances. This vision, in turn, overwhelms all that lay behind it and forces our imagined eyes to leave the body in search of remaining shapes. They peer at the pillow; and there, reaching out like tentacles, are the shocks of the indigo hair, ready to entangle the finest among Israel' (Jack Sasson, 'A Major Contribution to Song of Songs Scholarship', *JAOS* 107 (1987), pp. 733-39 [737-38]).

80. Black, *Artifice of Love*, p. 135.

81. Black, *Artifice of Love*, p. 135.

> In conjunction with *midbar, na'weh* refers to an oasis... Thus the youth
> is saying, in playful hyperbole: you are so lovely, so flawless, that what-
> ever part of you might in comparison with other parts be reckoned a wilder-
> ness, as somehow defective—even that 'wilderness' is an oasis, fresh and
> refreshing.[82]

Fox's comments capture the spatial undercurrents in v. 3 rather neatly. These
undercurrents arise from the poet's curious choice of words and images. So,
even in what is arguably the least geographical verse of 4.1-7, it is possible to pick up (along with several commentators—Hess notes these spatial
referents as well as Fox and Black)[83] the presence of boundaries, and of the
marking out of territories, and of the wilderness.

The spatial and topographical images used to compose the woman's
body build up into a kind of merismus. In chap. 4, for example, the woman
is comprized of goats on a mountainside, the washing of flocks (Keel suggests a waterhole by extension),[84] a mouth that doubles as a desert, natural
produce, the tower of David, gazelles feeding on lilies, a mountain of frankincense, and a mountain of myrrh. In chap. 6 her beauty is as the cities of
Tirzah and Jerusalem, the once southern and northern capitals respectively.
Her body in chap. 6 is largely a repeat of chap. 4, though this time the lover
goes so far as to evoke the luminaries that wheel above him: 'who is this
that looks forth like the dawn, fair as the moon, bright as the sun' (6.10). In
chap. 7 this woman is comprized of various harvests from the land (wheat,
wine, jewels), as well as an ivory tower, pools in Heshbon, a tower of Lebanon overlooking Damascus, and Carmel. As the images collide we begin to
see that the land is as encompassing an image as the woman herself. Landy
sums it up well:

> The image is that of the kingdom, the woman as the land of Israel. The
> images are topographical, even where the referent, like the ivory tower, is
> unknown. Together they compose a collective portrait—the tower of Leba-
> non sticks up like a nose, the head protrudes like Carmel, the eyes glitter
> like pools [of Heshbon], from a bird's eye perspective. The localities are
> all northern and peripheral; geographical inference would situate the wom-
> an's pudenda around the centre of the country, near Jerusalem. The images
> give an impression of the life of the country—the watchful tower, the pop-
> ulous city, the exploitation of the sea. The military outpost in the far north,
> the remote city on the edge of the desert, the uncompromising headland,
> assert boundaries, the limits of the land, and also the possibility of influ-
> ence beyond it, for example in the sea, or through trade, [and] the busy traf-
> fic of Heshbon...[85]

---

82. Fox, *Song of Songs*, p. 130.
83. Hess, *Song of Songs*, p. 132.
84. Keel, *Song of Songs*, p. 142.
85. Landy, *Paradoxes of Paradise*, p. 82.

While not all the images in the body-texts are geophysical (the pomegran-ates of 4.3, for example, are not particularly spatial images, nor are the doves of 4.1), all the images tend to invoke a something of a living con-text. In 7.3, for instance, when the male creates the woman's belly out of 'a heap of wheat', her body becomes part of the land's harvest; her navel, full of wine a stanza earlier, is secreting very pastoral juices. As Landy puts it, 'The image of the Beloved as the land of Israel is a specialization of the image of the woman as earth or earth-mother'.[86]

Put this way, the landscape from which this woman is composed is just as encompassing as the body it forms. This landscape is a fantasy, natu-rally. Israel, and the specific features that the lover mentions, no more fits together like this than gardens dissolve into cities. The poem is not map-ping a landscape but conceiving of a deterritorialized landscape. The lov-er's geomancy is done with willful disregard for the maps in the backs of our Bibles, true, but it is fashioning a world with its own kind of coher-ence.[87] The bodies in the Song, as LwOs, thus swing between two poles, the bodily organization into which they are recoiled and on which they submit to numerous interpretations and translations on the one hand, and, on the other, a plane of consistency on which they unfurl and open up to, and as, the world. The Hebrew speaking male character who composes these texts speaks of the Hebrew landscape in his evocations of a love. He seems to be constantly seeing his lover as he looks at his world. Her body is that open, and the landscape he creates is that available for poetic experimentation. Or, to put it slightly differently again: the body and the landscape do not function as discrete entities here. There is only a contin-uum of plateaus in the text, a series of nexuses of relationships, jumping off places for a myriad of interpretative leaps. These can be used to fold the landscape into an Organism (the Prior Body), or to unfurl the organism into a landscape of the kind Landy alludes to, and moreover, of the kind Deleuze and Guattari describe:

> Dismantling the organism has never meant killing yourself, but rather opening the body to connections that presuppose an entire assemblage, circuits, conjunctions, levels and thresholds, passages and distributions of intensity, and territories and deterritorializations measured with the craft of a surveyor.[88]

86. Landy, *Paradoxes of Paradise*, p. 82.
87. The synthesizing of landscape is nicely summed up in a question posed by Leo Krinetzki, who rhetorically asks, Du bist eine echte Tochter des Landes, in dem du geboren und aufgewachsen bist, in dir vereinigen sich alle Vorzüge dieses Landes in letzer, beglückendster Synthese? Krinetzki, *Das Hohe Lied*, p. 216.
88. Deleuze and Guattari, *A Thousand Plateaus*, p. 177.

Measuring Territories and Deterritorializations

If we return to Song of Songs 7 we can see how the female body of the Song also emerges, like the BwO, as a series of complex deterritorializations and reterritorializations which 'can be measured with the craft of a surveyor'. For starters, the Song's textual organs exist as part of a topographical network that transcends the boundaries of the body itself:

> Your two breasts are like two fawns,
>   twins of a gazelle.
> Your neck is an ivory tower.
> Your eyes are pools in Heshbon,
>   by the gate of Bath-Rabbim.
> Your nose is like a tower of Lebanon
>   overlooking Damascus.
> Your head crowns you like Carmel
> And your flowing locks are like purple;
>   a king is held captive in the tresses.

Here the eyes are not just pools, they are pools *in Heshbon*. The nose is not simply like a non-descript tower but is 'of Lebanon'. It enjoys views over Damascus. The toponyms do not 'apply' to the woman so much as build up to form a collection of images in which the male discerns his beloved's face. In other words, these apparently redundant features in the verses suggest a wider network within which the organs are being delineated. What does Bath Rabbim 'attach' to on the body? What does Damascus denote? How would a nose overlooking another city differ from the woman's nose here? Would a nose overlooking the Bronx be distinctive from this one? If so, how? The pools in Heshbon have been uprooted from their context by the male's perception, and yet they retain their nominal connectedness, the lines of flight that lead us back to the geophysical world they have been extracted from; they are still near Bath Rabbim.

These bits of the land do not 'become' organs or parts thereof, but they are still involved in the organ's constitution in the text (they cannot simply be divorced from the Song). And how we figure that connection contributes to the organ, even if we cannot definitively say *how*. These extraneous details tie the body into a broader spatial network and imply a wider world from which the images are drawn, and, importantly, *to which they might be returned*. The body may be formed as an open network of meaning, but it forms part of another open network: the landscape. The male's view of the connectedness of the landscape is transposed, turned into the organs of the woman. She rises out of the land to meet him, and us, as a mode of his perception.[89] And the landscape, similarly, is laid down as a territorialization of

---

89. Whereas this is particularly easy to apprehend in these topographical verses, the same general principle holds for other kinds of images. The phrase 'two fawns, twins

his desire. Female embodiment is not framed in the Song in terms of a living system. She is not a bodily subject, nor a bodily object, but rather a network of intensities, defined by axes, vectors, gradients and thresholds that might be re-organized at will into wider assemblages. Her organs are, in Deleuze and Guattari's terms, pure intensities.

Like the organs in a BwO the woman's parts are also frozen just beyond the realm of functionality. Whatever the pools-as-eyes are for, they are not for seeing. The woman's eyes, like her body, are not unities but are formed from linguistic and metaphorical equivalencies: like her hair, teeth, lips, etc., the woman's eyes emerge as open networks of meaning: connections between images that must be negotiated. For instance, the images of pools and eyes could be connected in all kinds of ways to give rise to the organ. They might be linked by wetness, by cavity, or to the imagery of military encampments, or to drinking, to fishing, to reflection, to the biblical trope of the sexual female at the well. But however we figure these reservoirs, it is difficult to see them as having ocular uses. The tower of the next line might be employed because of its height, its beauty, its colour, or its display of awesome architectural prowess, but it certainly does not smell anything. Towers, however stunning, do not have olfactory functions. It is difficult to know what to *do* with the female bodies in the Song of Songs because they never function *as* bodies in any meaningful way.[90] So, while the organs in the Song are not obvious visual cues—as their various reading traditions aptly demonstrate—they do not perform their 'favourite' bodily functions either.

These organs are caught on the cusp of various meanings; they are zones from which one could 'read' in various unorthodox directions. The organs of the lover are suspended as an intense nexus of potential relationships. Favourite 'lines of flight' (connections, relationships that define) have been employed to 'decode' them, to, in other words, form a bodily constellation

of a gazelle' (v. 4), implies a life cycle: a male deer and his—ultimately satisfactory— copulation with the gazelle, a gestation and a double labour. That is, the breasts of the woman become an extension of the processes of the gazelle's body. The breasts retain these numerous connections, and others alongside them, betraying a world beyond the body, a world that has been summoned up in order to bring this woman into being. The problem with the bodily images is not how to begin 'translating' them, but where to stop. Similar contextual networks hold for other non-topographical images too: the shorn ewes of 4.2 (who have not miscarried); the threads of 4.3 (dyed and spun); the cut/ split pomegranate of 4.3; the mining/cutting, harvesting and grape pressing in the earlier part of Song 7. The connections-between, the Other spaces and associations, remain in the text but sit beyond the form of the organ, forcing each organ to betray the openness of the network—the wideness of the world—from which it is has been formed and *as which* it might be unfurled.

90. Indeed, while Black attempts to outline the image of the body-in-*process* in her discussion, it is only ever the processes of the *land* that are made explicitly visible in her discussion of the text.

that fits with the Theological demands of one particular reading community or another, but these organs are always suspended in such a way as to allow numerous possible reading trajectories. These bodily bits and bobs exist in the moment before interpretation is possible, where a network of potentialities thrives but where meaning inevitably eludes us. The organs do not mean. They are concentrations of readerly potential. The woman's body is a continuum of these intensities. One can take the watery eyes, the architectural nose, the ovine hair and one can push these organs into being different colours, different consistencies, as having entirely different functions (poetic and bodily). On the lover no organ is necessarily constant as regards either function or position; erogenous organs sprout everywhere— her whole body is a kind of diffusion of erotic potential, as Landy has noted. The entire 'organism' changes colour and consistency in the split second adjustments of the reader. One might therefore suggest that the 'bodies' of the lovers in the Song are occlusions or singularities pinned between ever divisible organ-ness and ever expandable world-ness. They come into being as a kind of 'stratum' as we readers experience the pressure exerted between organ-ness on the one hand and spatiality on the other.[91]

As I pointed out earlier, Dali's Mae West has no body *per se*, but her form—the manufactured plastic formation of female celebrity—emerges from the parts and then claims originality over them. Mae does not exist beyond the half-and-half 'organs'—sofa lips, painting eyes, curtain hair— that we, as onlookers, must connect and collate in order to 'make' her a body. These organs do not function as hair, or nose, or lips, of course. She does not speak or kiss or eat. But the organs *do* function as pure connectivity, frozen as they are at a point exactly between soft tissue and soft furnishings. These particles can be grouped together into different kinds of strata: viewed as a subjective bodily portrait, or else, and with a different sense of scale, as a setting for that body. Mae West's bodily presence on the canvas and the surrealist apartment are nothing more than the reader's inhabitation of the 'text' re-imagined. Mae and her apartment are an open network, a continuum that can be pushed one way or the other by virtue of how we lodge ourselves within it as readers.

---

91. Or as Deleuze and Guattari say: 'The organism is not at all the body...rather it is a strata on the BwO, in other words an accumulation, coagulation, and sedimentation...' Or, again: 'The strata are bonds, pincers'. Or again, 'God is a lobster, or a double pincer, a double bind'. The body, the arch 'theological' allegory of the text, only comes into being in the pressure exerted between these pincers, of bodily expectation on the one side and of spatial experience on the other. This woman is always poised on the edge of meaning, on the edge of unfurling out as the cosmos—like Calvino's Mrs Ph(i)Nk$_0$ in the spatial story that we looked at in Chapter 2—and on the edge of being recoiled into a formation, an Organism, as she is in Song scholarship; see Deleuze and Guattari, *A Thousand Plateaus*, p. 176.

The woman in the Song of Songs has no body and the male speaker has no landscape, but each incomplete network borrows from the other. The woman does not exist beyond the half-and-half organs—thread-bare lips, dove eyes, goat hair—that we, as readers, must connect and collate in order to make her a body. These organs do not function to cover or smell or speak, but the organs do function as connectivities between the lover and the land. The body-texts thus represent the painting of a portrait and a landscape all at once and on the same canvas. Does the spatiality of the text grow wider after 4.1, does it zoom out beyond the limitations of specific referent settings—house, vine-yard, city—to place the lovers in a kind of 'national' context? Or does the spa-tiality of the text narrow, zooming in to focus on a single human body and a handful of specific anatomical features? The Song does both, and neither. The Song evokes bits and pieces of a landscape on the one hand, and, on the other, it evokes bits and pieces of a body. The feral body emerges as readers orient themselves towards one network of connections in the text:

> If the woman's body is represented by the animals and buildings of the land, it also comes to be identified with the land itself. On her animals are herded (4.1-2); on her, animals feed and might be hunted themselves; on her are built the structures that both decorate and aid in her defence.[92]

And, as readers privilege the other network of associations, a landscape emerges:

> …the life of the country—the watchful tower, the populous city, the exploi-tation of the sea. The military outpost in the far north, the remote city on the edge of the desert, the uncompromising headland, [these] assert boundar-ies, the limits of the land, and also the possibility of influence beyond it, for example in the sea, or through trade, [and] the busy traffic of Heshbon…[93]

If, in Dali's piece, Mae West and the apartment's features are always laced with unreality because of their duality, the figurations of lover and land-scape cannot entirely shake the other in the Song either. The female body is always tellurian and the landscape is always a kind of benevolent 'earth mother' (Landy's very next words in the citation above). The two networks are mutually constituting, a self-sustaining milieu. She is his world, and in her the whole world is concentrated. Indeed, world and woman are always already an interpretation of each other.

Lodged 'in' a Boundless Text

This is part of what makes interpretation of the body so tricky and so vari-ous in the text: it is an open site of connectivity, not a plane to be interpreted

92. Black, *Artifice of Love*, p. 135.
93. Landy, *Paradoxes of Paradise*, p. 82.

by readers so much as a series of strata we must negotiate. In that sense we
follow the male lover's lead. He climbs inside the woman by fashioning her
from his landscape. We climb inside her by inhabiting the connections by
which she is constituted. The Song's bodies seem to be structured in such
a way as to capitalize, even rely upon, the reader having to 'inhabit' a sed-
imentary set of connections in order for the lovers to gain their bodies, to
gain their own agency to 'inhabit' the text. The Song seems to have followed
Deleuze and Guattari's instructions for the fashioning of a BwO to the letter:

> Lodge yourself on a stratum, experiment with the opportunities it offers, find
> an advantageous place on it, find potential movement of deterritorialization,
> possible lines of flight, experience them, produce flow conjunctions here and
> there, try out continuums of intensities segment by segment, have a small
> plot of new land at all times. It is through a meticulous relation with the strata
> that one succeeds in freeing lines of flight, causing conjugated flows to pass
> and escape and bringing forth continuous intensities for a BwO. Connect,
> conjugate, continue: a whole 'diagram' as opposed to still signifying and
> subjective programs. We are in a social formation; first see how it is stratified
> for us and in us and at the place where we are; then descend from the strata to
> the deeper assemblage within which we are held; gently tip the assemblage,
> making it pass over to the side of the plane of consistency. It is only then that
> the BwO reveals itself for what it is: connection of desires, conjunction of
> flows, continuum of intensities.

Lodging himself at the stratums of the landscape and the body, the speaker
experiments with the opportunities afforded by an open network. The body
texts that are produced find various potential movements, deterritorializations and possible lines of flight between bodily and non-bodily spaces. The
speaker experiences them, tries out continuums of intensities (organs) segment by segment, and has new plots of land ready to explore at all times.
The body-texts free lines of flight, cause conjugated flows of meaning to
flow, pass and escape; they bring forth not a body but a BwO, the earth and
the body as self-constituting milieus. The poetic voice connects and conju-
gates; what emerges is embodiment as diagram (as map?) rather than embodiment as a subjective programme. The Song works from a particular social
formation—the Kingdom of Israel and its environs—and descends the strata
into a deeper assemblage. At the same time, the poem works from a particular social formation—the body—and ascends the strata into a wider assemblage. In so doing the speaker reveals the poem's approach to embodiment
for what it is: a connection of desires, a conjunction of flows, a continuum of
intensities. The woman is not a collection of memories, a primordial One to
be psychically recovered, but an open network, a 'world-wide intensity map'.

Thus, while we can liken the Song's bodies to Dali's portrait of Mae West
and to Deleuze and Guattari's BwO, in another sense the LwO's amenability to folding and unfurling makes her like Calvino's Mrs. Ph(i)Nk$_0$, of
whom I made significant mention in Chapter 2. There, the unified cosmic

point exploded from a state of punctiformity into one of spatial possibility as Mrs. Ph(i)Nk$_0$ made room for sexual desire (and tagliatelle). In the Song the sexual desire of the speaking lovers has achieved something similar: the LwO situates the lovers and transcends them all at once; the LwO is folded into a circumscribed object of desire and yet also expands to become her lover's, and our, context. The strange bodily performativity of the Song, is, like Mrs. Ph(i)Nk$_0$'s, a symptom of the Song's paradoxical spatiality, and a summary of it. This (con)fusion of scales, this performance of textuality, this self-inhabitation, is visible everywhere.

'The Patient Labyrinth of Lines Traces...'

Methodologically, this chapter has set out to approach the issue of the body through the quasi-surrealist view of Deleuze and Guattari, and via the more explicitly surrealist project of Dali in his 1935 portrait of Mae West. The surrealist flavor of this chapter thus ties the Song's bodies into the Benjaminian concerns that have been governing the overall direction of my discussion and allows me to begin to bring together some of the strands I have been working with throughout the book as a whole.

For Benjamin, surrealism and the visual spatiality of images combines in an attitude toward the body that is reminiscent of the LwO. In her recent work on urban imaginaries, Mary Mills puts Benjamin's attitude to the body in these terms:

> For Benjamin this connects with Surrealism and the importance of the visual sign: what matters is not words but the visual space of images. Benjamin wants to create an immediate interaction with the past, in time's intersection with space...disparate material objects are held in relationship by virtue of occupying a common place. The image-space is 'understood as a dialectic at a standstill; is transformed into writing'.[94]

There is an obvious echo here with the LwO, which is, in Deleuze and Guattari's terms, also 'frozen' at a point of potentiality. In this state of dialectic standstill the Benjaminian body shares its conceptual space with various disparate objects, and becomes re-imagined as a result of the (potentially shocking) connections that might be made within it, and using it. As Mills goes on to say, this sense of Benjamin's attitude toward the body is described by Bernd Witte as an 'attempt at dialectical fantasy'.[95] Certainly, the spoken,

---

94. Mills, *Urban Imagination in Biblical Prophecy*, p. 29; the citation in Mills's summary here is by Sigrid Weigel, *Body-and-Image-Space: Re-reading Walter Benjamin* (trans. Georgina Paul *et al.*; New York: Routledge, 1996), p. 52.

95. Mills, *Urban Imagination in Biblical Prophecy*, p. 30, citing Bernd Witte, *Walter Benjamin: An Intellectual Biography* (trans. James Rolleston; Detroit, MI: Wayne State University Press, 1991), p. 91.

discursive LwO of the Song, opened out into a fantasy homeland and col-
lapsed down into a fantastical body all at once, is itself a kind of dialectical fantasy, and one that produces quite admirably the kinds of Benjaminian
shocks I described in Chapter 1. If, for Benjamin, 'image-space conjoins with
body-space'[96] in order for embodiment to function, then the Song seems to
embody Benjamin's sense of embodiment. Readerly inhabitation and 'body-
and-image-space' in the text conjoin, each actualizing the other.

Thus Benjamin's sense of body-and-image-space directly relates to what
I have just been hinting at with regard to the LwO as a kind of cipher for the
spatiality of the Song as a whole. As Sigrid Weigel points out in his book
Body-and-Image-Space:

> This scene, this (revolutionary) moment in which image-and body-space
> coincide, signifies as it were Benjamin's *idea* of *Aktualität*. For Benjamin,
> the representation of an idea can, as he sets out in *The Origin of German
> Tragic Drama*, 'under no circumstances be considered successful unless the
> whole range of possible extremes it contains has been virtually passed in
> review…The idea is a monad—that means briefly: every idea contains an
> image of the world. The purpose of the representation of the idea is nothing
> less than an abbreviated outline of the image of the world.'[97]

Benjamin's sense of ideas as miniaturized contexts, or, as I put it in Chapter
1, Benjamin's ability to find within the emblem the whole world contained,[98]
helps us with the sense of the Song's bodies and how they fit into my overall discussion over the last few chapters. In the Song, the body contains an
image of the world, and the world bears the imprint of the body: descend
into either one of these matrixes and one finds the other; this is spatiality
functioning with a suspension of the rules of scale, with realities enclosing
themselves; the body in is an abyss (*en abyme*).

What is at stake is not simply the ready lines of connection that run
between the Song's bodies and Deleuzian theory. My foregoing observations on the body are important in the context of this volume not because I
am especially interested in using Deleuze *qua* Deleuze to read the Song, but
because the aspects of the textual bodies that Deleuze draws our attention
to—namely, their nature as continuums of becoming, as nexuses between
potential categories, as malleable acts of readerly capture, as potentially
illegitimate, anti-theological phenomena—are familiar ones. Previous
chapters of this thesis have sought to address directly these very issues, and
the LwO re-expresses, indeed gives further language to, those features of
the Songscape we have already considered. Like my discussion of the body

96. Weigel, *Body-and Image-Space*, pp. 8-9.
97. Weigel, *Body-and Image-Space*, p. 9, citing Benjamin, *The Origin of Tragic
Drama* (trans. John Osborne; London: New Left Books, 1977), pp. 47-48.
98. See p. 25 above.

above, my preceding chapters have sought not to decipher meanings in the text (the significance of the garden or the city, say, or of the masculine or the feminine principles of the poem) but rather to map the forces of attraction and repulsion by which these categories are constituted. The LwO and my discussion of it are somewhat fragmentary, but they are also unifying phenomena within the discourse

The openness of the lover's body to the landscape is really no different from the openness the exists between the positions of reader and lover that I looked at in Chapter 2, for instance. The duality of the lovers/landscape that we have seen in this chapter is an hallucination of the 'space of two' from that discussion. Lovers and readers, like the lover and her landscape, are a self-constituting milieu in the midst of which a 'corpus' comes into being. In the end, figuring the text as a site of becoming rather than as a locus of meaning is the same as figuring the text as a phantasm rather than a dream. We do not observe dreamy meanings and chase their interpretation, but we participate in an open network of phantasmic images. We do not step into the text's world to observe love's oneiric truths but we fashion ourselves as lovers by engaging with the spatialities implied by text's ideological production numbers.

One might tie the systemicity of the lovers' bodies to the spatiality of the Song in more specific ways as well. It seems fitting for example to note the equivalencies between the idea of the body as an act of capture and my suggestion that gendered roles come into being in the text only through certain modes of readerly organization. The same might be said of my crtique of the figurative line that runs between garden and city. The view taken in this chapter that every ('bodily') stratum always backs onto another into which it might be incorporated, seems particularly poignant in light of these discussions. As I have been at pains to point out, spatialities do not ground ideas in the biblical text, they function only as further acts of readerly capture. And just as the surfaces of the lovers' bodies are delineated only because of the folding of strata, so too the divisions we draw between urban and rural, between inside and outside, between one lover and the other can be unzipped, unfurled and unfolded. Ideologies can be made to transcend their spatial boundaries as we use space to reconfigure them.

More important even than the diaphanous nature of the Song's categories is the way in which various layers of the Song's textuality are duplicated within the text itself. The Song is in Derrida's words an 'indefinitely multiplied structure—*en abyme*', a structure in which parts of the text reproduce the entire structure of that text within themselves ('within the idea is an image of the world').[99] We saw in Chapter 2 how the lovers figure their relationship as a literary endeavor, duplicating in the text the very processes

99. Derrida, *Of Grammatology*, p. 163.

of us reading it. The bed described on the page comes to be mistaken for the page itself, two blank oblongs of figurative recreation and sexual adventure; the lover locked out of the boudoir in Song of Songs 5 projects his desire onto another oblong—that of the door—in the manner of an interpreter trying to make sense of an obscure text; the city and the garden come to stand in for the self-referential space of the poem as a whole.

The LwO of this chapter might, therefore, be considered a further multiplication of the Song's textuality. The mixture of subject and context—of lover with landscape—duplicates the (con)fusion of read text and readerly context that we have already seen at work in the Song. The spatialities of the Song's readers and of its internal lovers' bodes rub up against each other in the same way that Mae West and Dali's apartment do. Reading body and read body are mutually sustaining elements of the process of apprehending the Song. The LwO is a microcosm that swallows what it maps and the Songscape is, once again, figured as a space that does not describe sexuality so much as narrate the structure of textuality more generally. In other words, if there is no outside-text then perhaps it holds too that *il n'y a pas de hors-corps.* The corpus knows no bounds.

This book has been concerned with two interlocking issues. First, I have been attempting a spatial reading of the Song of Songs that takes space as seriously as it takes ideology. I have, in other words, been looking to investigate the problems, partiality and multiplicity of the Song's spaces without simply falling back into ideological reduction as a kind of analytical coping strategy (pitting in versus out, male versus female, intimate space versus threatening society, and so forth). In asking why the Song is impossible to put on a map, I have found myself giving an account of the overlapping spaces of the text and of how spatial questions foreground the self-referentiality of the biblical love poem, but in the process I have also caught myself reimagining, or perhaps simply re-apprehending, what maps are. The 'map' represented in this book, very idiosyncratically *my* map, is not what we might usually expect a map to look like, nor does it makes the claims maps usually seem to make. It is not graphical, for one. It is not a controlled exercise in miniaturization, nor is it an intellectual seizure of the Song's territories. My map is instead something of an open site of collapsible 'points', a site in which a number of contemporaneous reading trajectories can be plotted, a place of launching off—a plateau in the Deleuzian sense. The second issue I have been concerned with, intimately connected with this very general sense of the map, is the modelling of a somewhat broader range of biblical spatial approaches than we have been used to in the guild. In this second endeavour I have very consciously sought to disrupt the controlling methodologies in the field. Put simply, Lefebvre's Marxism encourages us to describe a certain modality of power using space rather than to experiment with space in order to play with our own sense of how power is constituted within a given system. This seems to be a hangover left from the kind of evangelical Marxism that Lefebvre espouses, and my mapping has demanded something quite different. Instead of parsing out power within spatial relationships, I have sought to demonstrate the malleability of space, and so power, and the more subjective dimensions of their operation within literature.

Recourse to the work of Walter Benjamin as an alternative way into questions about space is not coincidental, of course. As another European scholar, another cultural critic, and another unorthodox Marxist, Benjamin provides a neat counterpoint to Lefebvran politics, and his use in these pages demonstrates, I hope, just how prescriptive biblical scholars' approaches to spatiality have become. Benjamin proves that critical, culturally attuned, emancipatory, left wing projects are possible outside of Lefebvre's *La production de l'espace*. More importantly, Benjamin's suspicion about the project of history makes his work far more applicable to literary projects, and his propensity to 'shock' readers makes it far more useful. Rather than circumscribing biblical space, Benjamin opens it up to experimentation and thus to re-inhabitation. As I have said, the results of these experimentations are not intended as sensible fixed meanings or new orthodoxies but they are able, at least in places, to disrupt traditional approaches to a text, to suspend certain expectations of the way the textual system functions.

A foundational argument of mine in this regard has been that using the term 'dream' as shorthand for the Song's tricky spatiality has implications for the way we conceive of the Song as a whole. The language of the oneiric at work in Song scholarship has perhaps played a particular role in the interpretation of the poem, making the Song's spatiality appear culturally intelligible while exempting scholarly discourse from the problems involved in critiquing its conceptual underpinnings. Benjamin's phantasmagoria, as a critical tool designed to disrupt the dreamer, provides an alternative mode of understanding the spatiality of the text. This phantasmagoria, and the spaces of projection and scrim that it posits for us, allows us to chart the raw spatiality of the Song on the one hand and, on the other, the spatiality of language in general. In practice, the position of reader comes to be mapped on to the position of 'lover' in the context of the Song and this equivalency is in turn suggestive of the ways in which the Song describes textuality as much as sexuality. The Song's lovers love in the 'gap', as I termed it in Chapter 2, between language and page. The paramours love in an abyss, that is, *en abyme*.

Most of the preceding chapters have developed these themes by playing with the possibilities opened up by taking the Song as a projection that plays with light and dark (rather than as an interpretable dream). So, for instance, the Song's garden has a shadow side upon which its sunlit rills depend. The sunny enclosures of the Song's wonderland are predicated on a politics of manipulation, control and the prescription of (female) bodily performativity. Similarly, the city is not the two-dimensional obstacle to love that some scholars have described. The Song's capital is not even a vaguely ambiguous space. It is instead a kind of literary concretization of the uncanny, a spatializing of the politics of revisiting, hallucinating, and of being shocked by the familiar, which, in fact, the technical manifestation of the phantasmagoria actually implied in its original context. I have argued that these twists and turns of the Songscape's labyrinthine city lead back in the end to the garden's undergrowth and that the Song's two most iconic spaces overlap and describe each other. In a sense the uncanny city is itself an uncanny repetition of the garden. The configurations of power that lie in the Song's individual scenes thus seem to bear out the phantasmagorical operations I describe as underwriting the text. The Songscape enacts a phantasmagorical blurring of the familiar and the novel, one image becoming another, each new, each already known. As I have already discussed at the end of the last chapter, these processes are borne out again in my two readings of gender performativity in the Song (Chapter 4) and in the continuum of the lovers' bodies (Chapter 5), which do not embody the Song's lovers so much as our own readerly inhabitations of the text.

These readings reiterate the idea that the Song seems to merge the spatiality of its own textuality with the spatiality of its lovers. When we read about their love, we find ourselves, structurally speaking, reading about our own reading process. This cross-over between textuality and sexuality is the natural product of three particular facets of the poem that I have been coming back to again and again in my various discussions, (1) The poem's own prioritizing of the power of poetic speech (2) the poem's sense of language as having power to constitute worlds and (3) the poem's confusing of writing/reading with being in love. In the Song, the result is a literary world that represents the representational, that functions by means of a staging of stagedness, a read landscape where space principally describes the spatiality of reading. If the lovers borrow the spatiality of our reading, coming alive through it, we similarly use them to break the boundaries of the text giving us entry into their rose-tinted world.[1]

This brings us back to the work of Derrida I began with in Chapter 1. For Derrida, these kinds of unfoldable self-referencing structures are a fundamental operation of all text, 'where one can read a book within a book, an origin within an origin, a centre within the centre'.[2] For Derrida, all text is a space of repetition and the splitting of the self:

> An entire theory of the structural necessity of the abyss will be gradually constituted in our reading: the indefinite process of supplementary has always already infiltrated presence, always already inscribed there the space of repetition and the splitting of the self. Representation in the abyss of presence is not an accident of presence; the desire of presence is, on the contrary, born from the abyss (the indefinite multiplication) of representation, from the representation of representation, etc.[3]

1. In literary readings we participate in the world of the lovers, of course; in allegorical reading it might well be the case that the inverse idea is in play: we allow the paramours out to inhabit our own cosmological system (whatever that might be).

2. Quoted in Lucien Dallenbach, *Le recit speculaire: essai sur la mise en abyme* (Paris: Seuil, 1977), p. 216.

3. Derrida, *Of Grammatology*, p. 163.

The Song too fits this mold quite nicely as a space of repetition and of the splitting of the self. Recognizing this is the key to mapping the Song as site of infiltrated presence, with the reader infiltrating the lovers' relationship, and the lovers infiltrating the spatiality of the reading process itself. So, while spatial theory forces us to come to the Song afresh, to think about its cities, its gardens, its gender ideologies, and its so-called dreamscape in different ways, it is also true that the Song's modelling of Derridian concerns about text and space prompts some key questions for spatial reading more generally.

The Song reminds us that if we take the assertions of contemporary spatial theory at their word—if we consider space as both a social product and as a concretization of social forces—when we consider space in texts we are always and inevitably looking at the representation of representation. We make our analyses, and ourselves, sites of the multiplication of textual structure—spaces where the edges of textuality breakdown to inaugurate yet more spaces. For what I have been demonstrating throughout the book is that text is not, indeed it cannot be, a 'supplement' to explicate historical space. Nor indeed is textual space an axis on which fixed literary 'meanings' can be plotted. *Texts are, in fact, re-performances of the spatialities by which texts come into being.* By the same stroke, space is a re-performance of the textualities by which spaces comes into being. The interplay, or better: the intercourse, that takes place between these two projects is in a sense the very heart of the Song's sexual discourse.

I suggest that the role of spatial analysis is not to apprehend space, to find three simple steps by which it can be tamed. The role of spatial analysis is to experiment with textual systemicity. The potential problem with this figuration is that all such experiments might well lead back to the self-multiplying structure of space and text. Derrida insists, after all, that these processes are alive in all textual systems. But mapping the varied and vibrant ways in which textualities and spatialities go about duplicating themselves within a given corpus has its own virtues. The conceptual maps we produce will not behave; they will not sit flat (or still) on the interpretative table. Their production remains important, however, because their value does not lie in their obedience but in their ability to shock, to disrupt, and to multiply our current modes of reading. The literary maps we must aim for are, in Derrida's terms, the 'signifying structure[s] that critical reading should *produce*...a space of reading that I shall not fill here: a task of reading.'[4] In the end this is what the Songscape concretizes for us, it is this principle that the poem takes and fashions into hills and vistas, cities and trembling bodies: 'a task of reading'. And, surely, many waters cannot quench that.

---

4. Derrida, *Of Grammatology*, p. 158.

BIBLIOGRAPHY

Adorno, Theodor, 'Letters to Walter Benjamin', in Fredric Jameson (ed.), *Aesthetics and Politics* (London: Verso, 1977 [1935]), pp. 110-33.

Almog, Yael, 'Flowing Myrrh upon the Handles of the Bolt: Bodily Border, Social Norms and their Transgression in the Song of Songs', *BibInt* 18 (2010), pp. 251-63.

Alter, Robert, 'The Garden of Metaphor', in Harold Bloom (ed.), *The Song of Songs* (New York: Chelsea House, 1988), pp. 177-94.

Arbel, Daphna, 'My Vineyard, my Very Own, Is for Myself', in Athalya Brenner and Carole R. Fontaine (eds.), *A Feminist Companion to the Bible (Second Series)* (Sheffield: Sheffield Academic Press, 2000), pp. 90-103.

Assis, Elie, *Flashes of Fire: A Literary Analysis of the Song of Songs* (The Library of Hebrew Bible/Old Testament Studies, 503; London: T. & T. Clark, 2009).

Bachelard, Gaston, *The Poetics of Space* (trans. M. Jolas; Boston: Beacon Press, 1994 [1958]).

—*La terre et les reveries du repos* (Paris: Corti, 1946).

Bar-Efrat, Shimon, *Narrative Art in the Bible* (London: T. & T. Clark, 2004 [1989]).

Barnett, Clive, 'Review of Thirdspace: Journeys to Los Angeles and Other Real-and-Imagined-Places', *Transactions, Institute of British Geographers* (1997), pp. 529-30.

Benjamin, Walter, *The Arcades Project* (trans. Howard Eiland and Kevin McLaughlin; Cambridge, MA: Harvard University Press, 2002 [1927–1940]).

—*Illuminations* (trans. Harry Zohn; New York: Schocken, 1969).

—*The Origin of German Tragic Drama* (trans. John Osborne; London: Verso, 1998 [1928]).

—*Reflections, Essays, Aphorsms, Autobiographical Writings* (trans. Edmund Jephcott; New York: Schocken, 1978).

—*Selected Writings, 1913–1926* (2 vols.; trans. Rodney Livingstone; Cambridge, MA: Belknap Press, 1996).

—*Walter Benjamin's The Archive: Images, Texts, Signs* (London: Verso, 2007).

—'Problem der Tradition I', in Rolf Tiedemann and Herman Schweppenhäuser (eds.), *Gesammelte Schriften* (Franfurt am Main: Suhrkamp, 1974), pp. 1229-55.

—'Surrealism: The Last Snapshot of the European Intelligentsia', in M.W. Jennings, H. Eiland, and G. Smith (eds.), *Walter Benjamin: Selected Writings. II. 1927–1934* (Cambridge, MA: Harvard University Press, 1999), pp. 207-21.

Bergant, Diane, *The Song of Songs* (Berit Olam: Studies in Hebrew Narrative and Poetry; Collegeville, PA: Liturgical Press, 2001).

Berquist, Jon L., and Claudia V. Camp (eds.), *Constructions of Space. I. Theory, Geography and Narrative* (Library of the Hebrew Bible/Old Testament Studies, 481; London: T. & T. Clark, 2007).

—*Constructions of Space. II. The Biblical City and Other Imagined Spaces* (Library of the Hebrew Bible/Old Testament Studies, 490; London: T. & T. Clark, 2008).

Bishop, Elizabeth, *Complete Poems* (London: Chatto & Windus, 2004).

Black, Fiona C., *The Artifice of Love: Grotesque Bodies and the Song of Songs* (JSOTSup, 392; London: T. & T. Clark, 2009).

Black, Fiona C., and J. Cheryl Exum, 'Semiotics in Stained Glass: Edward Burne-Jones's Song of Songs, in J. Cheryl Exum and Stephen D. Moore (eds.), *Biblical Studies/Cultural Studies: The Third Sheffield Colloquium* (Sheffield: Sheffield Academic Press, 1998), pp. 315-42.

Blanchot, Maurice, *The Space of Literature* (Lincoln, NE: University of Nebraska Press, 1989).

Bloch, Ariel, and Chana Bloch, *The Song of Songs: A New Translation with an Introduction and Commentary* (Berkeley, CA: University of California Press, 1995).

Bloch, Ernst, 'Erinnerungen and Walter Benjamin', in Theodore Adorno and Rolf Tinnermann (eds.), Über Walter Benjamin (Frankfurt am Main: Suhrkamp, 1968), pp. 16-23.

Bloom, Harold (ed.), *The Song of Songs* (New York: Chelsea House, 1988).

Boer, Roland, *Knocking on Heaven's Door: The Bible and Popular Culture* (Biblical Limits; New York: Routledge, 1999).

—*Marxist Criticism of the Bible* (London: T. & T. Clark, 2003).

—'The Bowels of History, or The Perpetuation of Biblical Myth in Walter Benjamin', *Journal of Narrative Theory* 32 (2002), pp. 371-90.

—'Henri Lefebvre: The Production of Space in 1 Samuel', in Berquist and Camp (eds.), *Constructions of Space* II, pp. 78-101.

—'Keeping it Literal: The Economy of the Song of Songs', *JHS* 7 (2007), pp. 1-14.

Borges, Jorge Luis, *Dreamtigers* (Austin, TX: University of Texas Press, 1985 [1960]).

—*Labyrinths: Selected Stories and Other Writings* (London: Penguin, 2000 [1964]).

Brenner, Athalya, *The Intercourse of Knowledge: On Gendering Desire and 'Sexuality' in the Hebrew Bible* (Biblical Interpretation Series, 26; Leiden: E.J. Brill, 1997).

—*Song of Songs* (Sheffield: Sheffield Academic Press, 1989).

—'Aromatics and Perfumes in the Song of Songs', JSOT 25 (1983), *pp. 75-81.*

Brenner, Athalya (ed.), *The Song of Songs: A Feminist Companion to the Bible* (Sheffield: Sheffield Academic Press, 2001 [1993]).

Brenner, Athalya, and Fokkelien van Dijk-Hemmes, *On Gendering Texts: Female and Male Voices in the Hebrew Bible* (Biblical Interpretation, 1; Leiden: E.J. Brill, 1993).

Brenner, Athalya, and Carole R. Fontaine (eds.), *The Song of Songs: A Feminist Companion to the Bible (Second Series)* (Sheffield: Sheffield Academic Press, 2000).

Burrus, Virginia, and Stephen D. Moore, 'Unsafe Sex: Feminism, Pornography and the Song of Songs', *BibInt* 11 (2003), pp. 24-52.

Butler, Judith, *Bodies that Matter: On the Discursive Limits of Sex* (New York: Routledge, 2007 [1993]).

Calvino, Italo, *Cosmicomics* (trans. William Weaver; London: Penguin, 2011 [1976]).

Camp, Claudia V., 'Introduction', in Berquist and Camp (eds.), *Constructions of Space*, II, pp. 1-18.

Carr, G. Lloyd, *The Song of Solomon: An Introduction and Commentary* (Leicester: InterVarsity Press, 1984).

Carroll, Lewis, *Alice's Adventures in Wonderland and Through the Looking-glass* (London: Vintage, 2007 [1865]).

Castle, Terry, 'Phantasmagoria: Spectral Technology and the Metaphorics of Modern Reverie', *Critical Inquiry* 15 (1988), pp. 26-61.

Certeau, Michel de, *The Practice of Everyday Life* (trans. Steven Rendall; Berkeley, CA: University of California Press, 1984).

Clairvaux, Bernard of, *Sermons on the Song of Songs* (4 vols.; Kalamazoo, MI: Cistercian Publications, 1976).

Clines, David J. A., *Interested Parties: The Ideology of Writers and Readers of the Hebrew Bible* (Sheffield: Sheffield Phoenix Press, 2009).

Cohen, Margaret, 'Walter Benjamin's Phantasmagoria', *NGC* 48 (1989), pp. 87-107.

Colbrook, Claire, *Gilles Deleuze* (New York: Routledge, 2001).

Conan Doyle, Arthur, *The Lost World* (London: A.L. Burt Company, 1912).

Cook, Albert, *The Root of the Thing: A Study of Job and the Song of Songs* (Bloomington, IN: Indiana University Press, 1968).

Cooper, David, 'The Poetics of Place and Space: Wordsworth, Norman Nicholson and the Lake District', *Literature Compass* 5 (2008), pp. 807-21.

Dallenbach, Lucien, *Le recit speculaire: essai sur la mise en abyme* (Paris: Seuil, 1977).

Dault, Meredith, 'The Last Triangle: Sex, Money and the Politics of Pubic Hair' (Unpublished MA thesis; University of Ontario, 2011).

Davidson, Ian, *Ideas of Space in Contemporary Poetry* (Basingstoke: Palgrave Macmillan, 2007).

Davidson, Richard, 'The Literary Structure of the Song of Songs *Redivivus*', *Journal of the Adventist Theology Society* 14 (2003), pp. 44-55.

Davies, Philip, 'Space and Sects in the Qumran Scrolls', in David M. Gunn and Paula M. McNutt (eds.), *'Imagining' Biblical Worlds: Studies in Spatial, Social and Historical Constructs in Honor of James W. Flanagan* (Sheffield: Sheffield Academic Press, 2002), pp. 81-98.

Deckers, M., 'The Structure of the Song of Songs', in A. Brenner (ed.), *A Feminist Companion to the Song of Songs*, pp. 185-89.

Deleuze, Gilles, and Felix Guattari, *A Thousand Plateaus: Capitalism and Schizophrenia* (London: Continuum, 2011 [1987]).

Delitzsch, Franz, *Proverbs, Ecclesiastes and the Song of Solomon* (trans. James Martin; Grand Rapids, MI: Eerdmans, 1980 [1872]).

Derrida, Jacques, *Of Grammatology* (trans. Gayatri Chakravorty Spivak; Baltimore, MD: Johns Hopkins University Press, 1997 [1974]).

—'The Double Session', in *Dissemination* (trans. Barbara Johnson; London: Athlone Press, 1981), pp. 187-237.

—'Signature Event Context', in *Limited Inc* (Evanston, IL: Northwestern University Press, 1977), pp. 1-25.

Descartes, René, 'Principles of Philosophy', in J. Cottingham, R. Stoothoff, and D. Murdoch (trans. and eds.), *The Philosophical Writings of Descartes* (Cambridge: Cambridge University Press, 1985), vol. 1, pp. 207-52.

Diamond, Irene, and Lee Quinby (eds.), *Feminism and Foucault: Reflections on Resistance* (Boston, MA: Northeastern University Press, 1988).

Donald, James, *Imagining the Modern City* (London: Athlone Press, 1999).

Dorsey, David A., 'Literary Structuring in the Song of Songs', *JSOT* 46 (1990), pp. 81-96.

Driver, S.R., *An Introduction to the Literature of the Old Testament* (Edinburgh, 7th edn, 1898).

Elkins, James, *Landscape Theory* (New York: Routledge, 2008).

Elliott, M. Timothea, *The Literary Unity of the Canticle* (*Europäische Hochschulschriften*, 371; Frankfurt: Peter Lang, 1989).

van Erp-Houtepan, A., 'The Etymological Origin of the Garden', *Journal of Garden History* (1986), pp. 227-31.

Eslinger, Lyle, 'The Case of the Immodest Lady Wrestler in Deuteronomy XXV 11-12', *VT* (1981), pp. 269-81.

Exum, J. Cheryl, *Song of Songs: A Commentary* (Louisville, KY: Westminster/John Knox Press, 2005).

—'Developing Strategies of Feminist Criticism/Developing Strategies for Commentating the Song of Songs', in David J.A. Clines and Stephen D. Moore (eds.), *Auguries: The Jubilee Volume of the Sheffield Department of Biblical Studies* (Sheffield: Sheffield Academic Press, 1998), pp. 206-49.

Falk, Marcia, *Love Lyrics from the Bible: A Translation and Literary Study of the Song of Songs* (Bible and Literature, 4; Sheffield: Almond Press, 1982).

Fauconnier, Gilles, *Mappings in Thought and Language* (Cambridge: Cambridge University Press, 1997).

Fisch, Harold, 'Song of Songs: The Allegorical Imperative', in *Poetry with a Purpose: Biblical Poetics and Interpretation* (Bloomington, IN: Indiana University Press, 1988), pp. 80-103.

Fischer, Stefan, *Das Hohelied Salomos zwischen Poesie und Erzählung: Erzähltextanalyse eines poetischen Textes* (Tübingen: Mohr Siebeck, 2010).

Fokkelman, Jan P., *Reading Biblical Narrative: An Introductory Guide* (Louisville KY: Westminster/John Knox Press, 1995).

Fontaine, Carole R., 'Watching out for the Watchmen (Song of Songs 5.7)', in C. Cosgrove (ed.), *The Meanings We Choose: Hermeneutical Ethics, Indeterminacy and the Conflict of Interpretations* (London: T. & T. Clark, 2004), pp. 102-21.

Foucault, Michael, *The History of Sexuality. I. The Will to Knowledge* (London: Penguin, 1976).

Fox, Michael V., *The Song of Songs and the Ancient Egyptian Love Songs* (Madison: University of Wisconsin Press, 1985).

Fraser, Mariam, and Monica Greco (eds.), *The Body: A Reader* (New York: Routledge, 2001).

Freehof, Solomon B., 'The Song of Songs: A General Suggestion', *JQR* 39 (1949), pp. 397-402.

Freud, Sigmund, 'The Uncanny', in *The Uncanny* (trans. Donald McLintock; London: Penguin, 2003 [1919]), pp. 121-62.

Frye, Marylin, *Politics of Reality: Essays in Feminist Theory* (Trumansburg, NY: Crossing Press, 1983).

Fuss, Diana, 'Inside/Out', in Diana Fuss (ed.), *Inside/Out: Lesbian Theories, Gay Theories* (New York: Routledge, 1991), pp. 1-10.

Galbraith, Deane, 'Review of Luke Gärtner-Brereton, *The Ontology of Space in Biblical Hebrew Narrative: The Determinate Function of Narrative 'Space' within the Biblical Hebrew Aesthetic*', in *Bible and Critical Theory* 5 (2009), pp. 45.1-45.3.

George, Mark, *Israel's Tabernacle as Social Space* (Ancient Israel and its Literature, 2; Atlanta, GA: Society of Biblical Literature, 2009).

—'Space and History: Citing Critical Space for Biblical Studies', in Berquist and Camp (eds.), *Constructions of Space. I. Theory, Geography and Narrative* (London: T. & T. Clark, 2007), pp. 15-31.

Gerhards, Meik, *Das Hohelied: Studien zu seiner literarischen Gestalt und theologischen Bedeutung* (Leipzig: Evangelische Verlagsanstalt, 2010).

Gerleman, Gillis, *Ruth, Das Hohelied* (Neukirchen–Vluyn: Neukirchener Verlag, 1965).

Gide, Andre, *Journal 1889–1939* (Paris: Gallimard 1951),

Ginsburg, Christian D., *The Song of Songs: Commentary, Historical and Critical* (London: Longman, Brown, *et al.*, 1857).

Gordis, Robert, *The Song of Songs and Lamentations: A Study, Modern Translation and Commentary* (Texts and Studies of the Jewish Theological Seminary of America; New York: Ktav, 1974).

Goulder, Michael D., *The Song of Fourteen Songs* (Sheffield: JSOT Press, 1986).

Graham, Susan, 'Justinian and the Politics of Space', in Berquist and Camp (eds.), *Constructions of Space.* II, pp. 51-77.

Grosz, Elizabeth, 'Woman, *Chora, Dwelling*', in *Space, Time and Perversion, The Politics of the Body* (London: Routledge, 1996), pp. 111-24.

Gunn, David M., and Paula M. McNutt (eds.), '*Imagining' Biblical Worlds: Studies in Spatial, Social and Historical Constructs in Honor of James W. Flanagan* (Sheffield: Sheffield Academic Press, 2002).

Haraway, Donna, *Simians, Cyborgs, and Women: The Reinvention of Nature* (London: Free Association Press, 1991).

Harding, Kathryn, 'I Sought Him but I did not Find Him': The Elusive Lover in the Song of Songs', *BibInt* 16 (2008), pp. 43-59.

Harvey, David, *Social Justice and the City* (London: Edward Arnold, 1973).

Hermann, Wolfram, 'Gedanken zur Geschichte des altorientalischen Beschreibungsliedes', *ZAW* 75 (1963), pp. 176-96.

Hess, Richard S., *Song of Songs* (Grand Rapids, MI: Backer Academic, 2005).

Hill, Leslie, *Cambridge Introduction to Jacques Derrida* (Cambridge: Cambridge University Press, 2007).

Hill Collins, Patricia, *Black Feminist Thought: Knowledge, Consciousness, and the Politics of Empowerment* (London: Harper Collins, 1990).

Honeyman, A.M., 'Two Contributions to Canaanite Toponymy', *JTS* 50 (1958), pp. 59-61.

Hook, Derek, 'Monumental Space and the Uncanny', *Geoforum* 36 (2005), pp. 688-704.

Horst, Friedrich, 'Die Formen des althebräischen Liebesliedes', in Rudi Paret (ed.), *Orientalische Studien Enno Littmann zu seinem 60. Geburtstag* (Leiden: E.J. Brill, 1935), pp. 43-54.

Hubbard, Phil, Rob Kitchen and Gill Valentine (eds.), *Key Thinkers on Space and Place* (London: Sage, 2004).

Huggett, Nick (ed.), *Space From Zeno to Einstein: Classic Readings with a Contemporary Commentary* (Cambridge, MA: MIT Press, 1999).

Huie-Jolly, Marie, 'Language as Extension of Desire: The Oedipus Complex and Spatial Hermeneutics', in Berquist and Camp (eds.), *Constructions of Space.* I. *Theory, Geography and Narrative* (London: T. & T. Clark, 2007), pp. 68-86.

Hussey, Edward, *Aristotle's Physics: Books 1 & 2* (Oxford: Clarendon Press, 1983).

Irigaray, Luce, *Elemental Passions* (New York: Routledge, 1992).

—*Je, tu, nous: Toward a Culture of Difference* (New York: Routledge, 1993).

—*Speculum of the Other Woman* (trans. Gillian C. Gill; Ithaca, NY: Cornell University Press, 1985).

Iser, Wolfgang, *The Act of Reading: A Theory of Aesthetic Response* (Baltimore, MD: Johns Hopkins University Press, 1980).

Jacobs, Carol, *The Dissimulating Harmony* (Baltimore, MD: Johns Hopkins University Press, 1978).

Kant, Immanuel, *Critique of Pure Reason* (trans. Marcus Weigelt; London: Penguin, 2007).

Keel, Othmar *The Song of Songs: A Continental Commentary* (trans. Frederick J. Gaiser; Minneapolis, MN: Fortress Press, 1994).

Krinetzki, Leo, *Das Hohe Lied: Kommentar zu Gestalt und Kerygma eines alttestamentlichen Liebesliedes* (Düsseldorf: Patmos, 1963).

—'Die erotischen Psychologie des Hohenliedes', *TQ* 150 (1970), pp. 404-416.

LaCocque, André, *Romance, She Wrote: A Hermeneutical Essay on The Song of Songs* (Harrisburg, PA.: Trinity Press International, 1998).

Landy, Francis, *Paradoxes of Paradise: Identity and Difference in the Song of Songs* (Bible and Literature Series, 7; Sheffield: Almond Press, 1st edn, 1983).

—*Paradoxes of Paradise: Identity and Difference in the Song of Songs* (Classics Series; Sheffield: Sheffield Phoenix Press, 2nd edn, 2011).

—Review of M. Timothea Elliot, *The Literary Unity of the Canticle*, *Biblica* 72 (1991) pp. 570-72.

Lefebvre, Henri, *The Production of Space* (trans. Donald Nicholson-Smith; Oxford: Blackwell, 1991).

Lenhardt, Christian, 'Anamnestic Solidarity: The Proletariat and its Manes', *Telos* 25 (1975), pp.133-54.

Longman III, Tremper, *Song of Songs* (New International Commentary of the Old Testament; Grand Rapids, MI: Eerdmans, 2001).

Lopez, Kathryn Muller, 'Standing Before the Throne of God: Critical Spatiality in Apocalyptic Scenes of Judgement', in Berquist and Camp (eds.), *Constructions of Space* II, pp. 139-55.

Maier, Christl, *Daughter Zion, Mother Zion: Gender, Space and the Sacred in Ancient Israel* (Minneapolis, MN: Fortress Press, 2008).

Mariaselvam, Abraham, *The Song of Songs and Ancient Tamil Love Poems: Poetry and Symbolism* (Analecta Biblica, 118; Rome: Pontifical Biblical Institute, 1988).

Marx, Karl, *Das Kapital: Kritik der politischen Ökonomie* (Berlin: Otto Meisner, 1867).

Massey, Doreen, *For Space* (London: Sage, 2005).

—*Space, Place and Gender* (Minneapolis, MN: University of Minnesota Press, 1994).

Massumi, Brian, *A User's Guide to Capitalism and Schizophrenia: Deviations from Deleuze and Guattari* (Cambridge, MA: MIT Press, 1992).

McKay, George, *Radical Gardening: Politics, Idealism and Rebellion in the Garden* (London: Frances Lincoln, 2011).

McNutt, Paula M. '"Fathers of the Empty Space" and "Strangers Forever": Social Marginality and the Construction of Space', in Gunn and McNutt, *'Imagining' Biblical Worlds*, pp. 30-50.

Meek, Theophile J., 'The Song of Songs: Introduction and Exegesis', *IB* 5 (1956), pp. 91-148.

Mehlman, Jeffrey, *Walter Benjamin for Children: An Essay on his Radio Years* (Chicago, IL: University of Chicago Press, 1993).

Meissner, Bruno, *Babylonien und Assyrien*, I (Heidelberg: Carl Winters, 1920).

Meredith, Christopher, 'A Case of Open and Shut: The Five Thresholds in 1 Samuel 1.1–7.2', *BibInt* 18 (2010), pp. 137-57.

—'The Lattice and the Looking-glass: Gendered Space in Song of Songs 2.8-14', *JAAR* 80 (2012), pp. 1-22.

Merleau-Ponty, Maurice, *Phenomenology of Perception* (trans. C. Smith; London: Routledge, 2002 [1964]).

Merrifield, Andy, 'Henri Lefebvre: A Socialist in Space', in Mike Crang and Nigel Thrift (eds.), *Thinking Space* (New York: Routledge, 2000), pp. 167-82.

—'Lefebvre, Anti-Logos, and Nietzsche. An Alternative Reading of "The Production of Space"', *Antipode* 27 (1995), pp. 294-303.

Meyers, Carol, 'Gender Imagery in the Song of Songs', in A. Brenner (ed.) *A Feminist Companion to the Song of Songs*, pp. 197-213.

—'"To Her Mother's House": Considering a Counterpart to the Israelite *Bet 'ab'*, in Normal K. Gottwald, David Jobling, Peggy Lynne Day and Gerald T. Sheppard (eds.), *The Bible and the Politics of Exegesis* (Cleveland, OH: Pilgrim Press, 1991), pp. 46-47.

Miller, William R., 'A Bakhtinian Reading of Narrative Space and its Relationship to Social Space', in Berquist and Camp (eds.), *Constructions of Space*, I, pp. 129-40.

Mills, Mary E., *Urban Imagination in Biblical Prophecy* (London: T. & T. Clark, 2012).

Moore, Charles W., William J. Mitchell and William Turnbull (eds.), *The Poetics of Gardens* (Cambridge, MA: MIT Press, 1993).

Morely, Ian, and Colin Renfrew (eds.), *The Archaeology of Measurement* (Cambridge: Cambridge University Press, 2010).

Müller, Hans-Peter, *Vergleich und Metapher im Hohennlied* (Göttingen: Vandenhoek & Ruprecht,1984).

Munro, Jill, *Spikenard and Saffron: The Imagery of the Song of Songs* (JSOTSup, 203; Sheffield: Sheffield Academic Press, 1995).

Murphy, Roland, *The Song of Songs: A Commentary on the Book of Canticles or the Song of Songs* (Minneapolis, MN: Fortress Press, 1990).

Noegel, Scott, and Gary Rendsburg, *Solomon's Vineyard: Literary and Linguistic Studies in the Song of Songs* (Ancient Israel and its Literature, 1; Atlanta, GA: Society of Biblical Literature, 2009).

Økland, Jorunn, *Women in their Place: Paul and the Corinthian Discourse of Gender and Sanctuary Space* (JSNTSupp, 269; London: T. & T. Clark, 2004).

Ostriker, Alicia, 'A Holy of Holies: The Song of Songs as Countertext', in Brenner and Fontaine (eds.), *A Feminist Companion to the Bible (Second Series)*, pp. 36-54.

Owens, Craig, 'Photography "en abyme"', *October* 5 (1978), pp. 73-88.

Pardes, Ilana, *Countertraditions in the Bible: A Feminist Approach* (Cambridge, MA: Harvard University Press, 1992).

Perec, Georges, *Species of Spaces and Other Pieces* (trans. John Sturrock; London: Penguin, 1997 [1974]).

Phipps, William, 'The Plight of the Song of Songs', in Harold Bloom (ed.), *Song of Songs*, pp. 5-23.

Pile, Steve, *Real Cities: Modernity, Space and the Phantasmagorias of City Life* (London: Sage, 2005).

Pinder, David, 'Urban Encounters: Dérives from Surrealism', in E. Adamowicz (ed.), *Surrealism: Crossings/Frontiers* (Oxford: Oxford University Press, 2006), pp. 39-64.

Pippin, Tina, 'The Ideological of Apocalyptic Space', in Berquist and Camp (eds.), *Constructions of Space* II, pp. 156-70.

Plato, *Timaeus* (trans. H.D.P. Lee; London: Penguin, 1965).

Polaski, Donald, '"What will ye see in the Shulammite?" Women, Power and Panopticism in the Song of Songs', *BibInt* 5 (1997), pp. 64-81.

Pope, Marvin H., *Song of Songs* (AB, 7; New York: Doubleday, 1977).

Prescott, Holly, 'Rethinking Urban Space in Contemporary British Writing' (Unpublished PhD Thesis: University of Birmingham, 2011).

Rabin, Chaim, 'The Song of Songs and Tamil Poetry', *Studies in Religion* 3 (1973–74), pp. 205-219.

Rabinbach, Ansom, 'Critique and Commentary/Alchemy and Chemistry: Some Remarks on Walter Benjamin and this Special Issue', *NGC* 17 (1979), pp. 3-14.

Rendall, Jane, Barbara Penner and Iain Borden (eds.), *Gender, Space, Architecture: An Interdisciplinary Introduction* (London: Routledge, 2000).

Riley, Robert B. 'Flowers, Power and Sex', in Mark Francis and Randolph T. Hester, Jr (eds.), *The Meaning of Gardens: Idea, Place and Action* (Cambridge, MA: MIT Press, 1995 [1990]), pp. 60-75.

—'From Sacred Grove to Disney World: The Search for Garden Meaning', *Landscape Journal* (1988), pp. 136-47.

Robert, André, and Robert Tournay, *Le cantique des cantiques* (Paris: J. Gabalda, 1963).

Rogerson, John, and John Vincent, *The City in Biblical Perspective* (Biblical Challenges in the Contemporary World Series; Sheffield: Equinox, 2009).

Romdenh-Romluc, Komarine, *Merleau-Ponty and Phenomenology of Perception* (New York: Routledge, 2011).

Rose, Gillian, *Feminism and Geography: The Limits of Geographical Knowledge* (Cambridge MN: University if Minnesota Press, 1993).

Rosenthal, Judah, 'Rashi's Commentary on the Song of Songs (from Mss. Edited and Annotated)', in S. Bernstein and G.A. Churgin (eds.), *Samuel K. Mirsky Jubilee Volume* (New York: Jubilee Committee, 1958), pp. 130-88 [Hebrew].

Sasson, Jack, 'A Major Contribution to Song of Songs Scholarship', *JAOS* 107 (1987), pp. 733-39.

Schipper, Jeremy, *Disability Studies and the Hebrew Bible: Figuring Mephibosheth in the David Story* (Library of Hebrew Bible/Old Testament, 441; London: Continuum, 2009).

Shea, William, 'The Chiastic Structure of the Song of Songs', *ZAW* 92 (1980), pp. 378-96.

Shelly, Mary, *Frankenstein: Or, The Modern Prometheus* (London: Penguin, 2007 [1818]).

Shields, Rob, 'Henri Lefebvre', in Phil Hubbard, Rob Kitchen and Gill Valentine (eds.), *Key Thinkers on Space and Place* (London: Sage, 2004).

Soja, Edward, *Post-modern Geographies: The Reassertion of Space in Critical Social Theory* (London: Verso, 1989).

—*Thirdspace: Journeys to Los Angeles and Other Real-and-Imagined-Places* (Oxford: Blackwell, 1996).

—*Postmetropolis: Critical Studies of Cities and Regions* (Oxford, Blackwell, 2000).

Soulen, Richard, 'The *waṣfs* of the Song of Songs and Hermeneutics', in Brenner (ed.), *A Feminist Companion to the Song of Songs*, pp. 211-24.

Stadelmann, Luis, *Love and Politics: A New Commentary on the Song of Songs* (New York: Paulist Press, 1992).

Tacitus, *The Annals of Imperial Rome* (trans. Michael Grant; Harmondsworth: Penguin, 1972).

Thacker, Andrew, *Moving through Modernity: Space and Geography in Modernism* (Manchester: Manchester University Press, 2003).

Thöne, Yvonne Sophie, *Liebe zwischen Stadt und Feld: Raum und Geschlecht im Hohelied* (Berlin: Lit Verlag, 2012).

Trible, Phyllis, *God and the Rhetoric of Sexuality* (Overtures to Biblical Theology, 2; Philadelphia, PA: Fortress Press, 1978).

Tschumi, Bernard, 'Questions of Space: The Pyramid and the Labyrinth (or the Architectural Paradox)', in *Studio International* 190 (1975), pp. 136-42.

Tuan, Yi-Fu, *Dominance and Affection: The Making of Pets* (New Haven, CT: Yale University Press, 1984).

Warner, Maria, *Phantasmagoria: Spirit Visions, Metaphors, and Media into the Twenty-first Century* (Oxford: Oxford University Press, 2006).

Weigel, Sigrid, *Body-and-Image-Space: Re-reading Walter Benjamin* (trans. Georgina Paul; New York: Routledge, 1996).

Werth, Paul, *Text Worlds: Representing Conceptual Space in Discourse* (London: Longman, 1999).

Whiston Spirn, Anne, 'The Poetics of City and Nature: Towards a New Aesthetic for Urban Design', *Places: Forum of Design for the Public Realm* (1989), pp. 82-93.

Wiley, Michael, *Romantic Geography: Wordsworth and Anglo-European Spaces* (Basingstoke: Palgrave, 1998).

Winterbourne, Anthony, *The Ideal and the Real: An Outline of Kant's Theory of Space, Time and Mathematical Construction* (Dordrecht: Kluwer Academic, 1988).

Witte, Bernd, *Walter Benjamin: An Intellectual Biography* (trans. James Rolleston; Detroit, MI: Wayne State University Press, 1991).

Wohlfarth, Irving, 'Walter Benjamin's Image of Interpretation', *NGC* 17 (1979), pp. 70-98.

Würthwein, Ernst, 'Das Hohelied', in Otto Eissfeldt (ed.), *Die Funf Megilloth* (Tübingen: J.C.B Mohr, 1969), pp. 25-71.

Young, Ian, 'Biblical Texts Cannot Be Dated Linguistically', *Hebrew Studies* 46 (2005), pp. 341-51.

Young, Ian, and R. Rezetko, with the assistance of Martin Ehrensvärd, *Linguistic Dating of Biblical Texts* (2 vols.; London: Equinox, 2008).

Zakovitch, Yair, *Das Hohelied* (Freiburg: Herder, 2004).

INDEX OF BIBLICAL REFERENCES

OLD TESTAMENT

INDEX OF AUTHORS

Lightning Source UK Ltd.
Milton Keynes UK
UKOW050701210613

212563UK00004B/27/P